DARING TO PLAY

Translated into English for the first time, *Daring To Play: A Brecht Companion* is the study of Bertolt Brecht's theatre by Manfred Wekwerth, Brecht's co-director and former director of the Berliner Ensemble.

Wekwerth aims to challenge prevailing myths and misconceptions about Brecht's theatre, instead providing a refreshing and accessible approach to his plays and theatrical craft. The book is rich in information, examples and anecdotal detail from first-hand acquaintance with Brecht and rehearsal with the Berliner Ensemble. Wekwerth provides a detailed practical understanding of how theatre operates with a clear perspective on the interface between politics and art.

Warm and engaging, while also being provocative and challenging, *Daring to Play* displays the continued vitality of Brecht's true approach to theatre makers today.

Manfred Wekwerth worked in the Berliner Ensemble as assistant and co-director with Bertolt Brecht, and was the Ensemble's principal director after Brecht's death. He founded the first school of director-training in the German Democratic Republic in 1969, and directed throughout Germany and Europe in such theatres as the Schauspielhaus, Zürich, the Burgtheater, Vienna and the National Theatre in London. He led the Berliner Ensemble as Intendant from 1977 until 1991 and, until 1990, was President of the Akademie der Künste of the GDR.

DARING TO PLAY

A Brecht Companion

(Originally published as *Mut zum Genuss – Ein Brecht-Handbuch für Spieler, Zuschauer, Mitstreiter und Streiter*)

Manfred Wekwerth

Edited with an Introduction by Anthony Hozier
Translated by Rebecca Braun

Routledge
Taylor & Francis Group

LONDON AND NEW YORK

First published 2009 in German as *Mut zum Genuss* by Kai Homilius
Verlag, Werder
This English translation first published 2011
by Routledge
2 Park Square, Milton Park, Abingdon, Oxon OX14 4RN

Simultaneously published in the USA and Canada
by Routledge
711 Third Avenue, New York, NY 10017

Routledge is an imprint of the Taylor & Francis Group, an informa business

British Library Cataloguing in Publication Data
A catalogue record for this book is available from the British Library

Library of Congress Cataloging in Publication Data
Wekwerth, Manfred.
    [Mut zum Genuss. English]
    Daring to play : a Brecht companion / by Manfred Wekwerth; edited
with an introduction by Anthony Hozier; translated by Rebecca Braun.
        p. cm.
    Includes bibliographical references and index.
    1. Brecht, Bertolt, 1898-1956–Dramatic production. 2. Brecht, Bertolt,
1898–1956–Criticism and interpretation. 3. Theater – Germany (East) –
History – 20th century. 4. Wekwerth, Manfred. I. Hozier, Anthony. II. Title.
    PT2603.R397Z894513 2011
    832'.912 – dc22
    2010049615

ISBN: 978-0-415-56968-2 (hbk)
ISBN: 978-0-415-56969-9 (pbk)
ISBN: 978-0-203-81471-0 (ebk)

Typeset in Times New Roman
by Taylor & Francis Books

MIX
Paper from
responsible sources
FSC® C004839
www.fsc.org

Printed and bound in Great Britain by
TJ International Ltd, Padstow, Cornwall

CONTENTS

CONTENTS

ILLUSTRATIONS

ACKNOWLEDGEMENTS

I particularly wish to thank Professor Nesta Jones and the Research Committee of Rose Bruford College for generously providing a grant towards this translation. Manfred Wekwerth has had a close relationship with the college since he was invited to lead its Symposium on Brecht in 2000 and was awarded an Honorary Fellowship in 2002. It is fitting, therefore, that the college should now be able support the translation of the first of his books to appear in English.

It has been a great pleasure to work with Rebecca Braun on this translation. Through our continual dialogue her care and attention to detail has enabled me to learn so much more about the things I thought I knew. I know that Rebecca herself, in turn, would like to thank Tom Kuhn and Ritchie Robertson for their advice in response to occasional issues of translation.

For permission to include photographs, I would like to thank the following: Vera Tenschert, Hilda Hoffmann, Manfred Wekwerth, Tassilo Leher, Getty Images and ArenaPAL. I would also like to thank the following people for their help in tracing images: Frau Uta Kohl and Dr Asja Braune of Bertolt-Brecht-Archiv/Akademie der Künste, Grischa Meyer and Amy Stolarczyk. Every effort has been made to seek permission to reproduce copyright material before the book went to press. If any proper acknowledgement has not been made, the publisher would invite copyright holders to inform them of the oversight. I would also like to thank the staff of the Library of Rose Bruford College for their support in tracking texts and other material.

At Routledge, I would like to thank Talia Rodgers for her enthusiasm, great encouragement and advice, and Niall Slater for his unfailing support and guidance.

I owe thanks to Bernd Keßler and Chris Baldwin, theatre directors and friends, who brought Manfred Wekwerth to lead a symposium in the UK a decade ago. Finally, I want to express my gratitude to two people who have been particularly generous with their time and help: to Grit Eckert for her boundless patience and support in assisting me in correspondence; and to Angelika Haas for her friendly advice on many matters and for all she has done in helping me to secure illustrations for this book.

AH

INTRODUCTION

It is remarkable how little of Manfred Wekwerth's published writing is available in English. So much continues to be written about Brecht, yet the work of his assistant, leading collaborator and successor at the Berliner Ensemble, though often quoted, remains largely untranslated. None of Wekwerth's half dozen books on Brecht and theatre is available in English – and less than a handful of his numerous articles on theatre, culture and politics.

This matters because Wekwerth is one of the last of Brecht's key assistants and co-directors at the Berliner Ensemble to have remained consistently active in the theatre. (Or alive; others – like Besson, Rülicke, Monk, Palitzsch, together with leading actor Ekkehard Schall – have now gone.) He therefore represents a direct link for us with Brecht's own mature practice.

Wekwerth was taken on by Brecht as a student at the Berliner Ensemble in 1951 and he went on to assist and or co-direct with Brecht on such productions as *The Caucasian Chalk Circle*, *Winterschlacht*, *Katzgraben* and *The Mother*. Considered by Brecht to be one of his 'most talented directors' and by critic Kenneth Tynan as 'the most gifted' of his successors, Wekwerth's international reputation was made when the company was led by Helene Weigel in the years after Brecht's death with acclaimed productions first of *The Resistible Rise of Arturo Ui* and then of *Coriolan*[1] (described by Peter Brook as 'a triumph').

He left the company in 1969 because of Weigel's resistance to renewal and change, and directed productions for theatre, film and television in Germany and internationally, including *Coriolanus*[2] at the National Theatre in London, with Anthony Hopkins in the title role. During these years he completed his doctorate, wrote several important books and articles on Brecht, and established the first institute of director-training in Berlin.

Brecht's heirs[3] wanted to ensure that the Berliner Ensemble would maintain the strongest continuity with Brecht's work, and Wekwerth was brought back as Intendant of the Ensemble in 1977. Since then Wekwerth has been Brecht's foremost advocate and interpreter in the theatre – loyal but also sceptical and questioning. Theoretically and politically he has remained one of the most informed and articulate of all commentators on Brecht. He went on to run the Berliner Ensemble for well over a decade, and received some of the highest honours and awards in the GDR.

With the disintegration of the GDR in 1989 and the re-unification of Germany, his position became untenable. Inevitably, however critical he may have become about the GDR, his relative seniority in the cultural establishment exposed him to hostility in the – particularly western – press, and he resigned from the Berliner Ensemble and stepped down as President of the Akademie der Künste. After leaving the Berliner Ensemble he continued – often working with his wife, actress Renate Richter – to direct, write, and contribute internationally to workshops and conferences.

The implications of the collapse of the GDR in 1989 were as radical for Wekwerth as for Brecht. With Marxism called into question, Brecht's reputation also became a casualty of the failure of Communist East Europe and the USSR, and of two ensuing decades of triumphalist free-market capitalism and global domination by neo-conservatism. Wekwerth himself, like many leading artists and intellectuals in the GDR who were forced to leave their posts, shared the acute sense of frustration of many on the international Left in the aftermath of the collapse of functioning models (good or bad) of socialism. The whole period saw much of theatre culture retreat into political relativism, and the political significance of Brecht's own work marginalized. The result, as Wekwerth notes, was that Brecht gained museum status, became an academic classic, and one more commodity for the cultural market.

Wekwerth, however, remains a robust optimist, and what distinguishes his book is his continued responsiveness to the contemporary world. It is a measure of his approach that he prompts us to cross-reference what we read with what's going on around us, and re-evaluate Brecht in the light of the cultural impact of more recent global economic and political change. The book was completed during 2008, and up to its point of publication Wekwerth was adding amendments in response to swift-moving events as capitalist economies themselves entered their biggest crisis since the 1930s. Brecht's theatre for change in a changeable world became once more relevant when neo-conservatives were in retreat and when the USA – where some foretold 'the end of history' – elected a leader whose campaign keyword was 'change'. (A word that even the UK Right needed in its election rhetoric while planning for business as usual.) What makes Wekwerth's approach especially timely, therefore, is that capitalism is once more in question and, while political alternatives in the English-speaking world have yet to emerge, it is time to engage once more with Brecht's optimistic, playful and radical scepticism.

Wekwerth's book aims to cut through prevailing myths and misconceptions and provide a refreshing approach to Brecht's theatre, not as a reified body of theory and playtexts, but as a practical activity, as a way of questioning and challenging our own world through the pleasures of making theatre. 'Pleasure' and 'enjoyment' and 'play' lie at the thematic heart of this book, and the book's original title *Mut zum Genuss* – roughly meaning 'daring', or 'courage to enjoy' – reflects Wekwerth's intention to reclaim the Brecht he knew in the 1950s, the Brecht who had written on his post-war return to Europe:

> Let us therefore cause general dismay by retracting our intention to emigrate from the realm of the pleasing and let it be known, to even more general dismay, that we are planning to settle in this very realm. Let us treat theatre as a place of entertainment, as is only right when debating aesthetics, and examine what kind of entertainment most appeals to us.

The key, of course, is in the last words. Fundamental to Brecht's approach is a critical and questioning attitude to the world around us. Wekwerth subtitles his book *Ein Brecht-Handbuch für Spieler, Zuschauer, Mitstreiter und Streiter*, and intends it as a readable and useful companion to Brecht for theatre practitioners and people who share a level of political awareness and of engagement with their changing – and therefore changeable – world.

To that end Wekwerth has brought together a number of articles and talks, some recent and some from his time at the Berliner Ensemble. Where he has included older material, this has been revised and augmented in the light of events. The provenance of each article is identified in the book, and, for this English edition, the articles have been grouped into sections, each of which is preceded by a very brief introduction identifying some of its key ideas and practical concepts for English readers.

As an anthology the book mixes theoretical commentary, personal recollection and practical guidance, and Wekwerth's writing moves easily between the abstract-discursive and the conversational, its style reflecting the different contexts for which the various material was written. Wekwerth is widely read and an extensive range of political and philosophical theory informs his work. But he is a natural teacher and talker, and his text, mostly intended for talks or lectures, includes numerous quotations and passing references which cannot be given scholarly annotation in detail in this translation. Some editorial notes have been added, however, where names will be less familiar to English-speaking readers.

The book abounds in information, examples and anecdotal detail from first-hand acquaintance with Brecht and rehearsal with the Berliner Ensemble. This is its particular value. It is also a book about Wekwerth himself. As one of the last of Brecht's assistants and collaborators, his personal experience with Brecht and his continuing practice lend a particular authority to what he tells us of how things work – and how to make them work – in theatre. Beyond that, his political insights and clarity from a Left perspective are especially useful in relation to, not only Brecht's practice, but also the way our own theatre can engage with a world in need of change.

Anthony Hozier
2010

NOTE ON TEXT AND TRANSLATION

In addition to dividing the book into sections, each with a very brief editorial introductory note, some cuts have been made for the English edition. One short section of reviews of German theatre productions has been omitted because much of its commentary will be inaccessible to English readers. Where there are points of repetition in the text, some passages have been allowed to stand, while elsewhere a few small cuts have been made (indicated by square brackets).

A note on the translation of Brecht's key terms – '*Gestus*', '*Verfremdung*', etc. – is given at the point at which they are first used in the book.

In most cases quotations by other authors, even where they already exist in English, are translated afresh.

Titles of plays and books have been given where they exist in English, or otherwise translated within brackets.

Footnotes are by the author except where indicated.

AH

PREFACE

A Companion to Brecht?

Brecht is back in fashion. Intellectuals as well as politicians of every persuasion quote him to support their views. Likewise, his marketability seems assured, as the Brecht-Institute at the University of Karlsruhe has released an online communiqué bearing the title 'Brecht – the Goethe of the twenty-first century'.

This would certainly have amused Brecht. If you ever asked him why he enjoyed such popularity, he would reply quite simply: 'Brecht's slogans are the best'.

But seriously: such attempts to neutralize Brecht by popularizing rather than ignoring him are not reason enough for a new Brecht Companion. The best way of countering such attempts effectively is to let Brecht himself answer. His texts, whenever quoted and to whatever purpose, always speak for themselves.

But as far as theatre practice is concerned, in the course of recent workshops in Leipzig, Graz, London, Istanbul and Havana one thing has struck me in particular: questions are once more outnumbering opinions. This would appear to prove one of Marx's encouraging theses, that 'it is not enough for thought to strive for realisation, reality must strive towards thought'. You simply cannot ignore any longer how bleak the social, political and cultural landscape has become. But bleak conditions specifically do not – as many theatres today are claiming and marketing – axiomatically lead to bleakness (and thus to acceptance); rather they raise the question as to why something must be bleak in the first place. And here there is no way round Brecht. In response to such questions the old dialectician virtually demands to be heard, as he claims in his poem 'To Those Born Later' ('An die Nachgeborenen'), that it is not injustice in the world that makes him despair but 'if there were only injustice and no anger'. The world is getting anxious again. And anxiety is spreading. And with it the interest in Brecht.

But another thing struck me as well: within the theatre too knowledge is on the decline. Being willing by no means translates into being knowledgeable. Instead, there is widespread ignorance of what is unknown. Thus drama students about to graduate were not at all troubled that they had never heard of names like Therese Giehse, Helene Weigel, Charles Laughton, Laurence Olivier, Fritz Kortner, Buster Keaton, Yves Montand, Giorgio Strehler, Ekkehard Schall, etc. They simply had no idea these people had ever existed. But where knowledge is absent, opinions begin to rule, and where opinions rule, the media rule, and where the media rule, the mainstream rules. And the mainstream has dictated what should happen with 'Old Brecht': the writer is retained and admired (Goethe of the twenty-first century, and so on), and the thinker is avoided. For everything about Brecht's theory supposedly comes from a time when people placed a misguided faith in science as they unsuccessfully attempted to use it to force human progress, and tried 'to make theatre scientific' so that it could be used to support the ideological aims of a progress that was unreal. Thus theatre became 'Brechtian theatre'. However, 'Brechtian theatre', or so it is claimed, lost sight of reality by becoming too complex, and with this its sense for humanity's imponderables. Following this logic, 'Back to Brecht!' can only mean: away from his mistakes and back to his literature. Away from his commitment to collectivity, and back to freedom of the individual. The safest course of action: away with Brechtian theatre!

So to claim then, as this 'Companion' does, that Brecht simplified theatre in order to open it up to realities, must appear a little curious at the very least. And that is precisely my intention. My collaboration with Brecht, which lasted five years up to his death, and my examination of his work, which has lasted up to the present day, have led me to believe that 'wondering', finding things curious, actually *is* that very simplification. Or put in another, very 'un-Brechtian', way: the simple act whereby somebody wonders about something in the theatre is in fact the entire secret behind 'Brechtian theatre'. Aristotle wanted to arouse pity and fear in the theatre in order to purge the audience of pity and fear. Brecht 'merely' wants the audience to wonder. For wondering purges the spectator of his tendency to take things for granted, a tendency whereby familiarity stops him from seeing things as they really are. Thus one discovers for example that something that seems unchangeable has actually only been unchanged for a long time. Or that eternal truths are the gaps that time inflicts in our knowledge.

For as long as man could remember, it was taken for granted that an apple should fall to the ground until, so the story goes, one day Isaac Newton wondered in his garden why it is that an apple falls down and not up. He discovered gravity. If Aristotelian pity really arouses fear and suffering in the spectator, Brecht's wondering is by contrast a rather cheerful affair, because it leads to discoveries. And discoveries tend to satisfy curiosity, meaning they are fun.[1] And that's why I am claiming that 'Brechtian theatre' should above all else be fun. And that for example Brecht's entire engagement with science and politics, an engagement that is in truth not uncomplicated, did not make theatre more complicated, but rather quite the opposite, *more theatrical* (also so that politics and science can gain more from theatre again).[2] For, whatever it does, theatre must remain theatre, meaning a luxury. But it is said that luxuries are what makes life worthwhile. Or, as you can read in Brecht: 'What is the point in achieving something if it affords no reward to you?' And in theatre people afford themselves precisely the luxury of a 'premonition of the human condition' (Bloch) and then as a result inspire and encourage themselves to set about making this condition a reality.

To be sure, this aim is even further away today than in Brecht's time; but shouldn't that be a greater reason for taking it on? And sure, there is much we can't yet afford today and much we can no longer afford; yet that is another reason to insist on it. 'Whoever fights, can lose; whoever does not fight has already lost', Brecht believed in the thirties, responding to the defeat that back then was staring everybody in the face. Ernst Bloch spoke in 'dark times' of the 'ontology of not-yet-being'. And Ernesto Guevara, the revolutionary 'Che', only called a realist someone who attempts the impossible.

For the coward not only has no future, he also has no fun. But as history shows us, without fun no serious problem has ever been solved in this world, at least not seriously.

And so this Companion aims to gather together facts, views, experiences, stories, observations, ways of thinking, suspicions, errors, and reports on rehearsal practice and experiments that stem from my time working with Brecht and later my work with his theatre, in an attempt to prevent them from being forgotten and to make them available to everyone who is interested in Brecht and wants to use him in their work. I also consider where and how Brecht can be found, or not found, in contemporary theatre. And it offers those who reject Brecht the chance to reject the right thing.

And perhaps I will manage to apply Brechtian *Verfremdung* to Brecht himself to encourage us all for a change not, as I have often done myself, by drawing primarily on the aspect of deliberate 'interventionist thinking' to describe his theatre, but simply by daring better theatre. In short: to dare to enjoy and to play.

Manfred Wekwerth
Berlin-Grünau, February 2009

1

BRECHT'S THEATRE

An Extended Overview

Taken together, the three articles in this part – all of them extended lectures – form more than half the book, and the longest of these by far is the first, 'Brechtian Theatre Today', the Stockholm Seminar. This is one of the most sustained and comprehensive single accounts that Manfred Wekwerth has written about Brecht. Dating from the late 1970s, it appears here substantially revised. Of the other two pieces, 'Brecht's Simplicity' was written for a conference in 2006, and 'Brechtian Theatre – an Opportunity for the Future?' – though parts date back to the late 1990s – was primarily written for a theatre colloquium in Cuba in 2004. These pieces have been grouped together because they provide an overview of Brecht and a detailed discussion of key aspects of his work. All three reflect Wekwerth's review of Brecht in the light of the changes following 1989 and the crisis that has overtaken capitalist economies since 2007.

The 'Stockholm Seminar' begins with a brief Marxist analysis of capitalism. However, recognizing that Brecht's Marxism is an integral element of his approach, Wekwerth bases his commentary on the economic and political insights of, not so much the failed institutional Marxism of the GDR, but the liberating Marxism and socialism of a variety of thinkers from Benjamin and Gramsci to Habermas, Chomsky and Brecht himself. Wekwerth takes the prevailing myths and misconceptions about Brecht and systematically disposes of them. He then sets out to explain what Brecht was really doing. His account of Brecht's theatre is then enhanced by inclusion of personal memories of his experience of working with Brecht himself. He demonstrates that Brecht's theatre is not a matter of now all-too-familiar techniques but a critical and playful attitude and an engaging way of challenging and questioning our own changing world.

Readers interested in Brecht's practice will find that he provides useful explanations of some key aspects such as the following:

- the relationship to Stanislavski's approach to acting
- 'naivety' and Brecht's 'philosophical folk theatre'
- taking a critical stance or attitude ('kritische Haltung')
- showing the world as changing and changeable
- developing the 'Not-But' in events and the prompting of alternatives
- *Verfremdung* and *Verfremdungseffekt* – the technique of 'making things strange'
- historicization, and developing the tension between actuality and the fictional analogue
- developing the *Fabel*, the story-telling dramaturgy
- the principle of 'one-thing-after-another'
- the *Gestus* of showing and what is shown
- dialectical thinking – seeking and highlighting contradictions
- the active role of the spectator
- the politics of theatre
- and, above all, pleasure, playfulness and enjoyment – and the value of comedy.

These aspects are explained, not in isolation, but as part of Brecht's whole approach to theatre.

AH

BRECHTIAN THEATRE TODAY

An Attempt in Seven Days

Stockholm seminar[1]

Day one

'Brechtian Theatre Today' – I don't much like this title (even though I approved it). It's a title that doesn't see fit to ask what exactly Brechtian theatre is. Often enough 'Brechtian theatre', which everyone thinks they know plenty about, is considered a question of social conscience, fashion, or taste, but not a scholarly concept.[2] Yet again, the scholarly language to talk about theatre is missing. Indeed, most theatre practitioners refuse to talk about theatre in theoretical terms, just as lyric poets are upset if you talk objectively about lyric poetry, and not lyrically. The logical consequence of this would be that in order to talk about operas you have to sing. So we really do need some theoretical concepts in order to understand what we are doing when we engage in theatre, and why what we are doing gives other people pleasure. The theoretical concepts we use might not be entirely free from contradictions, but they at least should not be made to mean the exact opposite of themselves. That begins with the concept 'Brechtian theatre'. Like so many things today, it has been sorely abused by creative writers and critical commentators. For one group, Brechtian theatre is the trite problem-solver of past times, when there was still hope for the future; for the other it already is this hoped-for future. Both are equally off the mark. They are mere speculations.

First: Brechtian theatre, before it is anything else, is theatre. Not just a specific theatre that only produces works by Brecht, but – as should be the case for a 'proper' theatre – a theatre that seeks to entertain its audience with everything that world literature can offer.[3] When Brecht returned from exile to Berlin at the end of 1948 and began writing theatre once more, people expected him, in the light of 'the rubble not just on the ground but also in everyone's heads', to produce *Lehrstücke* (learning plays), similar to his work from the 1930s, where pedagogy was substituted for pleasure. Brecht himself had contributed to this with his radical polemic against 'the culinary'. *The Short Organum for the Theatre*, written shortly before his return to Berlin, begins however with the following words:

> Let us therefore cause general dismay by retracting our intention to emigrate from the realm of the pleasing and let it be known, to even more general dismay, that we are planning to settle in this very realm. Let us treat theatre as a place of entertainment, as is only right when debating aesthetics, and examine what kind of entertainment most appeals to us.

In Brecht's theatre there will not be any pedagogical instruction that isn't entertaining. No philosophy that isn't enjoyable, and no politics without pleasure. Pleasure not just in the light-hearted, but also, as Schiller had already envisaged, in *the tragic* too. While working in 1953 on Erwin Strittmatter's comedy *Katzgraben*, the first 'contemporary play' produced by the Berliner Ensemble and which describes the history of a GDR village at the time of the land reform, Brecht went one step further:

> It is not asking enough when one only asks of theatre that it provide realizations, insightful representations of reality. Our theatre must inspire joy in the act of realization, guide people's pleasure in changing reality. Our audience must not merely hear how Prometheus is freed from his chains, they must also be schooled in the joy of freeing him. All the joys and pleasures experienced by inventors and discoverers, the liberators' sense of triumph, these must be taught by our theatre.

If you look through Brecht's texts with an eye not to the content but to statistical probability, that is to say not considering what they mean but how often individual words appear in them, you will make a curious discovery: 'recognizing', 'changing', 'producing' seldom appear on their own. Mostly you will read: 'the joy in recognizing', 'the passion in producing', 'the fun in changing', 'the wit in making about-turns and jumps', 'the gratification in discovering and inventing', 'the pleasure in the instability of things'. These concepts – pleasure, joy, gratification, fun – tend to be overlooked or consciously omitted.

Because they correspond better to the false image of Brecht the rationalist, 'pure' productivity, 'pure' realization, 'pure' thought are adhered to – without the theatre. In one of the last conversations I had with him in autumn 1956, Brecht complained that people don't approach his theatre *naively*. Rather, they view it as 'a means of producing ideas', or 'a place for trying out thought-experiments', or even as a 'political reform centre'. As if he wanted to replace feelings and fun in his theatre with thoughts and morals, and pleasure with pedagogy. Or indeed theatre with scientific discourse. He claimed to have had recourse to science in order to help theatre become more theatrical, and with that more enjoyable, something which – in Brecht's opinion – had got lost in bourgeois theatre. He felt that bourgeois theatre – admittedly with a number of major exceptions – was increasingly engaging in phoney substitutes. It was replacing art with artifice, storms with storms in a teacup, and catharsis, so important to everyone, was in reality now just a cheap massage of the soul. Out of variety had come a superabundance, stories were interpreted before they had even been told, and everywhere an arty sense pregnant with presentiment was covering up meaningless nonsense. Shakespeare too eventually turned to scholarship in order to find his way back to strong stories that would actually interest people and were no longer being delivered by the court theatre.

Certainly in Shakespeare's day Plutarch, for example, was translated into English for the first time and Shakespeare used his *The Lives of Great Greeks and Romans* directly as the basis for his plays *Coriolanus* and *Julius Caesar*, passionate pamphlets about the value and danger of great men in history. Or let's take the example of the philosopher Thomas More, author of *Utopia* and a contemporary of Shakespeare. His biography of King Richard III (a falsification, incidentally) was used by the young Shakespeare immediately after its publication for his work *The Life and Death of King Richard the Third*, probably one of his most influential plays. And Brecht likewise used for his theatre the scholarship of *his* time, which was influenced by the natural sciences, economics, behavioural research, linguistics, but above all the dialectics of Hegel and Marx. The philosopher Wolfgang Fritz Haug[4] is even of the opinion that it was his engagement with scientific discourse, in this case Marxism, that allowed Brecht to overcome, also with regard to his literary output, the crisis of his individual anti-bourgeois protest which had run its course by the mid-1920s. Brecht appears to confirm this thesis in an entry to his work notebooks from 1928: 'When I read Marx's *Capital*, I understood my plays.' So Brecht was not interested – contrary to all rumours – in making theatre more academic, or more political; rather, he wanted to make *more theatre*. More specifically, he wanted to return to great theatre – with the help of scholarship and politics. He wanted to return to enjoyment.

'Enjoyment' is something that those on the political Left have only ever spoken about occasionally, and then with some embarrassment, because they consider enjoyment to be a luxury, and luxury to be a bourgeois excess. The 1968 revolutionaries went even further: they cast out aesthetics of any description as complicit with the 'repressive tolerance' with which they claimed the bourgeoisie tried to divert attention from the contradictions of reality. They went so far as to demand a 'revolutionary ban on culture', which was supposed to counter the 'autonomy of the cultural'. The aim was to say what had to be said in an 'elementary' fashion, without 'trivializing it through the transformations of art'. Yet enjoyment is one of the founding precepts of Marxism. A Marxism, however, that stems from Marx and which Brecht strictly differentiated from 'Murxism',[5] which was also popular in the GDR: 'Marxism, in its current widespread form of Murxism, is terrible because it makes asses unbeatable in debate'. Enjoyment can be found in Marx where you would least expect it: in his *Contribution to the Critique of Political Economy*. Here Marx argues that man's purpose isn't to produce, but rather that the purpose of all production is man alone. Man, in his 'conscious everyday activity', is the sole purpose of this activity. He isn't working for a higher being, nor does a higher being work him. He works for himself, and with this he also produces himself. And because man, through his activity as a social being, produces himself as he develops, he produces – without knowing or wanting to – precisely those 'higher beings' who reign over him and whom he has to serve 'in Heaven as on earth'. In reality however, Marx claims, it is man himself who makes 'God in his own image'. But in order to realize this, a long evolution across history is necessary. Marx believes that if man is to conceive of himself as a 'higher being' and use this realization to his advantage, then enormous 'efforts within society' are necessary, ultimately 'revolutionizing society from the bottom up'. Only in this manner can be formed the 'associations of free producers', which, by socializing the means of production, overcome the absurd contradiction of capitalism which allows communal production on the one hand and private ownership on the other. With this, the false belief that man is from birth onwards the subject of some kind of 'higher being' would also be rejected. The condition for realizing this state of affairs and putting such knowledge to good use is a 'general equality' between people. Not, Marx warns, in order to make everyone the same (as is usually suspected), but to give them the same chances. For social equality does not mean making people the same and eradicating their individuality (as is repeatedly claimed). On the contrary. 'Only when everyone is standing on the same footing can differences become apparent', Brecht writes in his *Me-Ti: Book of Changes*. Extending an individual's social relations, precisely by enabling equal opportunities, also extends his scope for personal fulfilment. Marx writes in the *Contribution*:

> And so the old understanding, whereby man, in whatever narrow-minded national, religious, or political context he places himself, appears to be the purpose of production, may seem considerably superior to the modern world, where production now appears to be the purpose of man, and wealth the purpose of production. But if we look beyond the narrow-minded bourgeois context, what is wealth other than a universality of needs, skills, pleasures, and the productive capacities of individuals that is attained through universal exchange?

Marx valued enjoyment (and more precisely 'human' enjoyment, which he distinguished from the 'primitive' or 'that of beasts') as something essential to man, something that ultimately makes man man. Enjoyment for Marx allows man self-affirmation. Or as he puts it: 'self-affirmation as man's sensual appropriation of his humanity'. Man recognizes himself in the works he has created and enjoys his ability to realize himself in objects. This differentiates him from a purely 'natural being', such as an animal, which in order to survive has to adapt to its environment and in so doing develops extensive adaptational skills. The philosopher Wolfgang Harich[6] writes:

> Man is not just biologically but above all historically conditioned. The more he produces, the more he loses his natural ability to adapt to his environment and, as a result of this 'biological deficiency', is forced to create a 'cultural environment' for himself. [I like the tangible scope of the concept 'culture' as it is used here, MW.] Man as a historical being does not adapt to his natural environment, but instead he changes it (whereby of course he never stops being a part of nature). And as he changes the world, he changes himself. For every appropriation is also always a production. Satisfying his needs, man constantly creates new needs. This is interesting: Marx does not consider man's first historical deed to have

been the satisfaction of pre-existing needs, but rather the creation of new ones.

And Wolfgang Harich, whom I particularly admire, even suggests that man is faced only with the alternative 'create more, or perish'.

However, in the 'pre-history of man' (Wolfgang Harich), in the greatest part of our history, therefore, during the course of which man and his labour eventually become commodities in their own right, the results of man's own work strike him as independent objects that remain foreign to him. This puzzling interpretation, which people were long at a loss to explain without mystifying it, was revealed by Marx to be a decisive phenomenon in social systems that are based on the production of commodities, including therefore today's capitalism. In the first volume of *Capital* he calls this 'commodity fetishism'. In taking on the form of a commodity, products created by one's own hand are no longer available for personal use, because their purpose is solely to be used by others, with whom they will be exchanged. The value of a commodity therefore does not emerge in its use but rather through exchange alone. However, those involved in the exchange experience this value, the product purely of human activity (production, exchange), as a quality of the work itself, just as it is a quality of sugar, for example, to be sweet. In today's bourgeois economy there is even such a thing as a 'pancake theory'. According to this, the value of a commodity is in the commodity itself, just as the sweet filling is in the pancake. With this, the relationship between people, production, and the act of exchange is 'objectified'. Something that man made by his own hand denies its human provenance: it becomes a fetish. These inverted relationships lend the fruits of human work a – as Marx terms it – 'ghostly objectivity'. And he writes: 'In this *quid pro quo* (exchange), the products of work become commodities, tangible, intangible or social objects […]. Nothing more than the specific social circumstances of man himself are in evidence here, but they take on the illusory form of a relationship between objects.'

Yes, the product of man gains power over man, as can easily be seen today in the totalitarian reign of capital finance, also known as 'the finance bubble'. It is capital's leap of faith towards complete independence, that absurd 'upswing' into the unreal, where man for a time can make more profit than is actually produced. Bankers, once the economy's servants, uncouple themselves from the 'real' economy and are able as speculators to turn even 'normal' capitalists into their disciples. Enormous profits derived from speculating bring in 'fictive capital' that is superimposed over the 'real economy' like 'finance bubbles', the economy becomes ever more heated as profits are made to bring in more profits, until eventually it bursts along with the bubble. It is absurd: even as it delivers an 'outstanding performance', capital devalues itself. Successes create crises. Capital is admittedly able to learn, but it is beyond instruction in this respect. Or as a clever economist expresses it (such a thing does still exist today): 'Capitalism shows itself to be meaningful on the small-scale and meaningless on the large-scale' (P. A. Baran[7]). Even though capitalism may appear perfectly rational in individual cases, it plays out an irrational cycle time and time again. Thus the next crisis follows on from the last. But this powerful capital, in whatever form it takes, this Mammon reigning over everything and everyone, is in reality nothing other than a social relationship between people. It is the exploitation of man by man, in a society that divides people into classes – those who own, and those who do not. One group, the owners, own the means to produce, while the other, the vast majority of the 'proletariat' (which translates as 'those who do not own'), does not own any means of producing and has to sell its labour in order to be able to work, and thus to live. (In this respect, the current argument that Marx, when he speaks of the 'working class', refers solely to industrial workers and is therefore losing his relevance in today's world where industrial work is increasingly being replaced by the services industry, is nonsense; Marx always associates the concept of the 'worker' with that of the 'proletarian', i.e. those owning nothing. And their numbers are growing out of all proportion today more than ever before.) The person who owns the means of production, the employer, mistakenly deemed to provide work, takes the worker's work from him, but does not pay (as it appears and the employers claim) for the work; rather, he pays for the labour. For the worker is forced to make his labour 'totally' available to the employer. For labour is a commodity that the worker sells to the employer; he doesn't have anything else he can sell. The price of the commodity labour is determined – as with every commodity – by what is necessary to produce it, so in this case the minimum amount of food, drink and sleep needed by the worker to keep replenishing his labour. This minimum, called a wage, is the tiniest portion of what a worker creates when he works. The tremendous difference between the wage that is paid and the values that are produced, the unpaid 'added work' or 'surplus value', is appropriated by the employer as his 'property'. So in reality he *takes on work* and the worker, who provides the employer with his work, *provides work*. The employer 'expropriates' the worker, he 'bleeds him dry'. And so the worker feels alienated not just from the product of his work, but also from his own work. With this, the worker feels alienated from himself, as he experiences an alienation from his everyday activity. (Incidentally, capital has a further strange quality: it is short-sighted. It is too quick in trying to make a profit and 'forgets' the consequences. So, for example, the employer 'forgets' that the person he 'bleeds dry' in the production process will later on be the purchaser of his products as they circulate around society. Only then periodically to realize that what the purchaser lacks in purchasing power is precisely the amount that the employer 'takes from him', the producer, at regular intervals. 'Tremendous crises, in cyclical rotation, resembling enormous / Invisible searching hands, take a strangling hold on trade, shake the businesses, the markets, the stores in silent rage / Hunger has always plagued the world when the corn silos were empty / But now, no one can understand it, we are starving because they are too full,' said Marx, put into hexameters by Brecht.)

Capital is precisely not, as it seems in our everyday understanding, something 'tangible', that is to say, simply 'monetary assets' or a 'conglomeration of values', or a 'means of production'; capital is, as Marx discovered, a 'value that conjures forth added value', and with this a relationship between people: the 'employer' and the 'employed'. It exists as long as 'the value provides value', and this is achieved by exploiting the 'employed'. Now, constant competition 'in the market' and constantly increasing levels of productivity, which result in constantly depreciating values for individual products (for example through automation and mass production), force the employer constantly to 'overhaul' production by rationalizing it. For 'overthrowing' is capitalism's way of life, as it must constantly 'revolutionize' production in order to 'maintain market position'. We know the results: mass redundancies, unfair wages, longer hours for less pay, 'deregulation' as agreed rates of pay are abolished, constant reduction in contributions to pensions and social security, right down to the legally approved poverty of those on the minimum wage and receiving state benefits. These cutbacks, cynically called 'reforms' today, are part of capital's 'normal' cycle, regardless of whether we are talking about a 'social market economy', a 'participatory workplace model', a 'shareholder society', a 'high-tech society', an 'information age', or a 'knowledge economy'. It is bad, and simply capitalism. Appealing to capitalism to refrain from 'profit dominance' (as leftwing parties' manifestos tend to state) is like appealing to the rain not to be wet. Recently the term 'grasshopper' has emerged. This refers to particularly 'greedy' employers, those 'high-yield hunters' of shareholder value, who act 'egoistically' and 'irresponsibly' towards society. They have been asked 'not to step out of line', but rather to feel responsible for others and to trade 'sensibly' like 'normal' capitalists, in order to avoid showing a 'lack of solidarity' and gambling with people's 'trust'. But this is to overlook (or to want to overlook) the fact that it is entirely 'sensible' for a 'normal' capitalist to behave 'irresponsibly' and with 'a lack of solidarity', that this is in fact one of the prerequisites of his existence. For it is neither the greed nor the bad character of the employer, that is to say the 'egoism underlying human nature' (as Friedrich Engels satirically observes), that determines 'entrepreneurial achievements', but rather the 'silent compulsion of economic circum-stances', as Marx puts it in his occasionally rather Shakespearean style. And that means that one's property and appropriating powers must be mercilessly secured. And Brecht, setting old Marx's texts to verse, continues in hexameters: 'The bourgeoisie's plans produce chaos. The more plans / The more chaos, need arises, where much is produced / To the vast majority the successes have become deadly / Society can no longer live in this system / Of ordered disorder and planned arbitrariness.'

As Brecht formulates it in his *Short Organum*, only by 'over-throwing society' can man's alienation from man gradually be reversed. But before such a revolution can be achieved (or also in times when successful revolutions are being tempered by a con-servative tendency), theatre – indeed art of any kind – can serve, as Ernst Bloch[8] says, 'as a premonition of the human condition'. Art can help to remove the sense that alienation is something entirely natural or God-given, and reveal it as yet another work of man. This makes it possible to criticize, and thus change, the process of alienation. Art can demystify to man's advantage. Above all, the 'premonition' gives man hope and courage to embrace his 'human condition'. The human condition entails the conscious wish and ability on the part of man to emancipate himself, that is to say to recognize his potential and be able to lead a self-determined life. And Marx's 'idea of emancipation' is by no means his only concept dealing with emancipation (and which bourgeois critics today keep strictly separate from his 'analysis of capitalism', in order to discredit emancipation as a revolutionary practice). On the contrary. In his very analysis of capitalism Marx *enacts* his 'idea of emancipation'. For only upon analysing capitalism and how it functions will those devoid of possessions be able to emancipate themselves as they realize the truth of their condition. And: 'How can he who has realized his condition be stopped?', Brecht's In Praise of Dialectics asks. Furthermore, Marx insisted that he wrote *Capital*, by all means a difficult, scholarly book, for the proletariat and not just for the 'educated', or indeed for those employers and bankers today who, fearing a terrible crisis, are all hectically turning to *Capital* in order to save their own capital.

This 'premonition of the human condition' does not just provide man with certain discoveries, it also affords him the enjoyment of being his own 'creator'. Human activity can be understood as the source of all 'creation' and – this is critical – also as the source of all change. For in creating his world, man is constantly changing it – consciously and unconsciously. 'The fact that changing one's circumstances is directly linked to human activity can only be construed as a "revolutionary practice" and understood rationally', according to Marx in his *Theses on Feuerbach*. This applies as much to social revolution as it does to the most mundane of daily tasks. Change is a fundamental part of human life. It turns man from a purely natural being into a historical one. 'To think is to break boundaries', Ernst Bloch contests. And 'enjoying' is also about realizing this; it is about affirming one's humanity to oneself and in so doing appropriating 'the human condition'.

Enjoyment as both the result of man's conscious everyday activity and the driving force behind further activity that has the power to change history and one's daily life alike – here is a key not just to understanding Marx, but also Brecht. These are the roots of his aesthetic: 'In art, people enjoy their life – art offers the artfulness of representations – art renders appearances meaningful – art allows positions to be justified – enjoyment strengthens one's desire to live', Brecht noted in 1956. In this respect, I believe 'Brechtian theatre' is – whether or not one wishes to admit this today – the theatre with the most future. It is not just a theatre among other theatres, that is to say a direction or a fashion; Brecht belongs to theatre like Einstein belongs to physics. For Brecht's significance for theatre is like a 'Copernican revolution'. His point of departure is no longer stated ideas, moralities, aesthetics, pre-formed opinions or ideologies, nor does it derive from abstract plans or moods in the world. Rather, it is the flesh-and-blood person who through his activity seeks to secure his basic needs not just in food, water, and shelter, but also in entertainment. That is to say, those things that make life worth living. 'For what is the point in achieving something if there's no reward for you?', as Brecht writes in his *The Days of the Commune*. For revolutions are not waged, as this play demonstrates, for the sake of waging a revolution, but rather in order to bring about a different human way of life as the tangible result of revolutionary upheavals. And here we should remind ourselves of what is written in the 'book of books', Matthew

4:4: 'Man does not live by bread alone.' The philosopher Wolfgang Heise[9] coined the phrase 'laboratory for the social imagination' for a theatre that unites work and play, realization and enjoyment, everyday life and history within a contradictory whole. Man really does design himself here, and he enjoys himself in the process. He 'plays' with his own self. Here you must dare not only to think interventionist thoughts but above all thoroughly to enjoy yourself. For without enjoyment there is – and not just in theatre – no thought. At least none that achieves anything.

So before we speak about 'Brechtian theatre', we must be clear that we mean 'proper' theatre. Fully fledged theatre with rounded, lively, contradictory, poetic stories and characters. And with effects that stem from light-hearted as well as serious pleasures. With grand feelings and dramatic emotions, then. When Angelika Hurwicz, who played Grusha in the premiere of *The Caucasian Chalk Circle* at the Berliner Ensemble in 1954, came to Brecht to apologize that she must have played her role poorly because the audience was crying at the end, Brecht comforted her: she had played her role well, for here the audience 'was crying in spite of itself'. The decision made by the paupers' judge, Azdak, not to give the child to the aristocratic mother, the 'owner', who 'forgot' it as she fled, but instead to let it stay with the servant, Grusha, who saved and raised it, would hardly have found approval in 'real life' among the largely bourgeois audience at the premiere. If these spectators did applaud it in the theatre, and were even moved to tears by the 'dispossession' of the rich governess, then this just shows what theatre can achieve. Here people were – perhaps even unconsciously – voting for a decision that would be unthinkable in their own lives, where maintaining their private property is God's first commandment.

'Brechtian theatre' is, regardless of all the suspicions levelled against it, theatre that aims to provide enjoyment for its audience. The bourgeois theatre has for a long time failed to create such enjoyment, and 'modern' theatre, misleadingly known as 'director's theatre', has particularly struggled in this respect. This begins with the craft of theatre, with the ability to observe realities and turn them into effective theatre. For example, staging the kind of chaotic situations that frequently occur in today's society not simply in a chaotic manner (which is fairly easy), but rather to use the art of theatre to convey chaos in such a way that the audience – either laughing or crying – understands its extent and the circumstances behind it. Mastering the art of theatre can make even boring stagnation, as characterizes our times, into exciting theatre. Great men of the theatre, if we think of Marivaux,

Ibsen, Chekhov or Beckett, have shown us how to do this. They turned the permanent boredom of their day into the welcome subject of exciting and comic theatre. For this, one must master not just the art of observation but also the craft of theatre itself; otherwise – as is today mostly the case – boredom on stage leads to terrible boredom in the stalls. Konstantin Stanislavski, for example, developed a whole array of 'artistic techniques' to stage boredom: the actor playing boredom shouldn't simply do nothing, but rather quite the opposite, beginning lots of tasks and finishing none. Lacking the basic craft (and necessary interest), directors of 'director's theatre' increasingly turn – even though (or perhaps because) they are talented – to phoney substitutes. Instead of showing processes, they engage in an interpretative acrobatics. The flesh-and-blood person, in as much as he still appears at all, is removed to the – as Walter Benjamin would say – 'icy wastelands of abstraction', where he is left to vegetate as an individual cut off from all society. But here also we are given interpretation instead of presentation: man's abandonment becomes the 'unavoidable price of civilization'; isolation is now 'freedom from peer-pressure', and loneliness 'the chance of lasting individuality'. The lack of social interaction, a problem for many today, is on stage turned into an absolute lack of interaction: the actors simply no longer interact with one another. They no longer say their lines to their partner, but deliver them instead, like arias in old-style opera, on the front of the stage towards the audience. And because people – so it is written in the programme notes – can no longer understand one another in today's 'repressive consensus', the actor speaks his lines so that the audience cannot understand him. (Although mumbling is certainly also a result of successful appearances in afternoon TV shows.) A Berlin production of Ibsen's *The Wild Duck* developed the 'modern approach' into a quasi degree course in the impossible (and was highly praised by reviewers). Ibsen reveals the 'life-lie' that links the Ekdal family's circumstances to those of an injured wild duck that they care for in their home and which gives the Ekdals, in spite of ongoing bitter family feuds, a sense of human and moral security. He does this by carefully building up the 'bourgeois façade' in order then equally carefully to pick it apart. Gradually the 'humanity' and 'morals' of this 'intact' family turn out to be products of its actual depravity. Just where the bourgeoisie thought they were on firm ground, an abyss is revealed. Destroying the 'bourgeois façade', though, is not just the hard critical edge that can be rediscovered in Ibsen, it is also the poetic attraction of his plays. This is what makes their disillusioning practices compelling even today. In

Berlin, however, the detour via Ibsen is avoided. The director gets straight to the point. The social criticism that is still considered relevant 'nowadays' should not be 'dressed up in bourgeois garb'. It should be 'naked'. This means 'total rejection' of the 'bourgeois façade'– and simply the absolute abyss. To this effect, an empty slope is erected, on which one quite literally slips into the abyss, for the actors have considerable difficulty standing on it. Rejecting 'bourgeois façade' (stage backdrops, etc.) of course means rejecting 'complex' acting. The audience mustn't be able to 'hide in bourgeois trimmings', it is confronted 'full on' with the message: everything is sliding into the abyss (slope). And with it, everything of any substance has been said about Ibsen's *Wild Duck*.[10] The 'deconstruction of bourgeois theatre', which the review pages thought to discern in these performances, turns out on closer inspection to be something completely different. It is the end of theatre, something that the puritans in England had already attempted to no avail over three centuries ago, as they tried to prevent people being distracted by the 'treacherous pretence of art' from their duties 'in this harsh life'. But for me, the high point of these 'natural' (or rather: naturalistic) inventions (morals going downhill = slipping down a slope) was a performance of Chekhov's *Ivanov*, also in Berlin. Here, in order to show the impenetrability of social relations 'without ideological masquerade', the whole stage was engulfed in a thick pyrotechnic smoke so that the audience really couldn't see the characters any more. Then, when the audience is left cold because they cannot even see the actors, never mind the point, the play is judged successfully to have portrayed 'man's utter helplessness in today's globalized world'. Techniques that were supposed to ban 'ideology' from the stage turn out to be ideological themselves: they are nothing more than interpretations of reality, without any reality to back them up. And, just like every false ideology, they make the paradoxes of our modern world even more confusing, rather than 'opening them up'. 'Director's theatre' reveals itself, in its 'naked' form, to be the opposite of what it intends: ideological theatre. But ideological theatre almost certainly entails losing the craft of theatre. Wherever showing is replaced by interpreting, craft is no longer required. 'Losing craft' according to Giorgio Strehler, probably one of the greatest theatre directors of the twentieth century, 'is losing the world'. Brecht incidentally also considered that an essential part of the craft of theatre was to avoid two 'simple' things that should absolutely never be allowed on stage: 'over-egging' and 'pre-empting'. 'Over-egging' is when, for example, an actor delivers a tragic speech in a tragic voice, while the stage is darkened to underline that this is a tragic moment, and tragic music is played to further emphasize the point. 'Pre-empting is', according to Brecht, 'quite simply theft'. Discovering in Ben Jonson's *Volpone*, for example, that the toadying Mosca's touching care and concern stem not from human kindness but from financial greed, is something that should be left to the audience. But in a recent production of it the audience was 'robbed' of its pleasure before the play had even started. For it was impossible to overlook that the whole stage scenery was blatantly built on a huge gold coin, making abundantly clear that this was all about money. 'Pre-empting is precluding' is an old theatre motto. This was also the case in an otherwise interesting and engaging theatre production of Choderlos de Laclos's epistolary novel *Dangerous Liaisons*. Here the moral depravity of the French nobility during the 'grand siècle' was conveyed quite simply by showing the characters in a poor light right from the start: in their clothes, language, and manners. With this, Laclos's extensive (and excellent) criticism of the nobility, who engaged in their crimes with the highest standards of elegance and behaviour and in a language that would honour Racine, was utterly wasted. Here too the audience is 'robbed' of the pleasure of discovering by itself that (like today) the 'elevated language' and 'impeccable manners' of those in charge almost certainly lead to them committing crimes while maintaining the 'greatest of claims to morality'. What may sound daring, bold, interesting, or even comical in this description is in reality elementary boredom. Visions become otherworldly, leaving the audience behind in the monotony of an eternal present. Imagination is now just an image, drawing a design, directing a director's idea. Whether spoken with approval or complaint, the stagnation of our world, and with this the end of history, is declaimed from the stage. The world – according to this message – has fallen apart into a superabundance of unconnected and unconnectable details. Everyone is on his own and looks only to himself. 'Liberalism' is the complete freedom to look after yourself entirely on your own. If you succeed in life you are a winner, if you fail no society is to be made responsible for the fact that you are a loser. TINA (There Is No Alternative)[11] is the new doctrine of salvation, invented by Margaret Thatcher, the first lady of a time that calls itself 'neo-liberal' because times never were so 'liberal' in turning everything, absolutely everything into money, people included. For man is – in life as in theatre – absolutely free to accept this situation. Or, as the review sections put it – fall into line with the 'pressure to conform to the majority'. This is a return to 'the state of self-inflicted immaturity', a state which Immanuel Kant did however urgently exhort us to 'exit'. For immaturity entails not just being unable to see certain things, but also being deprived of a number of enjoyments, including the most important of all: humour. The audience is left replete, but empty. And once you've had enough of these boring interpretative orgies, you sell it on by talking it up. For the value of an evening's theatre is determined – like the value of other commodities – by what people are prepared to pay for it. And so boredom too, when a corresponding investment has been made, becomes an artistic value that can be purchased with an overpriced ticket. Brecht's comment that he only invented his theatre because as a young man he was so bored by the theatre in Augsburg seems to be no mere anecdote after all. And his jokes about 'the bourgeois theatre's development from moronic to fine boredom' were also apparently not just jokes.

Day two

But back to 'Brechtian theatre'. Of course none of this has amounted to a definition yet. So what is 'Brechtian theatre'? And not just according to philosophers or *The Contribution to the Critique of Political Economy*, but in the theatre itself – that is to say, on the evening of a performance, in those 'windowless rooms' that claim to be the world? Brecht's penchant for pithy definitions is well known: 'What cannot be said in one sentence does not say enough.' Perhaps his answer to the question of 'Brechtian theatre' would have been: 'Theatre's noblest practice is to entertain the audience, and to do so as adequately as possible.' This in any case is what he says in his theoretical writings. But it leads straight to the next question: what is adequate? Before I try to say what it is, or might be, I would like to say what it *is not*. I want to set out three misconceptions, which are as widespread as they are false. In Stockholm when I held these lectures, the first question I was asked was always whether we worked in the 'Brechtian style' at the Berliner Ensemble. Because we didn't, I asked for an explanation as to what this style was. The answer came without hesitation: a grey, empty stage, a half-curtain, visible scene changes, sparse décor, sober acting, all passions and emotions avoided, enlightenment without any real suspense, an epic scope, and regular interruptions via scene titles and songs. In other words, educating the audience without any recourse to the 'culinary', or, in short, the way Brecht himself was believed to have produced *Mother Courage* as a 'model' play at the Deutsches Theater in 1949 post-war Berlin. I shall come back to this.

Misconception number one

The Brechtian style

For many, this is the main criterion for 'Brechtian theatre'. In England it has had disastrous consequences. When *Mother Courage and Her Children* was staged there for the first time in the 1960s, people were shocked that the audience laughed in a number of places. This was considered 'culinary'. Brecht supposedly wanted spectators who would learn from what they saw. And because no one could imagine that learning might be light-hearted, any kind of humour – and this in the land of Shakespeare – was distrusted. If there was any tension in the play – for example as a result of contradictory behaviour from the characters – people were equally shocked, as tension was considered to be the opposite of 'epic theatre'. Brecht has an exciting message in this play: that people 'naturally' learn as little from catastrophes as guinea pigs do from laboratory experiments, and that war, rendered possible only through their active participation in the first place, 'not only inflicts distress but also the inability to learn'. However, it was presented in such a simplified, black-and-white way that it was turned into unwitting praise for 'the human virtue of perseverance', for example when Mother Courage is considered at the end to return 'courageously' to war in spite of all the 'atrocities' she suffers. This is about the most boring message imaginable, proclaimed in every bourgeois second-rate theatre. As a result, Brecht already had the reputation of a 'great bore' before the Berliner Ensemble was ever invited to London. Directors, however, celebrated an asceticism that carefully avoided pleasure (and naturally resulted time and again in failure at the box office) as the right way of dealing with Brecht. They called it 'Brechtian style'. And it spells not just the end of Brecht, but of theatre itself. ('Brechtian style' was incidentally invented by the same people who nowadays damn him as outspokenly as they once revered him.)

The legendary performance of Mother Courage in war-torn Berlin of 1949 with which 'Brechtian style' is so popularly associated was in reality anything other than a demonstration 'without passion or emotion'. The style of this production, its aesthetic, was determined by its concrete circumstances. The audience, still caught in the Nazis' pathos-laden understanding of war, was to be confronted with the reality of the war that had just finished, and above all it was to be confronted with the futility of participating in war, as 'the ordinary man has little to win from the war of the great, but everything to lose'.

So the point was to tell the story of Mother Courage in such a way that those who at the end of the war saw themselves as merely having gone along with it, or even been its victims, realized their guilt in having made that war possible in the first place. The famous 'empty stage' was no empty stage, the backdrop was so to speak outside the front door, and the audience brought it into the theatre with them: it was the ruins of a whole city, the result of a war that Brecht had warned against in vain. The audience projected their own immediate experience of war onto the stage, and thus the empty stage was not empty for these people, it was filled with their personal 'images' of the war that had just passed. Certainly, *Mother Courage* was played in a 'sober' tone. But it was a 'sobering up', such as might be administered to drug abusers. Nazism was the drug, and in the theatre, or the 'Göring theatre' as Brecht called it, it had indulged in excesses of jubilation and teary pathos in order to carry on arousing feelings of grandeur even in respect of the bestial horrors of war. Even those who were mourning their fallen husbands and sons and beginning to see that war was a misfortune for them wanted the death of their husbands and sons at least to have had some point, for them to have fallen for the 'unfortunate fatherland'. Those who had little more than their grief wanted this grief, also after defeat, at least to be 'proud'.

Under these circumstances, having the courage to perform 'soberly', not to represent war as a victory fanfare or funereal lament but rather as 'nowt but business, and with lead, not cheese' stems not from 'the sobriety of Brecht the enlightener', but rather from his impassioned attack on the lie of war. And it was exactly this 'sobriety' that unleashed passions among his audience. People were passionately enraged by the way their 'heroes', who here only wanted to 'take their cut' from war, were made to lose face. Even members of the audience who had fought against Hitler protested. They wanted to have fought at least against 'lowly demons', not 'cheese merchants'. On one occasion, while on tour in Mecklenburg, the Berliner Ensemble showed *Mother Courage* as part of the trade union theatre weeks. People stormed the stage at the end and pulled down the half-curtain. They found the sobriety, or rather 'sobering up', so painful, that they were moved (intentionally) to protest in the strongest of terms, and in so doing slowly came to realize the truth of wars that are little more than 'bigwigs' pillaging. 'Sobriety' here was a deliberately chosen aesthetic technique, and a very effective one at that.

However, for many sobriety became the essence of 'Brechtian style'. They completely overlooked the fact that Brecht's production of *The Caucasian Chalk Circle* only several years later pulsated with a colour and an energy that had seldom been seen on the German stage before. The 'heroes' here were lovingly drawn characters who wanted not to win foreign lands but rather the favour of their fellow citizens by being useful. There's the servant Grusha, for example, who can't let anything go to waste. Neither the daily bread nor the governess's child, whom the 'bigwigs' 'forget' as they flee. These 'heroes' are cautious people who also have to be cautious with their own heroism. And so Grusha abandons the child she saved in order to free herself from danger, before she eventually takes him back in for good. These 'heroes' also have to think of themselves, as nobody else will. And – as the example of the paupers' judge Azdak demonstrates – you don't have to be born a hero in order to perform this 'heroism'. Goodness is not a God-given quality, but rather the result of good deeds. The development from *Mother Courage* to the *Chalk Circle* is often overlooked by those who only want to understand Brecht through his stylistics. Or take the example of the half-curtain, the so-called Brechtian curtain. It was supposed to help the audience question the realities presented on stage at a time when audiences were otherwise used to the heavy velvet curtain that, like a fateful guillotine, separated scenes and acts and allowed even the scene changes to seem the work of fate. Suddenly the audience saw scenery and props being changed, heard the noise of this work, and enhanced what they saw through what they experienced as partners and co-workers. The half-curtain signalled, even before it was raised: man is behind man's fate, also in the scene changes. Initially the audience was indignant that the 'cheap' curtain should replace the velvet one. Later on the opposite was the case. If we didn't hang the half-curtain, the audience would insist on having it back. Brecht needed a Brechtian curtain! It was turned into what it had been intended to destroy: a habit. But here too Brecht can help: 'The half-curtain, that linen drape fluttering lightly, should only be used as long as the velvet curtain is missed', Brecht noted once with some irritation; he had seen how the half-curtain was being turned into a Brechtian cliché.

However, there are also performances that come close to Brecht without realizing it. Indeed, they might even hotly deny playing 'in a Brechtian manner'. I am thinking of the performance of Beckett's *Waiting for Godot*, which I saw at the Dramaten in Stockholm.[12] Beckett, of all twentieth-century playwrights, is considered – if we follow the bourgeois classification of literature – to be Brecht's antithesis. But in the Dramaten Beckett was performed in such a manner that he came very close to Brecht. The play's absurdity was not some mythological abstraction of reality, but reality itself. The absurdities, that is to say the contradictions, observed by Beckett with the accuracy of a James Joyce, were shown here to be the behaviour of real people, derived from observing absurd situations. The clownish techniques that were used managed, contrary to the frivolity of other performances, to strengthen the presentation of reality with penetrating exactitude by giving the most ridiculous of situations a degree of normality that resulted in a particularly revealing kind of comedy. Neither fate nor the spirit of the age or the world were at work here, but two sad clowns – who did however have pretensions to being world spirits. In Germany, Beckett's *Waiting for Godot* was generally turned into the dark finale of an 'existential pessimism'. At the Dramaten, the sad state of being 'thrown into' absurdity resulted not in grieving over one's fate but in Swedish merriment: it is not that the world is absurd, but that people make it so. Those who are waiting for Godot to bring salvation are waiting in vain, for they are waiting for something that they themselves will not even do.

So Brecht's theatre cannot be understood with recourse to stylistic technique alone. Brecht himself constantly changed his techniques – as the examples of his productions of *Mother Courage* and *The Caucasian Chalk Circle* show. Brecht even suggested that with each play one should start again from scratch, that is to say, find the aesthetic techniques to arouse surprise, amazement, curiosity.

Misconception number two

It may seem correct to claim that **politics is a key criterion for Brechtian theatre**, but this is only the case at first glance. Of course Brecht's theatre is political theatre. With his *Lehrstücke* he was already directly intervening in politics in the 1920s. Later too it was intended that political processes on stage should lead directly to political action. Think of *Senora Carrar's Rifles*, written during the Spanish Civil War. Here we find in succinct terms: 'You cannot remain neutral!' Bringing current affairs to the stage, directly intervening in political battles, is of course political theatre, particularly in times of open struggles. But it is a widespread misapprehension that only political subjects can yield political theatre. There are of course Brecht plays with major political themes. Think of *The Days of the Commune*, or *Fear and Misery of the Third Reich*, or *The Mother*. But these plays aren't just political because they have a political subject or because political songs are sung in them, but rather because they adopt a certain political stance ('Haltung')[13] and want to spread the message: that social circumstances need to be changed. They aim to induce change, regardless of whether this is in the political or apparently private realm. Nor is *The Caucasian Chalk Circle* a political play just because it has a political prologue. Azdak's decision to award custody of the child not to its biological mother but to its foster mother is also a political stance: 'natural law' is broken in favour of productivity. But *The Caucasian Chalk Circle* also demonstrates – like many of Brecht's plays – characteristics of the parable. If the story of how a child is productively 'expropriated' is applied to a contemporary situation, its tremendous political repercussions quickly become apparent. In 1954 Brecht considered the play a contribution to the emotional debates that were running at the time about the Oder-Neisse border. At the end of the war, former German territories were awarded by the Allies to Poland. This was a good opportunity for reactionary circles to call upon 'natural law', 'patriotically' demanding the return of this territory – and it was not without effect on large parts of the population. It belonged to the Germans because it had always belonged to them, or so the argument went. They neglected to mention how this area had been made into German territory over the course of history, namely through violence. And that German imperialism had twice used the area as the marching ground for massive world wars. At that time, the young GDR accepted the verdict of the paupers' judge Azdak in respect of the Oder-Neisse question: 'That the things as are here should belong to those who do well by them.'

Inversely, an 'unpolitical' subject can be extremely political. Take *A Respectable Wedding*, one of Brecht's early plays, in which the word 'politics' is never mentioned. Many consequently doubt its political value. The 1968 student revolutionaries even rejected it as street theatre, on the grounds that it was petit-bourgeois because it had a petit-bourgeois subject. It does indeed play in a petit-bourgeois setting: a man, who is about to get married, places value on being 'his own master' in everything. So 'out of honour' rather than a lack of funds he constructs all his own furniture, even though he could have bought it cheaply round the corner. At the wedding feast everything falls apart, including the wedding party, for nothing had been properly stuck together. Beyond the situational comedy, the play takes on an eminently political aspect. It is a farce on the petit-bourgeois mantra, 'My home is my castle'. If one considers how many workers, including those here in the GDR who were supposedly living in socialist circumstances, lost all interest in 'the bigger picture' and withdrew into their family, back garden, car, and television, and if one considers what a loss this was not just for society but above all for these workers, then the play's political relevance quickly becomes apparent. Lenin once defined a communist as a lone producer who becomes interested in the entirety of the production process. In *A Respectable Wedding* the opposite happens. Chasing the 'honour' of being his own master, the worker robs himself of the opportunities that society affords him and flees, despite perfectly good furniture shops, into 'private' furniture construction. He emigrates from himself. In retreating out of society into the 'private' realm, he becomes not an 'autonomous individual', but an indistinguishable snob.

Brecht himself never measured the plays of his contemporaries, especially if they claimed to be political, by their 'political' subject, but rather by their political effect. A boring political play was for him an unpolitical play. For boring politics in theatre results in an entirely different political stance: an anti-political one. The political stance that Brecht had in mind doesn't just pertain to the political realm (especially as politics today is generally taken to mean party politics only). It equally pertains to the individual, the private, the intellectual, the emotional, the erotic, indeed even the esoteric if one so desires, and, last but not least, to the religious realms of human existence.

Today, however, many take for granted that political theatre is antiquated. It is believed to be hopelessly outmoded, if not plain risible nowadays. The latter point can't actually be entirely dismissed, if one understands as politics what the so-called 'political class', today's troop of politicians, presents us with, for this really is shoddy farce. But even if you just take Brecht's political theatre, his fate seems sealed. In recent years it was unable to prevent either the complete collapse of our social system, as witnessed by devastating mass unemployment, or the return of war as the continuation of politics, nor even the rebirth of fascism, even though during this time precisely those plays that directly seek to counter such developments were being performed, such as *The Resistible Rise of Arturo Ui* and *Saint Joan of the Stockyards*. But theatre practitioners' distrust, if not outright avoidance of, political theatre usually stems not from rejection on principle, but rather resignation. Its 'resounding ineffectiveness' has proved discouraging. In actual fact, however, such discouragement comes from overestimating theatre in the first place, from expecting it to be able to change the world all on its own. Brecht never claimed that theatre can change the world. Theatre can inflame political movements or dampen them down, but it cannot replace them. However, when it does inflame political movements it is capable of achieving more than all other art forms. Beaumarchais's *The Marriage of Figaro, or The Wild Day* hardly started the French revolution, but within the revolutionary atmosphere of 1784 it did give rise to a movement that directly anticipated the storming of the Bastille. Brecht's *Galileo* couldn't prevent the atomic bomb, but it surely diminished its number of supporters and awakened something of a conscience for the world in many of those who saw the play. A production of Brecht's *Turandot or The Whitewasher's Congress* hasn't managed to stop intellectuals in any society making their support available, at the right price, to the powers that be, but it did give us TUI, Brecht's inversion of the intellectual into a Tellect-Ual-In, a distorted image of the intellectual who will let himself be bought by rulers to carry out their trickery for them.

Theatre's political effects are long term. They can only be discerned in the short term when situations are 'speeded up', like in the French revolution of Beaumarchais's day. But the world is also 'changed' when, for example, audience members who saw Ekkehard Schall as Arturo Ui in the Berliner Ensemble come to realize years later that the production made it impossible for them to even begin to follow the 'nonsensical logic' with which wars today are once more presented as peace-keeping missions or help for the developing world. Certainly, people may also have been able to see through political stupidities before this production of *Arturo Ui*, but the desire to laugh at them straight away and in so doing render them completely powerless would have to count as one of the 'lasting' effects of the theatre experience.

Today much is made of audiences' increasing lack of interest in politics and how it is supposedly responsible for theatre's diminishing importance. Audiences are 'tired of politics'. And so, for example, when evaluating the 1968 student rebellion, people often come to the resigned conclusion that such a political impulse is almost entirely missing among the 'downtrodden' of today, where general acceptance that social circumstances are 'inalterable' has come to predominate. Accordingly, class struggle is deemed no longer to exist, while the employers and the employed alike have concurred with the 'constraints' of globalization. A former 1968 rebel, now a theatre director, seems to confirm this: 'Basically we've lost all our battles. We are broken. We've laid the ground for apathy.' Today's reality has become mired in this 'fog of resignation'. For the onset of such resignation has less to do with a weakening of the individual's will than with different social circumstances. Back in 1968, for example, the economy was 'booming'. True, one might end up in the clink after a 'demo', but never on the dole. In contrast to 1968, when the state openly tried to banish a 'rebellious ideology' with police truncheons on the street, today a 'rebellious ideology' has cleverly been turned into a 'constraint' of its own. It will result directly in you losing your job, if you have one to lose. The fear of ending up on benefits is greater than the anger caused by injustice. Today the state deals with fewer protesters against the 'system' on the streets, dealing with the individual 'at home' instead: he is simply deprived of the minimum required to exist. From there on in, existential angst determines all of his 'ideology', his behaviour included. The threat of being on social benefits is more effective than any police batons. Or, as the writer Heiner Müller put it in the 1990s: 'When unemployment is sufficiently high, there is no need for a state police.' Talk about 'the end of class struggle as a result of resignation from below' is itself nothing other than a new form of class struggle 'from above'. And there is a clear source for that 'fog of resignation': it spreads from the TV screen, the pulpit, and the lectern. The 'unpolitical audience' that is repeatedly invoked here and has apparently given in to its circumstantial 'constraints' should be the inspiration for a re-politicization of the theatre. The 'end of the class struggle' could be shown as an intensification of class struggle. If in times of open class struggles it was possible to presume the audience's interest in politics, because the messages were directly relevant to their daily battles, today this interest needs first to be aroused. But here precisely the 'unpolitical' attitude that is asserted everywhere could be a rewarding theme for political theatre, as it uses all available techniques to penetrate through that 'fog of resignation'. And it should do so by making special use of the most effective technique of all: humour. Brecht probably also meant something similar when, shortly before his death and envisaging what was to come, he described comedy as the most appropriate form of theatre for our times. For it is not just *what* is shown in the theatre, but above all the showing itself, the style, that is political. Theatre's social reality is not simply its existence in society, but its effect on society. It is not just measured in line with what happens on stage, but also with reference to the spectator. Consequently, theatre is not just a reproduction of society, it is above all a part of it. And this as the production happens. For here, as Dario Fo once said, 'laughter opens not just your mouth but also your brain'. Theatre ought, in any case, to show social struggles and use its own techniques to take part in these struggles. As indeed questions about theatre are not just 'questions for the theatre'. Here Georg Christoph Lichtenberg's words from 1777 are relevant: 'Whoever only understands a little about theatre doesn't understand it at all.'

Misconception number three

A final criterion that supposedly defines Brechtian theatre: **the actor's technique**. In mastering the *V-Effekt*, or *Verfremdungseffekt*,[14] the actor apparently demonstrates his character without in any way identifying with him, thus creating the necessary distance for the audience to be enlightened rather than emotional, and rendering it capable of responding critically to what it sees. 'Brechtian theatre' is considered to be less about 'rounded' characters than critiquing characters. The complete opposite of 'Brechtian theatre' is accordingly the 'Stanislavski system', which is still authoritatively represented by Lee Strasberg's school in the USA. Stanislavski, the great Russian theatre reformer, is said to demand complete identification of the actor with his character, in order to inspire a similar level of identification among the audience. This technique is known as 'empathy'. The aim, or so it is understood, is not to critique but to justify the character by having the audience share all his feelings and views. 'Brecht in one corner – Stanislavski in the other' was for a long time the call to arms invoked to cement insurmountable differences between them, and it is still heard today. Officially in the GDR the Stanislavski system was favoured, because it was believed that the process of identification in the theatre would also achieve an identification between the sceptics and the state – and after all Stanislavski carried a 'state blessing' in the Soviet Union, was practically worshipped there like a god, and was supposed to take on a similar position here (which incidentally, at least as far as theatre people are concerned, never happened, for the other 'god', Brecht, was far too present).

It is nonsensical to try to make technical processes (and acting technique is one of these) into a criterion for theatre. Of course the craft of acting underlies all theatre. But while theatre presumes craft, craft alone does not suffice to make theatre. Great talents often 'naturally' possess the right technique. And so Brecht also worked with actors who had never heard of his theory. They nevertheless performed the best kind of theatre in Brecht's sense, as talented actors are generally spontaneous observers of reality and in this sense realists, that is to say they understand people. But these are of course the exceptions. Stanislavski too spoke of how his 'system' (he always put 'system' in inverted commas) was rendered unnecessary by an actor who already possessed a great talent and a sense for realities. His system, he explained, was made for actors who were not in possession of this tremendous (and rare) talent, or for those who were not capable of reproducing with equal vibrancy for each and every performance the things they had practised over and over again in rehearsal. His 'system' was intended to help here. The reason that Stanislavski is mistakenly believed to demand that his actors identify completely with their characters in order to justify them from within lies elsewhere. It is simply ignorance. Clearly only Stanislavski's early writings are widely known, where he really does formulate these kinds of demands. The later writings differ quite considerably on this matter. Here, protocols of his theatre work in later years are available which make it apparent that he not only didn't practise absolute empathy of the actor with the character he was portraying, but expressly rejected it. It was now felt to 'lead to blindness in respect of other social relations which are not known to the character himself'. These relations however, even when the character is not consciously aware of them, are needed in order fully to understand a character's psychology. Stanislavski also considered the actor's starting point not, as is claimed, to be feelings, but rather actions. He calls this 'physical actions': before something can be felt, 'physical' action – concrete situations – must unfold on stage so that the relevant feelings can arise. Brecht follows exactly the same logic when he suggests that characters should be drawn from events, with their personal traits, including feelings, becoming clear in the process. And that a character's personality should not be 'fixed' from the outset, but rather developed as it acts out all its contradictions, and this in accordance with the principle of 'one thing after another'. Clearly, neither Brecht nor Stanislavski can be understood through purely technical criteria, nor can they even be properly distinguished from one another. For of course the views and intentions of the two great theatre practitioners who lived in quite different times are different, but precisely not when it comes to 'technique'. Likewise the claim, as popular as it is false, that Stanislavski demands the actor completely justify the character by completely identifying with him, whereas Brecht demands the character be critiqued, indicates that they have both been equally misunderstood. In one of the very few books that gives reliable information about Stanislavski's working practice, Nikolai Gorchakov's *Stanislavski Directs*, an interesting conversation from 1927 is recorded. It took place during a rehearsal of the revolutionary play *Armoured Train 14–69* and it concerned the presentation of 'negative characters', in this case counter-revolutionaries who were planning and carrying out murders.

OLGA KNIPPER-CHEKHOVA (ACTRESS): What? Then I'd have to kill someone myself first in order to be able to play this scene?

STANISLAVSKI: No, you have to play a so-called 'negative' character. I'm not reproaching you for wanting to make your characters politically and humanly plausible. Far from it. But here we are simply dealing with an actor's own emotion, with the fear of appearing before the audience as a 'negative character'. You'll have to get over this. A negative character commits a murder here.

KNIPPER-CHEKHOVA: No, I'm not capable of that. Take everything you want from me, but I'll never kill anyone.

STANISLAVSKI: But you don't need to kill anyone with your own hands. General Spasski's mercenary soldiers will do that for you.

KNIPPER-CHEKHOVA: I won't kill anyone by the hand of others, either.

STANISLAVSKI (ANNOYED): You are an actress at the Art Theatre and not landed gentry. And you will remain an actress from today when you play nobility from the past. In order to play nobility you don't yourself have to become spiteful and dangerous. It is the aristocratic lady, not you, that your audience is supposed to find spiteful and dangerous. And as an actress you can achieve this by not concealing your opinion of the lady, but by letting it come across even as you play her. You should be able to do this sort of thing, you're an actress after all.

Thus spoke Konstantin Sergeyevich Stanislavski in 1927.

As far as acting technique goes, there is not actually any technique that cannot be used in 'Brechtian theatre', provided it is suitable for revealing contradictions as they occur rather than covering them up. At the Berliner Ensemble we have tried out various techniques (or as Brecht called them 'acting styles'). In *Mother Courage* we reduced those who made much noise about their faith, maternal love, or duty to what they really are: hard-boiled business people. In *The Days of the Commune*, by contrast, we presented as 'extraordinary' those 'ordinary people' who did an extraordinary deed: for seventy-two days they took their fate into their own hands. The Council of the Commune that was elected by the population after the Parisian workers' uprising in 1871 called itself 'the commune of the unknown' in order to stop people feeling shy about refusing, if necessary, to re-elect them the next time round. Here we used the technique of 'making famous', a technique that Brecht liked to use when he was dealing with 'ordinary people'. We tried to show ordinary people as extraordinary, without having them stop being ordinary. We treated the unknown like stars, showed as much interest in Parisian workers as in the kings of Shakespearean history plays. We looked for the smallest behavioural traits in order then to present them as the greatest of character traits:

how do these people celebrate the Commune's election victory on the streets? How do they joke with one another? How do they dance? How does François, the student of theology, now allow himself to discuss sexuality? How does Jean, a young revolutionary, behave when his girl wants him all to herself at last following the victory of the revolution? These people are no 'born revolutionaries'. Quite the opposite. Brecht shows how they become revolutionaries only when no other option is available. Thus in the first scene 'Papa' enters the stage, a builder and member of the National Guard, plagued with rheumatism because, under order of the generals, he had to spend the whole night in the muck and cold, and was unable to see the point of this. The National Guard, primarily consisting of workers from the suburbs, was used by the generals as cannon fodder against the besieging Prussians in order to keep those workers out of Paris. 'Papa' is not thinking so much about revolution as the red wine, that he wants to have, as ever, in his bistro. And then, the ground slips from under him: coming back from battle, he is refused his wine because the price has risen overnight and his pay is no longer enough for even one glass of wine. Neither grand ideas nor programmes make him take to the barricades, just the wine he is refused. He joins the march to the Parisian Hôtel de Ville, and with this begins the revolution that was to last seventy-two days. (Of course, historically speaking this isn't the only reason, but the most immediate for 'Papa'.) When producing *The Days of the Commune*, we did something that is supposedly anathema to Brecht: we used techniques from Stanislavski. During rehearsal, as we constructed the characters, we looked for the most insignificant of details, opinions, moods that could here be the cause of a revolution. We tried to give the characters concrete biographies. In order to achieve this, the actors in rehearsal had to feel their way into the situations, using their observations and knowledge of human nature. The stage designer Karl von Appen drew detailed portraits of the figures before rehearsals started, pulling the 'unknown' out of their self-inflicted anonymity. The revolutionaries were to be shown as radical in the way they got straight down to business, and at the same time as 'endearing'. In Germany, where the revolutionary is a man with a knife between his teeth, this is sufficient to produce a real sense of *Verfremdung*.

We also experimented with 'historical' techniques. In Shakespeare's *Richard III* we used elements of old English folk theatre. Richard III is in bourgeois theatre the epitome of the psychological and physical villain. Famous actors have pulled out all the stops in order to inspire fear and trembling in the audience as early as the very first monologue: here a monster, deformed by a hunchback and a clubfoot, decides to take revenge on the world for his deformities. Oddly enough, this didn't prevent the monster from becoming one of the most popular characters. And this not just among the actors, but also among the audience. For Shakespeare had equipped the villain with far more charm and intelligence than any of the other characters in the play. For a long time this contradiction remained a puzzle. Until the Shakespeare scholar, Robert Weimann, secretly made a momentous discovery in the GDR: hunchback and clubfoot in the old English folk theatre were not at all signs of deformity, but, quite to the contrary, signs of one of the most popular folk characters: the 'Vice'. The Vice in the English folk theatre was the classic jester figure: playmaker, entertainer, sceptic and utopian in one. And just as in Italian theatre the Arlecchino can be identified straight away by his leather mask and patchwork clothes, the English audience recognized the Vice through his hunchback and clubfoot. Likewise, Richard's monologues were, as Weimann discovered, not monologues dripping with deep psychology, but direct addresses to the audience. This entailed a doubling effect: the actor left his character for a few moments, came to the front of the stage, and fraternized with the audience. In these passages, as Weimann proved, the text changes from one line to the next between the English of the courts and the English of the streets. Using this proletarian language Richard – acting now as the Vice – seeks to win the audience's favour to accompany him in his daring attempt to get the crown, that only God can bestow, all by himself – without God: sheer heresy in Shakespeare's day. By way of a comparison, Christopher Marlowe, a contemporary of Shakespeare who equally had his Doctor Faustus blaspheme against God, was sentenced to the dungeons for such heresy, only escaping because he was suddenly murdered. And Weimann made a further important discovery: from the fourth act on, the monologues abruptly stop. Another long-standing puzzle for Shakespeare scholarship, which even went so far as to write this down to the inexperience of a young Shakespeare who 'was running out of ideas'. Weimann had a different explanation: the end of the monologues, or rather the direct addresses, is the actual message of the play. A message that can be found in many other of the Elizabethans' plays: 'power corrodes power'. Having been brought to power by his wits, the first thing the powerful man loses is these very wits. Richard has nothing more pressing to do than to cover up the traces of his 'profane' rise to power so that he can then claim to have been divinely appointed (as US presidents still do today). King Richard insists that he has the crown directly from God and gets rid of everyone who knows anything about his godless rise to power: Lord Buckingham, the kingmaker on the stage, and the audience in the stalls. He has one beheaded, and he studiously ignores the other. It is a fantastic move on the part of Shakespeare to dupe his audience like this. Had they bet in the first half on the wit and charm of this brave 'enlightener' who rejects God, their disappointment in the second half is now all the greater. The same man, once in power, falls prey to the blind delusions conferred by the divine right of kings, just like all other rulers. The actor's technique of – as Brecht termed it – 'duping' causes the audience to identify with Richard in the first half (and the actor can use all his charm and wit to achieve this), only then to realize it has been duped in the second: how could we have trusted and followed such a man? With this, the audience is supposed to relive blow by blow Richard's experimental attempt to gain the crown without God and not initially – as in most productions – damn him as a murderer. That would in any case be an inappropriate interpretation of this play, for murder was a common occurrence among nobility of the time. Furthermore, other characters in the play have significantly more murders on their conscience than Richard (if they actually have a conscience). Weimann's discovery not only enriches our general understanding, above all it increases the possibilities open to the actor. Our 1972 production at the Deutsches Theater in Berlin with Hilmar Thate in

Illustration 1 Manfred Wekwerth in rehearsal of *Richard III*, Act I, with Renate Richter as Lady Anne and Helmuth Lohner as Richard, at Schauspielhaus, Zürich (1974). (Photograph in possession of Manfred Wekwerth.)

31

the lead role and which showed the 'double' Richard for the first time is still classed as legendary today. I have described the work on *Richard III* here in such detail because it shows how even the 'opposite of Brechtian technique', identification, can, under certain conditions, be used to produce *Verfremdung*. But if such a thing is possible, then acting technique alone can hardly be a criterion for 'Brechtian theatre'.

Day three

So what is 'Brechtian theatre', now that we know what it is not? I would like to list four points. Too insubstantial to define it, but perhaps enough to avoid floundering in a jungle of definitions.

Brecht's theatre is: **(1) marked by the standpoint it takes on the world**.

This is generally called a 'world view'. A useful concept, because it also emphasizes the action undertaken by the subject doing the viewing. A standpoint on the world, not a particular dramatic aesthetics, is the be all and end all of Brecht and his theatre. On the fiftieth anniversary of his death, critics once again tried with much to-do to divide him up into author, politician, dramatist, lyricist, the early and the late Brecht, Brecht the theoretician and Brecht the practitioner. This amounts to attempting to render absolute individual periods, remarks, stylistics, concerns, theses and mistakes, in order to avoid having to take the entirety of a work into account that points far beyond the individual man 'Brecht'. When the demand was raised at a Brecht colloquium in Frankfurt am Main to confront Brecht's work first and foremost with the man Brecht who clearly had not only written *Baal* but also lived the experiences within it, I was reminded of the Nazis' reproach that Marx had reduced work to the status of a commodity and himself had syphilis. Furthermore, I am not convinced that anything substantial would change in the theory of relativity if we knew that Einstein was unfaithful to his wife. Michel Foucault is quite right when he describes man as a gap in scholarship. In any case, when we are analysing a work the author's private person should be left to the biographers (after all, they make their living from this) and we should refrain from violently planting the author back into the middle of his plays or texts. I don't mean the subject of a work, but the person himself, about whom in this case we actually know quite enough already in order to understand his viewpoint on the world. Brecht was a communist. One of his favourite rules of thumb was 'to give a concrete analysis of a concrete situation'. And that comes from Lenin.

Brechtian theatre is: **(2) marked by the way it approaches theatre and the world.**

Brechtian theatre is: **(3) marked by the standpoint it takes towards the audience.**

The phrase 'theatre without an audience is nonsense' comes from Brecht – apparently a pleonasm. But there is a type of theatre that makes not winning over the audience but driving them away a criterion for its success. The reason: the audience that is driven away is 'petit-bourgeois'. Furthermore, from an 'intellectual' perspective, theatre is first and foremost self-discovery, that is to say production primarily for producers. The audience is at best tolerated here, and it is certainly not the main focus. In Frankfurt am Main I saw a production of Brecht's *In the Jungle of Cities* that was highly successful in this respect, for after the interval the seats were empty. I was among those who fled. The actors, however, carried on happily; they had after all managed to vanquish the petit-bourgeoisie even before the interval. Beating my retreat, I saw a poster hanging next to the exit which asked in capital letters: 'Can a production be so good, that there is no audience worthy of it?' But when the unworthy audience stayed away completely from the next showing, the artists were enraged; now it was the 'typical petit-bourgeois animosity to culture' that meant they had abandoned the theatre to its struggle for survival. Its attitude to the audience betrays much about a theatre's views and intentions. Brecht's theatre in any case cared about and still cares for the audience as a partner and co-player, for only the audience can put into action what the theatre intends.

Brecht's theatre is: **(4) marked by its way of working.**

With regard to (1)

Of course Brecht's theatre is a materialist theatre, that is to say its starting point is the primacy of the material world, or the well-known thesis: 'It is not people's consciousness that determines their existence, but conversely, their social existence, that determines their consciousness.' This is what Marx says. In Brecht's times it was in fact common knowledge among many theatre practitioners, but these days such an outlook has once again become the exception. For today not only modern theatre practitioners but above all modern philosophers have begun seriously to wonder whether perhaps it is in fact our consciousness alone that determines our existence, indeed whether anything even exists outside of our consciousness. Quite a lot depends on this question after all, in particular the market value of these practitioners and philosophers. For if consciousness (or, as they say, 'the spaces of the mind') is the only real thing in this world, then as the only real thing it should be reflected in their salaries. I am reminded here of a short story by Brecht from his *Me-Ti: Book of Changes* that also deals with the mind and the material:

> At a conference in the town of Wuhan near the banks of the River Yangdsidjiang some philosophers became locked in bitter argument as to whether things are outside us, existing for themselves alone, and without us, or whether they are inside us, existing for us, and not without us; so whether the River Yangdsidjiang really exists or is only present in our mind. The question could not be solved, as an unexpected thaw in the nearby mountains caused the Yangdsidjiang to burst its banks and the arguing parties were all drowned.

And yet: the materialist answer alone to what was known categorically in the GDR as the 'supreme question of philosophy', namely that our existence determines our consciousness, is not sufficient, indeed it is actually 'wrong'. For Marx only invokes it polemically against the idealistic assertion that our consciousness determines our existence. In any case, it is insufficient for the kind of materialism that one needs in order to understand Brecht's theatre. 'The Germans', remarked Brecht in his *Work Journal*, 'have little talent for materialism. Wherever they have any, they immediately turn it into an idea.' Certainly, the experience in the GDR shows how easily a materialist answer to the 'supreme question' can lead to pure idealism. 'Existence', which now rigidly had to determine consciousness, was itself turned over the course of time into a matter of (false) consciousness. It was increasingly made to overlap with the pure belief that something could be 'achieved once and for all'. And the 'supreme question of philosophy' was no longer answered in general philosophical but in contingent political terms. The rule was that 'what had been achieved must be maintained'. Any suggestions for change were not infrequently considered to be 'a disruption to stability' and criticism a hostile intention. The fact that what had been 'achieved' must at some point have come about by changing what had been 'achieved' before, that is to say through criticism, or 'people's conscious activity', was ignored. 'Idealized' materialism, however, turned the result of consciously subjective activity into the *idée fixe* of an 'objective given' which must now guide everything, including consciousness. Marx calls such a move 'the objectification of social relations'. Probably one of the reasons why in the history of the GDR the 'subjective factor', that is to say conscious involvement on the part of the producers in determining and maintaining the state, the industries, and the facilities – in fact a prerequisite of Socialism as an 'association of free producers' – was hardly developed at all. And yet conditions were objectively good, as the state, industries, banks, educational facilities, and the land and soil were all constitutionally 'property of the people'. They should have been made property of the producers not just *de jure*, but also *de facto*.

Brecht's materialist world view, as it concerns us here, is specifically not a case of merely viewing the world as an 'objective given', but asks about the 'subjects' who create the 'world'. It is a question concerning our 'conscious, objective everyday activity' ('bewussten gegenständlichen Lebenstätigkeit'). This has serious consequences for theatre, as theatre has its own means of uncovering the 'human everyday activity' in 'fixed' things and events. But in a negative scenario it can equally make them disappear, 'magic them away', so to speak, turning human activity back into a 'fetish'. Thanks to the 'magic' inherent in plays, also known as the art of deception, theatre is able to make something *really* happen on stage that does not happen at all in reality, but that seems real to the audience. This 'art of deception', a consensus reached with the audience as long as the theatre lasts, is one of theatre's greatest assets. The spectator is thus able to have real first-hand experience of risky situations without actually being exposed to reality. In 1954 Brecht noted on this point in his *Vergnügungen auf dem Theater* (*Pleasures in Theatre*): 'In this manner the spectator can experience more life than just his own and more curious connections between all lives than just at home, none of this with his own body, but all of it with his own eyes.' The theatre can stage murders that shock the audience like real murders but nevertheless make them clap rather than call the police. 'Aristotelian theatre' (which Brecht, drawing on Aristotle's *Poetics*, described as a form of acting that seeks, by encouraging the spectator to identify with the events on stage, to create pity and fear) uses this 'magic' to play the trick of a century: real human interactions are mythologized. The mode of presentation, relying as it does on identification, makes them appear unavoidable. Even everyday events are imbued on stage with the aura of a work of fate; there is no alternative because they seem beyond human intervention. The subjects, the characters acting, are 'objective givens' for the spectators, as the characters and their characteristics bear the stamp of completion right from the start: Othello represents 'jealousy', Coriolanus 'pride', Richard III 'the monster', etc. The spectator, in identifying with the hero, shares his fate as if it were his own and allows himself to be carried along through the highs and lows of the plot (as spectators in the theatre are only too ready to do, to judge by some of the successes). And thus the step from 'being led' to 'being misled' is small. For example when the subjective appearance of theatre is believed to be objective reality, and the effectiveness of theatre mistaken for existing reality. Brecht saw a great danger here that theatre (and art more generally) could be misused. Walter Benjamin speaks about 'aestheticizing politics'. For example when the Nazis – successfully, incidentally – led the world to believe in 'the fanatic will of a united people' in the way they stage-managed tremendous marching masses, gigantic 'light domes' fed by hundreds of floodlights, and the thundering rhythm of marches and marching feet at the Nuremberg rallies. Brecht called this 'the theatre of making-believe'. Today this 'theatre of making-believe' can be found, among other places, in election campaigns, where the illusion of real battles is created in order to make the public believe that there are real alternatives between the parties. Or in 'events', now gradually also taking over theatre, where we are made to play a substantial part in experiencing illusory realities that lack all substance. The very standpoint on the world taken by Brecht's 'non-Aristotelian' theatre, by contrast, does not allow it to accept events on stage as 'the work of fate' or 'objective givens'. Rather, it asks how things happen and, linked to this, how they pass away again, that is to say, their place within history. Something that demands to be seen as eternal and unique can be revealed as *just one* possibility among several, dependent on the life and times of man. And thus changeable by man. (Which is not just more insightful, but also more entertaining.) Brecht also made some entirely practical suggestions for this. For example, the theatre spectator watching a particularly well-known play should not let himself 'be gripped' by the plot during the play but – for his own satisfaction, of course – imagine additional possible turns of events to those depicted on stage. What would happen, for instance, if Othello let Desdemona live and believed her? How would the story continue? Or if Galileo did not retract his assertions? Would the church have the courage to burn the famous man as a heretic? So is Galileo unnecessarily fearful when he retracts? Or what if Godot actually did appear at the end of the whole play spent waiting for him? Would that change anything? And so on. In this way events can very quickly be made to lose their appearance as the work of fate, as the only possible outcome. They are 'historicized'.

'Historicizing' is key to 'Brechtian theatre'. Brecht by no means only 'historicized' historical plays; he also 'historicized' contemporary plays because contemporary subject matter, thanks to its routine, everyday nature, is particularly prone to escape its own historicity. It creates the impression of having always been as it is. It becomes, to use one of Brecht's favourite words, an 'ever-thus' ('Immeriges'). With this, it becomes an 'objective given' and escapes human interference. Now, to 'historicize' something means to understand it through its historical context, so how it came about and passed away again, and with this how it can be changed. Strictly speaking to 'historicize' is to apply Marx's first thesis on Feuerbach to theatre: 'The main flaw in all materialism up to now [...] is that the object, reality, sensuality is conceived only in the form of an object or opinion, not however as human sensory activity or as a practice; not subjectively.'

With regard to 'historicizing', today's theatre often has recourse to older times precisely when it is trying to be contemporary. Showing historical plays as if they were 'in the present' has become a ritual. Not only in costume and make-up, which can be legitimate, but in the way they are torn out of their historical field – supposedly in order to bring them up to date.[15] Thus a director introduced a murder to Ibsen's *A Doll's House* because for his 'contemporary understanding' an outstanding IOU note, and for such a small amount at that, was not a sufficient catalyst for a family tragedy of such proportions.[16] This dehistoricization makes the play difficult for a contemporary spectator to understand, precisely when it is supposed to be being made more accessible. The arrogance of the present means it is valued only in contemporary terms. The spectator not only loses all sense for the past, but also any active interest in it. He himself is 'dehistor-icized'. He becomes a faceless observer, for whom past happenings are incontrovertible facts. 'He sinks,' says Marx, 'into a state without history'. And Voltaire speaks of 'fatal contentment', mocking it in a variation on a quotation from Gottfried Wilhelm Leibniz: 'This world is the best of all worlds, provided one doesn't know any others.' Mis-guidedly rendering historical plays contemporary means they lose not only their dramatic tension – in the very way that tiny events can cause terrible tragedies – but also their contemporary nature. The spectator is no longer able to draw parallels between the alien hap-penings and his own situation, for they are already presented as his own. The happenings become incontrovertible. The present stretches out to infinity. It becomes an 'ever-thus'.

Likewise, if you want to question the present – with old or new plays – and 'mercilessly' criticize it, dehistoricization in the end leads to the opposite – to adaptation. Because it deactivates the spectator. In order to 'shock people out of their comfortable existences', social distortions, for example, are commonly shown with 'the most brutal degree of naturalness'. Artaud's 'theatre of cruelty' and Brecht's statement that 'shock is the first stage of knowledge' are the reference points here. Incorrectly, for both reckon with the effect of a particular aesthetic. These distortions, by contrast, invoke a brutal naturalness. This can – as is evident – have an extraordinary initial effect. But brutality soon becomes second nature to people. It shocks the audience, but with the kind of shock inspired by natural disasters. When a Munich production of Shakespeare's *Timon of Athens* tries to stage the 'bifold authority', the 'split personality' (in this play the major theme of the waning aristocracy that is split between the feudal demand for 'God's mercy' and an already well established bourgeois greed) by having the actors wear enormous heads that appeared to have been split by an axe, this may be a well-intentioned attempt to show the brutal 'splits' that also happen today. It says next to nothing about the reasons for such occurrences, however. Social brutality, which is the real brutality today but is not 'naturally' obvious, remains invisible. Furthermore, the shock caused by the gigantic split heads distracts us from the true horrors of our times: for example how man is constantly turned into 'human capital', how 'supporting the national interest' yields the systematic abolition of jobs, 'greater flexibility' is a return to medieval lawlessness, an 'efficiency cure' spells the mass destruction of existences, 'optimizing education' means radically reducing the options available and creating a general loss of perspective for young people, the marketization of everything, even language, destroys whole spheres of life, individualism, down to the level of sexual and dietary preferences, is eradicated by the norms dictated by the media, 'liberalization' has become the complete freedom from social securities, and existential angst is cultivated in order to render employees more productive. And when fear for one's job determines everyone's fundamental way of being, the state's continued existence is far better ensured than if violence were directly invoked. As noted earlier, Heiner Müller commented on this point laconically, 'When unemployment is sufficiently high, there is no need for a state police.' But these kinds of brutality remain 'invisible', because the screen, lectern and pulpit systematically present them as 'normalities' that we come to accept. They hide behind the drugs of an 'easy-living society' that includes shock as one of its favoured narcotics, those goose-bump-inducing creeps we get from the 'visible' acts of brutality deemed to be the actual crimes of our time. In this way social discrepancies, caused by the ruthless exploitation of capital, are turned on stage into unavoidable and never-ending crises of nothing less than the human condition. They lose their historical situation, and with this the idea that they can be changed. But if something cannot be changed then it becomes – whether so intended or not – part of the existing circumstances, even when these circumstances are being 'brutally' criticized on stage. The theatre of the century before last and its narrow-minded acceptance of fate is being given fresh wind from backstage, perhaps now with a red flag in its hand. For the 'postmodern radical theatre' wants to go beyond Marx in political and theoretical terms. While he may have unearthed the brutal alienation ('Entfremdung') of man, he is considered not to have had the courage to 'accept this as the inevitable side-effect of human socialization' in the eyes of Jacques Derrida, philosopher and, in his own words, someone who has 'thought Marx through to the end'. An even more recent Marx-perfecter by the name of Rohrbeck puts it more precisely again: 'We are not debating the question of alienation or how to resolve it, rather we must manage to deal with experiences of alienation as sensibly as possible and find a meaningful way of living in a world that seems strange to us.'

Staying with Marx, there is another phrase that I also consider key to Brecht's outlook on the world. Brecht would probably be less grand and call it a 'working hypothesis'. The sentence goes: ' "History" does not need man to function as a means for expressing its [...] designs, rather history is merely the activity of man as he follows his designs.' That is what Marx says in *The Holy Family*. Likewise, where history conjures up supernatural powers that control man, powers indeed that man fears and worships, these powers are made by man. They are also the result of human activity. And theatre is able to reveal these powers for what they are: man's 'congealed activity'. Even fate, tragedy, dreams, hopes, mistakes, moods, desires, jealousy, envy, the superego and the subconscious, libido and Thanatos – legitimate subjects of theatre – are in the end nothing other than people following their designs, or what they think of as their designs. Particularly in times of exaggerated mystifications, as have been brought about by all kinds of media as never before, and during which the edict that the world cannot be grasped 'shores up' the capitalist system on a daily basis precisely by making the world unknowable (this has also become the credo of many a theatre producer), 'Brechtian theatre' offers a suitable alternative. Where mystification has become exaggerated, theatre has a better chance of demystification. Theatre like no other art can tear asunder the 'objectively real fog' ('objektiv-realen Nebel'), for Ernst

Bloch a consequence of the normal way in which capital is used. One could also speak of a *Verfremdung* of social relations. Precisely when 'the inexplicable' takes over, it can give rise not only to fear but also to the desire to explain, while unknowability provokes the pleasure in making things known. For Brecht believes the world can be understood. Understood not in the sense that one can understand absolutely everything, but that it can be understood in principle. For each new realization also entails new gaps in one's knowledge and the realization that these gaps exist. The 'inexhaustibility of subject matter' prevents, as one can also read in Bloch, the 'sacred standstill of complete knowledge'. If there is any certainty, then it is that nothing is absolutely certain. Each certainty produces new uncertainties, each new solution new problems. And if there is a plan, then this is always a plan of possibilities. This was also incidentally the painful experience of those 'real' socialists who thought that secure planning alone would 'lawfully' guarantee certainty as to the way society would develop.

But Brecht not only believes that the world can be understood but also that it can be changed. Man understands the world by constantly testing out what he has understood in his daily practice, and, in so doing, modifying this knowledge. 'I only fully grasp what I have altered' – this statement from the young Brecht is probably a 'categorical imperative' of his entire work. Responding to Friedrich Dürrenmatt's question in 1955 as to whether the world can possibly be recreated in theatre, Brecht writes:

> For people of today, questions are valued for the answers they provoke. People of today are interested in conditions and events that they can do something about. [...] My opinion at least is that today's world can also be recreated in theatre, but only when it is understood as something that can be changed.

With regard to (2)

That is the way the world and theatre are approached – you can also call it Brecht's method (although Brecht himself did not like the term and preferred to speak of a 'way of working'). It is the method of materialist dialectics. It seeks to locate the driving force of things not in external agencies – whether God, a universal law, the principle of creation or a party programme – but rather in the things themselves. More precisely, in the contradictions that are inherent in things. Dialectics refers to the 'unity of opposites'. But unity – and this is also the key to dialectics – is also always a battle of opposites. As a result of this battle, things are in constant motion, as opposites can turn into their counterparts. But these transitions do not take place in a continuous and linear fashion, rather in leaps, in which quantitative changes eventually result in a new quality. Brecht (this time to his displeasure) also had to experience such a leap. As mentioned earlier, he invented the famous lightly fluttering curtain, the 'Brechtian curtain', in the 1920s to replace the heavy velvet curtain. The audience was supposed to be surprised when it was suddenly able to follow the scene changes through the half-curtain, and was supposed to realize, to its astonishment, that theatre too is 'the work of man'. The audience really was, as I have already detailed, not just astounded, but enraged. Brecht was content. But then Brecht was to experience the power of dialectics. Once the audience had got used to the 'Brechtian curtain' at the productions of the Berliner Ensemble, they were enraged whenever it was absent. If a Brecht play was showing, then people wanted the 'Brechtian curtain'. What had been intended to destroy conventions became a convention itself. Brecht counts 'dialectics', in a nice poem of the same name, to be one of his great pleasures; in the case of the 'Brechtian curtain' he wasn't so keen on it. For dialectics is 'to blame' that the 'half-curtain' was only used as long as the heavy velvet curtain was missed. Dialectics refers in these circumstances – and not without humour – to 'negating the negation'. Each new position results from the negation of another. Or put more simply: materialist dialectics teaches us to think in contradictions and to understand things fully as they are in motion. Even more simply: to think contradictions. Applied to society: the way society develops cannot be explained outside society, as no explanation exists outside man. The unity of the contradictions that comprise man's daily activities and the transformation of these contradictions into new qualities are the driving force behind human development. This is the case for the individual as much as for historical epochs. If we follow Marx, then none other than capitalism itself produces its negation and creates its own 'grave digger'. For capitalism must, in order to carry on extending its use of capital, constantly increase the numbers of its enemy, the proletariat, in order to 'extend' its ability to exploit it, as the proletariat alone creates added value. With this, capitalism creates its own opposite that will eventually turn into a new quality, that is to say the destruction of capitalism. Uniting contradictions, collapsing opposites into one another, making the leap of quantitative development that yields new qualities are for the dialectics of Marx (and thus also for Brecht) the law of motion underlying human society.

This realization can empower man vis-à-vis his own situation, but it also entails a great danger. If, for example, it gives rise to the belief that the laws governing how a society develops act like the laws of nature, 'objectively', meaning without human intervention. From this point of view, different kinds of society follow on from one another – the transition from feudalism to capitalism, or from capitalism to socialism, for example – like geological periods, or like good weather turning bad. Thus communism too is an unavoidable necessity, and its triumph is written in the law books. Such false certainty can have deadly consequences, particularly for people who subscribe to the idea of changing social relations. They rely on an 'objective' law that doesn't exist. They do not realize that reality is nothing other than a reality made by man. This is also the case for the 'objective', that is to say pre-existing, relations into which people are born. These too are ultimately nothing more than the 'congealed activity' of previous generations. Even people who claim, with recourse to Marx, that Marxism has given them access to the truth demonstrate a false 'objectification' of social relations. Such a 'flight into certainty' – as theologians would call it – has already led to many a catastrophe in the labour movement. For example, the leaders of the labour movement, including such excellent minds as Karl Kautsky, took up the fatal cry of Kaiser Wilhelm at the outbreak of war in 1914: 'I no longer see any parties, I see only Germans now', in the conviction that the war would lead 'with the force of law' to the end of capitalism. Likewise in the recent past, when the GDR reached a serious crisis point in 1989, the false certainty that socialism existed as if by the force of law and was incontrovertible led to the country's demise. 'The events of 1989,' writes the legal philosopher Uwe-Jens Heuer, 'must have caused the very last Marxist to question his understanding of history, according to which history is a necessary natural process that knows no alternatives and yet guarantees victory.'[17] Developments within society, such as socialism, are not some kind of necessity enacted by the laws of nature, they are great opportunities, and it is up to man to seize them or miss out. But a 'certainty' that relies on changes happening as if 'by law', actually weakens all change, because it weakens man's active involvement. When Brecht speaks of change, he means making it possible for people to make changes, to become 'active'. In theatre, this means making evident the contradictions within events by invoking the technique of *Verfremdung*, with the result that these contradictions are subjected to man's 'revolutionary practice', which is really just another word for social change. And changing society is really just another word for *Verfremdung*.

Verfremdung is probably one of those concepts that has caused the most confusion in Brecht's theatre. '*Verfremdung*' is first of all a word that does not exist in German. Many a computer today still marks it as incorrect and will replace it with 'befremden' or 'entfremden'. Translators too have 'corrected' Brecht in this manner. In England, for example, '*Verfremdung*' has been translated with 'alienation', in France with 'distanciation'. Both mean the opposite of what Brecht means, because both mean 'to distance'. This is probably the source of the resilient claim that Brecht just wanted his actors to show distance. The early Soviet study of art, which was however later 'forgotten' in the Soviet Union, came nearer the mark when it spoke of 'ostranenije'. This is because '*Verfremdung*' is not actually Brecht's invention at all, but rather comes from the philosopher and art theorist Viktor Shklovskij. In his essay 'On the dissimilarity of the similar', Shklovskij writes:

> In 1915 I created the term *Verfremdung* (ostranenije). In the way it works *Verfremdung* is like a puzzle. The puzzle is always a pretext for engaging in the pleasure of discovery. A puzzle, by hiding something that is known, forces you to revisit all the characteristics of that thing in order to guess what it is. And the technique of *Verfremdung* must show the world in such a manner that it is freed from its usual associations so that it can be seen as if for the first time.[18]

So *Verfremdung* is about better recognition, not just distance. The distance that is created is supposed to make the well-known object appear 'foreign' ('fremd'), in order to recognize it all the better. Distance is not the result of *Verfremdung*, but rather the beginning of this process. Because when this process is initiated, the object – 'freed from its usual associations' – appears not as it does in the familiar, everyday context, but as it really is. This is like the famous question about the number of windows in a house that you have been living in for years; it can only be answered if you look at the house 'as if for the first time' and count the windows.

But Brecht does not just treat *Verfremdung* as an aid for understanding the world; it also provides the opportunity to intervene in society. 'Brechtian theatre' is in actual fact applied materialist dialectics. *Verfremdung* is a classic example of 'negating the negation': distance is created in order to overcome distance. On stage this means allowing the spectator to grasp events that are shown not as part of a usual set of circumstances but rather as an unusual, contradictory mix that comes to light during the performance. Now, contradictions allow the spectator to understand things as they really are: that is to say, changeable. But precisely this quality, even though it is key, is covered over by the force of daily habit, it becomes 'invisible'. This is particularly so for things one believes one knows particularly well. 'What is well-known is, because it is well-known, not known' is a phrase from Hegel that is itself already so well-known that nobody really knows it any more, or at least no longer thinks what it means. Now, Brecht wants to 'reactivate thought' (or as he later terms it 'to dialecticize') and break habits by subjecting what is familiar to *Verfremdung*, or better: to disturb them by making the 'invisible' visible once more. For once you have got used to something, you accept it as it is, as if it were always like that and will always remain so. It becomes an 'ever-thus'. However, Brecht recommends not simply accepting the 'ever-thus' – at least for the duration of a theatre visit – but instead questioning it. Why is it as it is? Why not different? Will it always be so? And so on. In short, he suggests 'wondering'. For as the philosopher Wolfgang Fritz Haug correctly puts it: 'Believing that something is self-understood can be a way of getting used to not understanding anything.' Perhaps something that appears unchangeable will turn out simply not to have been changed for a long time? Or something that raises claims to eternity is perhaps just the product of specific circumstances and thus in reality has only a limited lifespan. Walter Benjamin, who probably knew Brecht like few others, put it succinctly: 'The art of Brecht's theatre is to provoke amazement instead of [...] empathy.'

In this context, Brecht was his own best spectator. I remember a rehearsal of Goethe's *Urfaust*. We were rehearsing the so-called 'religious discussion'. We thought the rehearsal was over, when Brecht suddenly began to wonder (which he really did do 'naively' and not on principle). He just couldn't, as he put it, 'get his head around' the idea that instead of answering Gretchen's question 'What do you think of religion?', Faust enters into a long disquisition on Spinoza's pantheism. Theatres tend to interpret it as the great scholar's special declaration of love for the 'simple' girl. When the actress playing Gretchen then nodded her head knowingly throughout the entire scholarly speech, it was too much for Brecht. He became furious: this petit-bourgeois girl couldn't have understood a word of it! And Brecht asked what we thought at the time to be an entirely inappropriate question: why didn't this man marry the girl? Because the question about religion, as any student of Catholicism will tell you, was clearly a question about the 'holy sacraments', so marriage. And he suggested the actress 'just speak plainly'. So asking, instead of 'What do you think of religion', 'What do you think of marriage?'. To our surprise, the otherwise thoroughly rhetorical scene blossomed. Faust's lecture about Spinoza could not possibly be a special declaration of love any more, on the contrary, it was simply a way of evading a question he didn't want to answer. Brecht's 'inappropriate' question led to a whole new way of seeing the play. For it brought to the fore the contradictions in Faust's character that bourgeois theatre, in its attempt to portray man as 'noble, helpful and good', had so gladly overlooked: Faust's 'path to truth' is in reality lined with corpses. The girl's mother dies from a poisonous sleeping potion that is given to her so that the lover can sneak into Gretchen's bed unnoticed; the brother, who catches Faust, is stabbed to death by him in a fight (in which Mephisto secretly wields the dagger); Gretchen becomes a child murderer. The famous 'love scene', when played 'properly', turned out to be, for all its poetry, a death sentence for the girl, for Gretchen will end in a dungeon waiting every hour for the executioner after she has killed the 'illegitimate fruit' that results from this love scene. Brecht's 'wondering' led to something else too: it revealed 'Goethinger's' humour (as Brecht the Bavarian liked to call Goethe the Swabian). For Goethe has the great scholar turn to Spinoza in his hour of need – at that time the most progressive world view, it is true – in order to get the girl into bed, but this bed is certainly not the marital bed.

Even if it sounds very simple: 'wondering' is the source of all discovery, all inspirations, all humour, in Brecht's theatre (and not only there). And thus also of all enjoyment. It would be interesting, but unfortunately beyond the scope of this study, to analyse *Verfremdung* not just from a philosophical point of view, which sees it as a way of changing the world by negating the negation, but from a 'naive' one. For the world is also changed in other ways that can indeed be more effective. Think of the economy, politics, the media, and political agitation. The 'naive' view, however, understands *Verfremdung* in its particular context, which is the artistic one. Here too the world is changed, but for enjoyment. Here *Verfremdung* is above all an extension of the ability to enjoy oneself. Philosophical descriptions often strengthen the suspicion that *Verfremdung* entails suppressing 'naive' pleasures in order to achieve certain understandings. A view informed by theatrical practice would have to argue the opposite, for *Verfremdung* can tremendously enrich the pleasure of theatre. And not just since Brecht. Repeatedly asked about '*Verfremdung*' (something that rather began to bore him as time went on), Brecht himself liked to refer to the clowns, especially Grock, the great Swiss musical clown.

Grock comes eagerly on stage, sits down at the piano, importantly lifts both arms in the air, like a virtuoso, spreads his fingers to begin – but he falters, he can't, the piano is too far away. Helplessly he looks at the audience, and after a while they helpfully gesture to him that he simply has to move a little closer. Of course he doesn't understand straight away, but then it finally dawns on him. A joyful 'aha!', and he pushes the piano, with great effort, towards his chair.

'Wondering' is probably the biggest difference between 'Brechtian theatre' and 'Aristotelian theatre', as Brecht rather simplistically termed the kind of theatre he criticized. For in his *Poetics* Aristotle characterizes the theatre as a place where pity and fear should be aroused in order to purge the spectator of pity and fear. Brecht's theatre, by contrast, is a place where one should learn not to fear but to wonder. It offers escape from the crippling sense that things are 'naturally' as they are, it renounces the much-loved 'flight into certainties'; it is uncomfortable when things are at a standstill; it casts doubt when everything seems clear. And this calls for a multitude of artistic means. Tragedy and clownery, history and parable, verse and slang, fantasy and documentary, emotions and coldness, the rational and the abyss, the obvious and the absurd, building things up and pulling them apart, everything is welcome that can playfully 'set in motion' things that appear to be at a standstill. The static contents of the Pantheon are to be made to move. 'Adequate pleasure cannot emancipate itself too much from fun, which plays a suitably important role in a materialistically minded society. And if the actor becomes too timid, how is he to raise the dark reserves of vitality (of a life force that has not yet been socialized) which also determine the asocial?' asks Brecht. When everything has been answered, then that is reason enough to ask questions. What has happened over the course of history should also be shown as what it is: something that has happened, so something that is ephemeral. What has been 'ever-thus' must get used to being deemed temporary, something that has been 'fixed-for-once-and-for-all' will now count as urgently in need of change. And this technique of uncovering what is hidden by wondering (i.e., *Verfremdung*), can in practice be achieved by various means. By a song, that interrupts the plot; by music that comments on events; by a scene design that 'narrates contradictions'; indeed even the very way a play is written can, through 'breaks' in the *Fabel*[19] and action, necessitate the active staging of contradictions. In Beckett's *Waiting for Godot* at the Dramaten, for example, a clown technique was used that resulted in genuine *Verfremdung* through the self-contradictory nature of form and content. Hegel calls this 'the contrast of the essential and its appearance, of the end and its means'. It is general inappropriateness. When the actors playing Vladimir and Estragon turn the simple act of eating a carrot into a problematic process, as if they were dealing with major problems of the universe, *Verfremdung* sets in: an inconsequential act becomes even more inconsequential, the more it is made to appear significant. An 'old trick' that every circus clown knows. Or when the actor playing Vladimir gives a ridiculous speech, in the tone of a well-versed parliamentarian delivering his political manifesto, declaring his considered intention finally to do something, only then to sit down and do nothing – here not only does Vladimir's inconsequentiality take on gigantic proportions, but so too does the parliamentarian's. Incidentally, Brecht would very much have liked, as he assured me in our last conversations at Buckow, to produce Beckett's *Waiting for Godot* as a realistic clownery at the Berliner Ensemble. He would have made Vladimir and Estragon into unemployed layabouts, who were absurdly waiting not for work but for Godot. But Brecht was not to manage this.

When thinking about *Verfremdung* in the theatre, it is often helpful and amusing to think about the *Verfremdung* of everyday things. Money, for example. Money appears to come from God, or at the very least from some universal law, and seems immutable. Marx refers to Shakespeare's *Timon of Athens* in his *Capital* when he says that money itself is a god: 'Money turns white black, beauty ugly, badness good, and lowliness noble, it tempts the priest from the altar, blesses the cursed, honours the thief and provides the spent widow with suitors.' (The total market economy follows Shakespeare to the letter.) In order to see this God in slightly more secular terms, another writer can help us. He describes a brilliant *Verfremdung* of money, or in this case gold. He is Daniel Defoe, with his *Robinson Crusoe*, hardly read these days, or if so, only as a children's book. The novel, written in 1719, contains along with Defoe's masterly narrative style an important contribution to political economy. Robinson's ship hits a reef and sinks. Robinson is the sole survivor and, leaving everything else behind, he manages to save two small barrels of gold. He hopes this will allow him to secure his survival on the lonely island where he is washed up. For gold, so his life up to now has taught him, is the most important substance because it is the most valuable. When he doesn't meet a single soul on the island he makes an amazing discovery: gold isn't worth anything. It only has a value if someone else is there to recognize it. Otherwise gold is just a measure of value that man introduced in order to exchange his goods with other people. A single measure was needed for that, and so a metal by the name of gold was chosen. Otherwise gold cannot, as Robinson had to discover to his dismay, even be used for tools, because it is too soft. The false certainty that gold is 'in itself' valuable, that is to say without the existence of people, arose because it was used in everyday trading as a 'measure of value', to the point that people eventually came to believe that this value was inherent in it. Only an experience of *Verfremdung*, as Robinson lands on an uninhabited island, can quickly destroy this pious belief. Robinson has to realize that gold is a useless metal, and that only human activity, here in the form of exchanging goods, endows it with value, making it into money. Historically, money came into the world along with the production of goods, and it will at some point disappear from it again along with the production of goods. Then gold will perhaps be just a pretty sight around the neck of a pretty woman.

Now that the dialectics of *Verfremdung* finally appear to be more or less clear, something unexpected crops up: dialectics. Its objection demands to be heard: the sentence, '*Verfremdung* breaks habits', is false. It is a simplification, maybe legitimate in theatrical rehearsals, but as an explanation of the dialectics of *Verfremdung* it is itself not dialectic. It is a paradox: *Verfremdung* cannot be understood without *Verfremdung*. Or put another way: the technique of *Verfremdung* must be applied to *Verfremdung*. For habits are not destroyed just for destruction's sake; as habits are destroyed, new ones should also be made. For habits are both a curse and a blessing. If, on the one hand, they cripple human activity by rendering transactions unconscious, on the other hand they are indispensable, as they form a part of the unconscious and thereby direct entire lives. Without the force of habit, it would be impossible to drive a car; one would otherwise have to reconstruct the technical process of each gear change beforehand in one's head. Even language would be impossible, as with each sentence one would have to think about the rules of grammar. The same is true of human behaviour. Behavioural norms which make collaboration between humans possible in the first place are only effective when they represent 'normality' for the individual, that is to say, they have become habit. Without this 'relief' human life and collaboration would be unthinkable. The 'norms' – fixed in laws and morals, customs and traditions – have to have become part of our 'flesh and blood' if they are to be effective in everyday life. Lenin, who correctly classed habits to be one of the most dangerous enemies of the revolution, in later years had to modify his repulsion towards them. When in a speech in 1921 to the youth association he made the revolution's continuation dependent on overcoming the cultural deficit of the masses, he said, 'In culture you can only consider you have achieved something when it has become part of everyday life, part of people's habits.' Here habits even act as a necessary pretext for social change. So, in contradiction with Brecht? Ultimately Brecht wants to destroy habits, precisely in order to bring about change. Something that is widely self-evident would be for Brecht – as the philosopher Haug correctly says – 'indicative of how people have got used to not understanding things'. But also in Brecht you find sentences like, 'There are few activities that so damage people's morals as being continuously concerned with morals. I hear, one must love the truth, one must keep one's promise, one must fight for what is right. But the trees do not say one must be green, one must let the fruit drop straight to the ground, one must rustle one's leaves when the wind blows.' Or. 'People will only really think when it is taken as read that they should think and they are ashamed not to do so.'

It may seem strange that Brecht, not generally known as a 'moralist', speaks here of morals. His aversion for Schiller's 'moral institution' and his opinion that ethics is nothing more than religion in disguise and 'the talk of "obligations and duties" ontological rubbish' are all well known. But to describe Brecht as an opponent of every kind of morality on these grounds is just as one-sided as making him an opponent of feelings and emotions. What bothered Brecht about Schiller's 'moral institution' is the claim to eternity. As if there were a moral code that were as fixed a quantity as the 'starred sky above me'. This in any case was how Immanuel Kant saw it, and Schiller admired him for his 'categorical imperative' that stated what one 'must' do, independent of time and place. And yet we know that for example in Pericles' Greece, today still a model for civilization and justice, killing a person was by no means immoral. On the contrary, someone who never killed was considered immoral. For the general good could only be maintained, according to the dominant moral code, if slaves, who were, also according to the dominant moral code, not people but property like houses, farms and animals, were deterred from any kind of insubordination by the yearly killing of at least one slave. Likewise, the 'terror' that counts as the pinnacle of immorality today was declared in the 1793 decree 'La Terreur', issued by the National Convention in France, to be the holy duty of every citizen so that the endangered revolution could be defended against Prussian-Austrian intervention. Brecht did not reject morality, but, as the philosopher Haug establishes: 'Like Marx, he rejects the foundational claim of ethics', because morals are not a basis, but a superstructure. 'The moral question must be treated,' Brecht wrote in the 1940 *Messingkauf*

Dialogues, 'as a historical question.' For Brecht, morality is 'a driving force for socially productive behaviour'. It can be different at different times, just as 'productive behaviour' can vary. 'History raises the question of the concrete form morality takes. It is an historical question in the sense of a history that unfolds as we act.' And morality is precisely most effective when it is no longer generally demanded, but rather self-understood on an everyday level, thus when it has become a 'good' habit. In *Me-Ti: Book of Changes* Brecht notes: 'One of the greatest sentences is the sentence: "I am ashamed". Almost everyone has a good voice when speaking this sentence.'

I must confess that I also felt, when I began directing Brecht, that breaking habits was the guiding purpose of his theatre. And so shortly after Brecht's death I directed *The Resistible Rise of Arturo Ui* as a general attack on mind-numbing conventions. Brecht was very careful with regard to the way this travesty of the Nazis' rise to power should be directed. The German audience should only laugh at 'the house-painter', as Brecht called Hitler, after they had first been deeply shocked once more. He made the performance of *Arturo Ui* dependent on the production of his play *Fear and Misery of the Third Reich*. This did not take place in Brecht's lifetime. Only immediately after his death did a collective of directors who had been pupils of Brecht direct *Fear and Misery of the Third Reich*, so that the path was clear for *Arturo Ui*.

At this time, many 'in the East' were also beginning to think that they had been completely unable to resist the suggestive power of Hitler who had possessed the demonic power of 'great criminals'. Names such as 'Napoleon' and 'Ivan the Terrible' were mentioned in this context. We wanted to destroy this belief as it was threatening to become an easy excuse. Using the technique of clownery we wanted to show that this 'great criminal' was nothing more than someone who carried out great crimes. We showed, 'in the style of a fairground freak show' that the rise of Hitler, who is here called 'Ui', was astoundingly similar to the rise of Al Capone, that gangster who through murder and blackmail managed the illegal alcohol trade in Chicago at the time of the prohibition. The audience's protest, with which we had fully reckoned, was provoked as early as the 1959 premiere. Even people who had not actively wanted fascism but had nevertheless tolerated it protested against the way the usual excuse that they had been forced to submit to a 'demon' was 'destroyed'. Now they were supposed to have been taken in by a street bandit! The farcical destruction of what had become a cherished, routine excuse instead of a source of shame was clearly timely back then. *Arturo Ui*

Illustration 2 Arturo UI in rehearsal with Siegfried Kilian, Hilmar Thate and Ekkehard Schall, Berliner Ensemble (1959). (Photograph courtesy of Vera Tenschert.)

enjoyed worldwide success. In 1961 the production in Paris won the Théâtre des Nations prize and the Parisian theatre critics' prize. But it does remain 'one-sided', albeit intentionally so. In later works I increasingly discovered the other side to Brecht. When we directed *The Days of the Commune* we were initially equally concerned with 'breaking habits'. In the debates that were being carried out at the time, above all by those on the Left, concerning the role of 'revolutionary violence', many people had 'got used' to the opinion that socialism, as the most humanitarian form of humanity, excludes violence of any kind. Such an opinion is clearly also the result of horror at the fascist acts of violence that took place. And here there was one particular sentence in the play that was hotly debated. As the commune looks set to be defeated, the revolutionary Langevin says to the teacher Genevieve, who rejects all violence, 'In this battle there are

Illustration 3 Ekkehard Schall as Arturo Ui (first performed 1959). (Photograph courtesy of Vera Tenschert.)

only bloody or dismembered hands'. But Brecht did not merely intend *The Days of the Commune* to 'destroy' false habits, it was also to represent his suggestions for constructing a new state that he had brought back with him from emigration. It was to help the governed, and even more the governors, to create 'new habits', because it was clear that old habits were quickly going to take hold again. Sentences such as the following were to guard against such danger: 'Let us not make any claim to infallibility like all the old governments do. Let us publish all our speeches and acts, let the public in on all our imperfections, for we have nothing to fear except ourselves.' *The Days of the Commune* was equally a great international success. Brecht's suggestions in respect of 'new habits' also received much applause from our 'governors'. Sadly only in the theatre.

Likewise in his previously discussed production of *Mutter Courage* (*Mother Courage*), set in the ruins of 1949 Berlin, Brecht was primarily concerned with destroying habits, including the most dangerous of all, people's tendency to accept war as an unavoidable natural event. People must finally realize that wars are the work of man and are started in the name of business. But Brecht's next concern – at least this is how I see it now – was to show how 'new habits' arise. Also in one's everyday life, for example, greeting with considerable distrust future social occurrences, injustices and developments that claim to be unavoidable 'natural events'. He called this having a 'critical stance'. Later, in the criticism of Stalin that Brecht formulated in response to a query after Khrushchev's revelations (for me an example of 'classic' *Verfremdung*), he first gives reasons to destroy the usual belief in Stalin's 'infallibility' and his godlike status by stating how he has come to realize that, 'One of the bad legacies of Stalinism is the decline of dialectics. Without knowledge of dialectics, transitions such as that from Stalin the engine to Stalin the brake cannot be understood.' But Brecht's aim was not just to destroy the belief in Stalin's 'infallibility' that had also taken hold of the labour movement; above all, new habits were to be established: 'Worshipping Stalin to lead (painfully) to a rejection of worship'.

The 'critical stance' – one of Brecht's favourite terms – is probably the shortest way of describing Brecht's approach to the world and theatre. And yet it too is the source of misconceptions. Although it is never missing in any scholarly publication on Brecht, usually the essential ingredient is missing: theatre. The 'critical stance' is understood as a theoretical approach to the world, art as at best a useful aid. For Brecht, by contrast, a 'critical stance' was a 'hugely aesthetic stance'. It is not first and foremost about recognizing how the world works, but rather enjoying this recognition. Enjoyment alone – in the theatre at least – makes insightful thought into 'interventionist thought'. Or as Brecht says in another context: 'Art is needed to turn what politics sees as correct into something that people see as exemplary.'

In one of our final conversations in Buckow, Brecht, to our surprise, kept on referring to 'naivety', and he complained that his works had been understood to date 'un-naively': as 'exercises in thought' or 'political enlightenment'. Certainly that was also in there. But without naivety art could not possibly be produced, and definitely not his theatre. He didn't mean primitive naivety that is the opposite of reflection. He meant naivety that follows analysis. It is not sufficient for a spectator to have achieved new insights at the end of a theatre performance. Other events can also convey such insights, and better. For example lectures, seminars, discussions. What theatre can do: transform insights into naive reactions: amazement, anger, shock, protest, agreement, unease, but also laughter, mockery, amusement, glee, courage, etc. And this as enjoyment. Only such naive reactions endow thought with what Benjamin called the 'practical glowing core of Marxism'. This new naivety is according to Brecht the real chance to dispense with the unholy opposition of thought and enjoyment. Thinking must itself become enjoyable by becoming action. And the place where this transformation takes place is the theatre. During this conversation I noted a comment that Brecht made more as an aside but that strikes me today, where everyone is busy 'theorizing' him, as important: 'We should stop all this talk of "psychology" in theatre, we should start – for a time at least – talking about "knowing people" instead.'

I actually wanted to finish this point about the approach taken to the world and theatre with a well-known quotation from 1954 where Brecht states that dialectical theatre is able to make dialectics itself enjoyable. In the admirable book *Philosophieren mit Brecht und Gramsci* (*Philosophizing with Brecht and Gramsci*) by Wolfgang Fritz Haug, I found another text instead. Haug quotes Günter Anders, who says in his piece *Bert Brecht – Gespräche und Erinnerungen* (*Bert Brecht – Conversations and Memories*): 'The pleasure that Brecht wants to create consists of delight in the way the world's changeability is enacted to us, and this delight in what is enacted is also precisely a happy anticipation of something real to come. At least the anticipation of possible realizations.' This text strikes me as more 'naive'.

Day four

With regard to (3): The third point is the effect Brecht's theatre has on its audience.

According to Brecht, two art forms need to be developed, the art of acting and the art of spectating. This doesn't just refer to theatre advertising and the need to ensure that there are spectators sitting in the auditorium (which is not always so easy). Brecht meant a basic principle that has clearly become so self-evident for theatres that nobody thinks about it any more: 'Without spectators theatre is nonsense.' This is not about filling theatre rooms or having 'talks with the audience' after performances, it is about the actor himself. For without spectators there is no art of acting. True, one can stand alone in front of a mirror and gesticulate, but the art of acting only comes into existence with the spectator. I will even go so far as to claim that it is not the actor who is the main player in the theatre, but the spectator. For Brecht, as we saw, 'the action' was *the* constitutive form in which a play's message resides. This does of course refer to the action on stage – what happens between the characters during the play – but it also, and above all, refers to the basic action in theatre: 'the fact that a person, or several people, get up on stage because they have something interesting to convey'.

Some time ago, I carried out an experiment in the Skara theatre school,[20] where a group of us had gone in order to teach the theory and practice of theatre. At the time, the 'theatre of the absurd' was enjoying great popularity, and the students saw Eugène Ionesco's *The Bald Primadonna* in their local theatre. They were fascinated by the way the play, the absurd events of which were completely incomprehensible in isolation, had such an effect. 'Nothing' happened on stage, and yet the play yielded gripping action. On the morning after the performance, the students hotly debated how this effect could have come about. Everyone agreed that the play's message was what made it gripping. Ionesco's philosophy that not the theatre but the contemporary world is in itself absurd and no longer comprehensible functions here directly as the 'exciting trigger' that keeps the spectators gripped throughout all the scenes. They could not be dissuaded from 'the theatrical effect of modern philosophy'. When there was still no overall agreement by lunch and the fronts had become entrenched, I decided to do an experiment. We asked a student, who so far had not shown any especial talent, to prepare himself to come on stage after lunch (which he understood as a distinction), describing it as 'a concentration exercise'. The other students would watch from the auditorium how long someone can concentrate on stage without doing anything at all. So how long he could just stand there, without saying, thinking, or feeling anything. In order to do this, he must be sure not to move or show any facial expression. The best thing to do would be to think – because it is hard not to think about anything at all – about something that was entirely unrelated, but as commonplace and harmless as possible. The student promised to do his best and went away to prepare himself. We didn't say anything to the other students, as it was usual to begin after lunch with a short performance. When all the students had made their way back into the auditorium, we gave a sign behind the stage and the performance began. We very slowly raised the curtain. Our accomplice in crime really did stand on stage and do *nothing*. He didn't pull a face, he didn't say anything, he didn't move, indeed he had a completely empty facial expression, nothing especially noteworthy, simply the kind of look you can often observe when someone is elsewhere. So there was no way you could claim that he was simulating 'nothingness', there really was nothing there. As the curtain slowly rose the loud conversations stopped. The audience fell quiet as a mouse. Completely gripped, everyone followed the events on stage. After *nothing* had been happening for about four minutes, someone began to laugh in the auditorium, because he thought he was witnessing something absurdly comical. The others joined in, and it was the kind of laughter that many a comedian would have envied. Our accomplice on stage handled it well: he didn't do anything now either, even though he had had such a 'success'. For he of course thought we wanted to test how long he could do *nothing* but just stand there. The auditorium fell silent again. And now the audience remained silently gripped for about ten minutes. After about fifteen minutes we closed the curtain. The experiment was over. To discuss it, we all sat in the auditorium, our accomplice included, whom we had meanwhile let in on the trick.

Our question to the spectators: what happened in those fifteen minutes on stage? The result was astounding: they had seen an incredible amount. Indeed, the most varied of spectators had seen the most varied of things. Everyone agreed there was a 'great' beginning. The student on stage had brilliantly showed the concentrated strain with which he was planning 'something'. Some even claimed to have seen what he had planned: representing a criminal, he had planned to give himself over to the police. Then he had become inwardly uneasy, because he regretted his plan. And the way that he had then, without moving, stuck out the arrival of the police for nearly ten minutes with iron resolve, was deemed brilliant. The students argued about why they had laughed. A few claimed it was because of the Buster Keaton expression he had worn to show that 'he couldn't give a toss' about anything. Others thought they had seen how he actually wanted to say something the whole time, but couldn't get the slightest sound out. They found that hilarious. A girl disagreed. She had seen the tragedy of man in our industrialized society. In spite of all the other people around him, he was alone and silent. His silence was a protest, etc. When we asked our accomplice to tell us what he had been 'acting', curious reactions ensued. Most of the pupils were angry. They felt duped. Some laughed and said now they knew how to pass the next test. But some were also thoughtful.

We decided to adjourn and not evaluate this curious experiment until the following day. We added that they had just witnessed something unusual and that everyone can only experience once in their lives (namely only when they don't already know it). They had experienced *theatre itself*. Although what they had seen was not yet theatre (after all, the actor hadn't acted yet), in their behaviour as spectators they had actually answered a critical question, which may not have even been a question for them up to that point, namely who actually acts in theatre. If they would have answered without any hesitation before lunch that it is the actor, now this answer was no longer so easy. Because the actor specifically *didn't act*. Of course they could say they were fooled. They read into something that wasn't actually there. (After all, Carl Orff wrote a whole opera on that with the nice title *Astutuli!*) But on the other hand they hadn't been fooled at all. For all the meanings they had attached to the silence were entirely *possible*. So it wasn't actually a case of being fooled, but of giving possible *interpretations*. And in this respect the personal experiences that every spectator brings to a play from his real life of course play a major role: his social background, his attitudes, his outlook, his emotional state. But one thing had become clear. The spectator by no means takes the silence portrayed on stage as the only given, but rather projects *his possibilities* into it. Of course the spectator knows that the actor, not he, is acting, thus someone else onto whom he is transferring his possibilities. But that is precisely what is so attractive. The actor lends him his reality, as it were, so that the spectator's *possible performances* can – as agreed – be made *real* for the duration of the performance, but without the *risk of reality*. The spectator can treat his *possible* performances as if they were *real*. But without being forced to react realistically, for in reality he would come to the help of the silent person and not just observe him. The action that had so moved our students in *The Bald Primadonna* was therefore action that they had created themselves and which the play, which contained true observations of absurd situations in contemporary reality, had encouraged them to make. For it has been a curious characteristic of theatre as long as theatre has existed: spectators turn everything they see on stage *into action*.

If you were to walk very slowly and completely silently up to another person on the street, that person would ask themselves, 'What does he want?' If a person on stage walks slowly and silently towards the audience, everyone is sure: 'He wants something!' So the spectator immediately assumes a certain 'standpoint' from the person on stage: Is he thinking about something? Is he planning something? Is he waiting for something? Is he unsure? Or is he just tired? Is he speechless? Or is he trying to hide something? So the spectator *expects* action. He is always looking for a story on stage. Everything that the actor does on stage, even if he is doing nothing, is interpreted by the spectator as action. Even if a director, following the contemporary mainstream, declares that he no longer wants to depict any action on stage because in reality too nothing is happening any more and the world is stagnating, the spectator (as long as the actors are good) will interpret precisely *that* as action. This 'general agreement' that is as old as theatre itself was what Brecht had in mind when he spoke about the art of spectating. The spectator must understand that he is not just a spectator in the theatre, but a 'maker'.

Meanwhile it had got late and it would have been inappropriate to interrupt proceedings. We carried on discussing the experiment right into the early hours of the morning. As the next day dawned, we felt as if we had both – teachers and students – experienced something essential about theatre. Certainly nothing that is completely new. After all, who doesn't know Brecht's line that two art forms must be developed, the art of acting and the art of spectating? But when we go to our place of work every day in order to rehearse, while we are ready to question everything that happens on stage, we take the stage itself for granted. We avoid naturalism *on* the stage, but our relationship to the stage is a naturalistic one. Just because theatre is our everyday business and we are paid for it, just because the actor learns a part and plays it to an audience he usually doesn't even know, just because the audience generally sits quietly in their seats and only 'reacts' every now and then, we had decisively, but incorrectly, concluded that theatre is made only by theatre people. Even though our aim is precisely to counter everyday habits, we had ourselves become used to the everyday business of theatre. The way daily life in theatre appeared had us wagging the dog by its tail. We thought it was our duty as theatre people to shake people out of their tendency just to 'sit there passively'. And in order to achieve this, we turned to all kinds of measures because we were dissatisfied with the way in which people had quietly sat there up to now. We 'exploded' the dividing-line between the stage and the auditorium by putting the stage in the midst of the spectators. We rolled whole rows of spectators onto our stage in order to 'involve' them in our act. We gave out pieces of paper and had a vote. We 'democratized' the theatre and set up discussions in the foyer after the performances in which primarily the spectators spoke. We even planned to interrupt the play on stage at important moments in order to lure the unsuspecting spectators into discussions about how it should develop. These measures were sometimes extremely refreshing even for the professional theatre. But we neglected to do one thing: to ask how the spectator is actively involved in the event of theatrical production itself. Not after or before the showing, not beside or behind the stage, but on stage, *during* the actual performance. And how this involvement is different to other events, for example discussions, meetings, conversations that are certainly important but can only enhance theatre, not replace it. In short: what the role of the spectator *really* is in theatre.

Our experiment produced a surprising answer. *The primary player in theatre is not the actor, but the spectator.* He isn't actually physically involved in the acting (and there is no break through on stage, not even a happening, that can achieve this). On the contrary, what attracts him to theatre is precisely that the spectator transposes *his plays*, that he must otherwise 'play' in his mind's internalized model of the world, onto the stage for the duration of the performance.[21] Here, they are *enacted by others* and so the spectator is able to watch them. Thus it is wrong to consider the so-called silence in the auditorium to come from an audience lazily wallowing in its emotions which political theatre must shake up if it wants an 'active' spectator. It is certainly true that this 'silence' was abused by bourgeois theatre in its attempt to declare itself sacrosanct. But in reality 'silence' in the first instance signals nothing other than that the spectator has begun to perform. *The action on stage becomes his action that he simultaneously plays out in an internalized model in his head.* As the two do not have to be identical, the tension thus produced has a 'transgressive' effect ('Überschreitung'). This consists of discovering 'other variants' while at play, that is to say, new possibilities. It is just as wrong to undervalue or devalue 'naive' reactions from the spectator, such as laughing, crying, clapping, etc., because they are too 'simple'. For they are not 'the only thing' the spectator is doing, even if 'the rest' is not immediately visible to the actor, because the actor is of course himself this 'rest'. *Reactions are the expressions generated by the spectator's play, not the play itself. They indicate that a play is being performed.* They are (or should be) feedback to the players on stage that the 'theatrical effect' has taken place. 'Theatrical effect' is what I call that 'general agreement' that is as old as theatre itself; namely that the spectator goes to the theatre in order to transform, of his own accord, the events that are shown on stage into his own behaviour. This he does for his own pleasure, whether he agrees, protests, is amazed, doubts, mocks, cries, laughs, etc. It would be pointless to expect the theatre of the future generally to expect or provoke other 'reactions', for example by spontaneously including the spectator in the play. 'Play' in theatre, including when it is spontaneous or improvised, will always be an 'agreed' kind of play. Its effect is generated when spectators and actors are aware of this 'agreement' and abide by it: as a general rule that allows theatre to exist at all (what I called the 'theatrical effect'), and as a specific principle that underpins a play as it is performed.

But precisely in order to give the spectator the *greatest possible amount of space for his play*, this space must be sufficiently *stable*. That is to say, it needs 'fixed points'. 'Fixed points' in the *Fabel*, genre, stage space, musical commentaries, indeed even in the lighting. Even improvisation must be 'agreed' if it is to inspire a similar kind of improvisation in the spectator. Indeed, in order to tease out *the greatest number of variations* from the spectator, the stage itself must be sufficiently *unvaried* and 'known' to the spectator even when the unknown is being shown. Precisely in order to awaken his spontaneity, theatre needs to strike him as sufficiently familiar, it needs 'tested' rules and practised 'tricks' that stand the test of time and can be learned (we have already spoken of how the art of acting *and* the art of spectating are needed). A completely different opinion has become widespread today, however. It counts as 'liberating' and aims to produce 'simplicity' for the theatre by radically simplifying its means. So greater variety through greater arbitrariness, more imagination through simple improvisation, greater freedom for the spectator through liberating him from every *Fabel,* an opening up by 'leaving open' absolutely everything. The philosophical 'support' for this comes from 'deconstruction'. It seeks to heal the world by splitting it up into unconnected individual events, as every 'order' is believed to be an 'ideology', and thus a lie. Only what resists the dictate of truth can now be considered 'true'. A forerunner of postmodernism, the French philosopher Jean-François Lyotard gives us this quotation: 'Let us struggle against the white terror of truth with and for the red cruelty of singularities.' In theatre such 'simplifications' often enough turn out to be complications – to the point of utter incomprehensibility. Absolute 'liberties' on stage trap the spectator in a state of perplexity: he becomes helpless. Goethe the theatre director already knew that when he praised 'complex' theatre over 'simple' theatre:

> The more complete a creation becomes, the less the parts resemble one another. In other cases, the whole is more or less the same as the parts; but here the whole is dissimilar to the parts. The more the parts resemble one another, the less they are subordinate. Only when the parts are subordinated can a more complete creation be discerned.

Only by making a 'detour' via an aesthetic process of realization is theatre able to show reality 'simply'. And by making this detour it really does bring about – imitating the different contexts of reality – *new contexts* and is able to 'create reality anew', and thus to change it. In short: theatre, as theatre, must itself possess enough 'reality' (as the art of theatre), for the spectator's 'play' to have a real chance. And this reality of the stage must be in itself stable enough (in terms of *Fabel*, *Gestus*[22] and action) to offer a suitable 'range' for the spectator's play. Stage reality always also entails a degree of realization from the spectator. That is the *realism* inherent in theatre. It is this aspect alone that allows theatre to show on stage *as real* things that do not exist in reality. For the measure of this reality is not how it directly corresponds with reality but *how the spectator realizes it. Something is real if it leads to reality by guiding the spectator towards his real playing.* Theatre's worth as a place of entertainment is secured if the spectator playfully transposes what is shown on stage onto the needs and experiences of *his* life. Brecht writes in his additions to the *Short Organum for the Theatre*:

> In order for it to be possible, in a playful manner, for the particular nature of the kinds of behaviour and situations shown in theatre to come across and be criticized, the audience composes other additional kinds of behaviour and situations in its head and contrasts them with those shown in the theatre as the action unfolds. With this, the audience itself becomes a narrator.

After this very detailed description of the Skara experiment, one could be forgiven for concluding that theatre 'makes itself'. In our experiment it really was the case that 'nothing' happened on stage. The 'theatrical effect', the spectator's playing and his 'reworking' of the events shown into a reaction took place apparently 'by law of nature', like an echo coming back out of the forest. But who has not heard of Brecht's 'categorical imperative':

> Without opinions and intentions it is not possible to make representations. Without knowledge, nothing can be shown; how are you supposed to know what is worth knowing? If the actor doesn't want to be a parrot or a monkey, he has to take on history's lesson about how humans live together by taking part in the class wars.

For Brecht did not demand no activity, but rather a very special one. If theatre wants to have some kind of effect, then this effect must be created 'artistically'. In short, it must use its techniques to bring 'opinions and intentions' into play. Brecht, not just a practitioner of theatre but also an expert on it, cleverly used that 'ancient' theatrical effect for this by suggesting that the actor must take account of the spectator throughout his performance. That is to say: *he must play with him*. Also in the sense that he deals with him 'playfully'. He must set his act up in such a manner that the spectator is constantly challenged and encouraged to join in. And this so that the collaborative play takes on a certain direction that is determined by the *Fabel*, genre, and intention of the play.

A further curious characteristic of theatre that Brecht uses and that is also as old as theatre itself is relevant here: the spectator wants to be wrong. Or, as Brecht puts it, the actor must want to 'fool' the spectator, because that is what is expected of him. The spectator doesn't just want events on stage, he wants *unexpected events*. Surprise is *the* 'magic formula' for theatre and the most elementary form of pleasure. People go to the theatre to be surprised. They expect the unexpected. Nestroy knew this every bit as well as Aeschylus. Brecht's achievement is to have formulated this 'ancient characteristic' of theatre as a theatre theory and to have developed a usable working method for it (which I will discuss in the next point). In rehearsal he called it, not without humour, 'the great Not–But'. The play must be performed, produced and written in such a manner that the spectator is surprised by the plot development and the characters' behaviour, because what he is expecting does NOT happen, BUT the unexpected occurs. That is to say, the actor must encourage expectations to develop in the 'wrong' direction: Faust does NOT, as expected, free Gretchen from the dungeon, BUT he delivers her into the hands of the executioner; after it has become apparent that Godot will never come and it is pointless to wait for him any longer, Vladimir and Estragon do NOT go away, BUT they carry on waiting; Galileo, who would let no one dissuade him from his theory that the earth revolves around the sun, does NOT stand up to the Inquisition, BUT he retracts his theory; Chaplin, with a newspaper in front of his face, does NOT fall into the open manhole that he is heading straight for, BUT, in spite of the paper in front of his nose, skirts around it; Coriolanus, unmoved by all the requests from his friends, does NOT ignore his mother's plea to spare Rome, BUT leaves with his whole army, their plan not executed. The expectation that is NOT fulfilled has to be built up by the actor and the accompanying production to such an extent that the BUT is a 'breath-taking' surprise. (Brecht's slogan for this: 'If you want to topple a monument, you have to build it up.') When the expected does not happen, then that is already a discovery: the expected was not the only possibility after all, there are others. The spectator is encouraged to bring lots of similar variants into play and not to keep his opinion to himself. (That is not a particularly 'intellectual' demand of 'Brechtian theatre', as is always claimed, but can be seen in every pub when beer-drinkers sitting round a table keep on interrupting each other with their own version of events.) The 'surprise', as both a comical and a serious twist, is thus also an effective means of provoking 'interventionist thought'. It prevents the spectator 'fatalistically' accepting something and forces him to ask why. *Why* does Othello kill Desdemona for no reason? *Why* doesn't Coriolanus, whose mother taught him to stand firm, resist this selfsame mother's plea when to relent will entail certain death? Surprise is above all the great pleasure provided by 'comical and tragic circumstances' that distinguishes theatre.

'So "Brechtian theatre" is also about deceiving and misleading the spectator!' I hear those people cry who passionately misunderstand Brecht. 'For if the spectator is deliberately misled and only finds out at the end that what he saw was wrong, then that is nothing other than that old chestnut, *catharsis*. Aristotle wanted to arouse pity and fear, in order ultimately to purge people of their pity and fear, and with Brecht you are supposed to be misled, in order to be freed from your misconceptions.'

I can't even say this is completely wrong. Brecht too must have sensed something like this. That is probably why he complemented his 'Not–But' with another suggestion: the play must be produced and acted in such a manner that the spectator sees a scene in a 'new light' after he has seen the next. And retrospectively he figures out where the concrete details were to be found in the preceding scene that indicated the surprising turning point ('Drehpunkt').[23] He called this 'leafing back' and deemed it to be a useful and extremely entertaining affair in his theatre that, for a time, he called 'epic theatre'.

The spectator as producer – this is how you could describe the effect on the audience that 'Brechtian theatre' aims for, starting out from the 'ancient' fact that a story will only become a reality in theatre if it is realized by the spectator. And thus Brecht also only considered a play completely written when it had been performed to an audience. The story, the *Fabel* that a play tells, is simply not a fixed 'substance' in a play, like it is a characteristic of a map to show roads and paths. Or, to adapt a phrase from Wittgenstein: 'The *Fabel*'s existence is its use'.

The mere fact that a play by Brecht is performed far from guarantees that Brecht is actually performed. When, in a performance of *Mother Courage and Her Children*, Mother Courage curses war at the end of the sixth scene because her daughter was attacked and disfigured for life, and the shaken audience breaks out in frenetic applause (as often happens), then Brecht has been left behind, even though he is being played, for here the 'great tragedy' has been overlooked: that people's participation is what makes war possible in the first place – it was the mother herself who, in order to make a profit and with no regard for the dangers, sent her daughter out to procure new goods.[24]

If people watching a production of Beckett's *Waiting for Godot*, the declared 'antithesis' of Brecht, after all, are not prepared in the end to share Vladimir and Estragon's fate of continuing to wait for Godot, but rather make fun of those who wait for something that they themselves will not do, then they have come considerably closer to Brecht (although I am not claiming that this is 'Brechtian theatre'). For the spectator is challenged not to follow the story on stage as if he were harnessed to it, but rather to narrate it to its end *as he sees fit*. On the basis of *his* sensibilities, *his* situation and *his* class experience. This can in the process go way beyond the author's intentions. As indeed a play's intention and its realism must by no means be identical. ('A play is not more faithful than it is true' was Brecht's often-repeated response to the question of 'being faithful' to a work.) The trigger for Shakespeare to write *Coriolanus* was doubtless his lament

Illustration 4 Mother Courage curses the war (Scene 6). (Copy by R. Berlau/ Hoffmann.)

that with the death of the great Queen Elizabeth the feeling for greatness had been lost in England, for now people thought only of 'the price of corn'. The people just seem too cheap for great heroes. But Shakespeare's realism far transcends his intentions. Politically, Shakespeare was closer to the monarchy than the rising bourgeoisie, the merchant classes (this is understandable when one considers that the first thing the puritans, or merchants, did after their victory was close the theatres because they 'distracted people from their work'). But that didn't stop the refined playwright from giving the merchants good arguments too, knowing that this only made his heroes all the greater. And Shakespeare's 'elementary realism' allowed us to say something quite different without changing the actual text: perhaps the hero is too dear for the people. In the history of theatre there are astonishing examples of audiences 'continuing the story'. It is almost incomprehensible today, but – as Stanislavski reports – when Chekhov's *Cherry Orchard* was performed in Moscow in 1917 it provoked such a revolutionary reaction among the spectators that they went directly from the Art Theatre onto the street and erected barricades. This is an effect that certainly does not reside in the play, which 'only' documents the decline of a bourgeois family, but in a specific context it did inspire the spectator to finish the story of the felled cherry orchard in a revolutionary way.

Day five

With regard to (4): Brecht's theatre is marked by its way of working

Here the first question is always: does 'Brechtian theatre' need a Brechtian actor? True, there will always be actors who are more experienced than others in dealing with Brecht. But I have my difficulties with the term 'Brechtian actor', implying as it does that 'Brechtian theatre' is a matter for specialists. These days there is no real theatrical talent that is entirely unaffected by Brecht. And vice versa, talented actors naturally bring something with them that Brecht particularly valued and which is indispensable to his theatre: a feeling for reality, the ability to take pleasure in observation and to enjoy contradictions, the desire and ability to reproduce all this. Brecht's theatre is no 'speciality' as far as I'm concerned. I consider his way of appropriating the world around him to be universal. In this sense it is applicable to all plays that report in a contradictory fashion on the world, regardless of whether they do so directly or fantastically, in ancient or in modern guise, as fact or as a dream, indeed even the absurd is welcome as long as it shows the people behind it. As one can read in Brecht's *Messingkauf Dialogues*, his notes about making theatre:

> Why should I want to silence the realm of suppositions, dreams, senses? People also deal with social problems this way. Supposition and knowledge are not opposites. Supposition leads to knowledge, and knowledge to supposition. Plans come from dreams, and plans are turned into dreams [...]

Such a work method is no specialist area, it applies to theatre generally. It is the attempt, through simplification, to make the possibilities of theatre richer again. For the 'simplicity' of theatre compared to the unlimited nature of television, for example, is also its advantage, 'forcing' theatre as it does to show everything 'only' as the behaviour of people. Even 'ghostly objectivity' can thus be understood as the work of man and is with this dependent on human intervention. Brecht's method assumes the 'simple' fact that there is not one actor on stage but at least two, who enter into a relationship with one another, causing a 'situation' to occur. This is also the case for example with monologues, where the speaker establishes a relationship with himself. Even prayers are a 'relationship for two', for here God is the partner. And in Brecht the situations follow on from one another to form the story, also called a *Fabel*. And from this follows theatre. Here, incidentally, Brecht realigns himself with Aristotle, his 'deadly enemy', as he himself called him, who in his *Poetics* calls the *Fabel* 'the soul of theatre'. So, before an actor does anything else on stage, he must take on a stance towards another individual. Brecht called the totality of stances taken over the course of the play the play's *gestic*[25] quality; but he termed an individual stance taken by a character a *Gestus*.

Brecht invented the term '*Gestus*', and to this day there is no plural form for it. '*Gestus*' – like '*Verfremdung*' – has been the cause of considerable confusion. Generally, *Gestus* is confused with gesture. Recently I heard a not unknown director in a not unknown theatre referring to Brecht as he staged the play *Das Herz eines Boxers* (*The Heart of a Boxer*) saying, 'Make a bigger *Gestus* for me and take a great swing before you knock him out.' But even respected scholars, whose contribution to Marxist thought is unquestioned, are not immune. In an essay entitled 'Zum Verständnis Bert Brechts' ('Understanding Bert Brecht'), none other than Leo Kofler writes:

Along with the well-known technique of *Verfremdung*, Brecht considers one of the most important guarantees of successful *Verfremdung* to reside in the gesture. It can ambiguously reflect human ambiguity and thus offers us an important tool for making discoveries. [...] It falls between physical expression and language. [...] Thus the gesture proves itself to be far more than the outmoded concept implies, more than mimicry, which up to now has tended to characterize its wider applicability.

Brecht must have suspected the mistakes to which his *Gestus* would give rise when he warned in his *On Gestic Music*:

> *Gestus* should not be confused with gesticulating; we are not talking about emphatic or explanatory movements of the hand. It is a matter of whole stances. A language is gestic when it draws on the *Gestus*, makes clear certain stances that the speaker takes on towards other people.

But as Brecht himself only spoke of a 'useful way of working', I only properly understood what the *gestic* actually means for theatre (and not just for theatre) from the composer Hanns Eisler, who has been said to understand Brecht better than Brecht himself. In a conversation with the dramaturg Hans Bunge he says at one point: 'The *gestic* is one of Brecht's inspired discoveries. He discovered it just as much as Einstein discovered his famous formula.' If you follow this logic, language, which Goethe in his *Rules for Actors* after all describes as 'of the greatest importance and substance' in theatre, is not in fact the 'language of theatre', at least not primarily. The spoken word is just one means, alongside gesture, facial expression, and movement, that the actor uses to make himself understood. The language of theatre, however – and this is Brecht's discovery – is the *Gestus*. The *Gestus* that the actor takes on as a 'whole stance' in a particular situation determines everything else: tone, gesture, bodily posture, movement. Indeed, even language, the spoken word, only becomes comprehensible when a certain *Gestus* underlies it. Only with this *Gestus* does the real content of what is spoken become clear, because its situation becomes clear: there is an argument, someone wants to convince, someone is being insulting, asking for something, demanding, rejecting, inviting, cursing, warning, ordering, flattering, judging, becoming enraged, seeking reconciliation, and so on. If someone is grateful to someone else, for example, he will say 'thank you' differently to someone who uses the same words to refuse to jump into cold water. The German word 'schön' ('fine') has in purely language-orientated theatre a single meaning, namely to be fine. Even at stage school, students are taught that the word 'fine' should be enunciated finely. Goethe also advises in his *Rules for Actors* that the content of a text determine the tone: 'He [the actor] uses a gruesome tone for the gruesome, a tender tone for the tender, a ceremonial tone for the ceremonial [...]'. So much for Goethe the theatre director. In *gestic* theatre, on the other hand, 'fine' can mean much more than just being 'fine', depending on the standpoint and context in which it is said. For example, if a man is asked by his friend if he can lend him his new car for the weekend, and the man answers 'fine', then he is certainly not expressing great pleasure. Likewise a father's exclamation, 'A fine job you've done there', when his son breaks a neighbour's window with his football, is hardly intended to convey joy. Not to mention the phrase, 'A fine cock-up'. Brecht describes his understanding of the *gestic* thus:

> A language is gestic when it is underpinned by a certain gestus that shows the stance taken by the speaker towards another person. The sentence in the Bible, 'Pluck the eye that offends you out' is poorer in gestic terms than Luther's translation, 'If thine eye offend thee, pluck it out'. In the latter example, the eye in question is mentioned first. The opening clause contains the clear Gestus that assuming the eye to be annoying is correct, while the liberating advice comes last, like an ambush.

It is interesting to note here how Brecht overlaps with the views of that well known linguist Ludwig Wittgenstein, who said of language: 'The meaning of a word is its use in speech'.[26]

Just as Einstein did not 'invent' relativity, but rather discovered something that had always been present in nature, the '*gestic*' is not – as is often claimed – Brecht's invention. He 'only' discovered what theatre had produced in its heyday and what bourgeois theatre, concerned more with mystification than enlightenment, had forgotten. Brecht once more mobilized the 'primitive roots' of theatre, so to speak, for his new intentions. Who in theatre has not experienced the 'mystery of fluffed lines', when an actor says the wrong lines on stage because he cannot think of the right ones, but the audience doesn't notice a thing. When I studied acting in the Köthen theatre under Herr Krienitz, the 'older leading actor' of the theatre, one of the first rules I had to learn was 'Wrong lines that nobody hears, means your acting gets the all-clear'. Famous 'mistakes' also happened at the Berliner Ensemble and were passed down like jewels from generation to generation. Helene Weigel as Mother Courage, for example, who after a 'Catholic' attack changes her flag but not her allegiance, was supposed to say: 'A trader's price is what matters, not his religion. And protestant trousers will keep you warm too.' But what she said was, 'A trader's price is what matters, not his religion. And protestant trousers taste good too.' The audience, listening intently, didn't notice a thing, for Weigel had said the wrong lines with the right *Gestus* of being 'absolutely in the right', so that the audience too was convinced she was right. Once the dominance of the *Gestus* even came to our rescue in an extremely embarrassing situation. In the 1960s the Berliner Ensemble was invited with its production of Brecht's *The Messingkauf Dialogues* to take part in the 'Experimenta' at the Schauspielhaus in Frankfurt am Main, where model scenes were also being shown from other plays. One of these was the concluding scene from Brecht's *The Mother*, where Weigel as Pelagea Vlassova speaks the famous poem, 'In Praise of Dialectics' at the end: 'Whoever is still alive, should never say "never"/ What is certain is not certain / Things will not stay as they are.' The performance took place in an extremely tense atmosphere, as before we arrivd the CDU[27] had posted bills with the words 'The Cossacks are Coming' all over Frankfurt, and the Junge Union[28] had formed a cordon all round the Schauspielhaus on the evening of the performance to prevent people from entering the building. This of course only increased the audience's interest, as they partly had to push their way physically in. When Weigel began her 'In Praise of Dialectics' there was consequently an aura of expectancy in the room. And, carried away by the revolutionary atmosphere, she didn't notice herself saying something quite different: 'What is certain is not certain / Things *will stay* as they are.' I wanted the ground to swallow me up, for I was the director, after all. But the audience was so convinced by the *Gestus* of maternal reassurance with which Weigel, red flag in hand, head cocked and leaning slightly forward into the audience, spoke her lines, that they thanked her with thunderous applause for the fact that the world will *not* stay as it is. How insisting on the text 'alone' can by contrast ruin a whole scene was something I was to discover when I directed *Coriolanus* at the Royal National Theatre in London, where I and my colleague Joachim Tenschert were invited by Laurence Olivier, director of the National in the 1970s. Coriolanus was to be played by the famous British-Canadian actor Christopher Plummer. He had badly wanted to work with the

'BE chaps' after he saw our Berlin production in London. But the collaboration failed in the first rehearsals, when Plummer refused in the very first scene to brandish his sword in order to disperse some plebeians who were staging a sit-in against army service. His opinion: why should a sword be necessary when a Plummer appears? All explanation was to no avail, he stuck by his refusal and explained why: If 'a Plummer' has to wield a sword in order to disperse plebeians, that would damage his market value. We, less bothered about market value, insisted on the sword and so it came about that we, to Plummer's surprise, took his threat that he would 'chuck it all in' seriously and asked an understudy to take Plummer's place. An understudy is someone who sits in on rehearsals and learn the lines 'just in case'. But 'Larry', as Olivier wanted to be called, who had himself played Coriolanus four times, felt the understudy was not aristocratic enough, not to mention the fact that he had a strong Welsh accent. We, on the other hand, liked the young man's real directness and so Coriolanus became this understudy's first big part at the theatre. His name by the way is Anthony Hopkins. Hopkins is a *gestic* actor through and through, it is in his nature.

Coriolanus's mother by contrast, the great American actress Constance Cummings, went 'completely by Shakespeare', which however, as we were to discover, only referred to the lines (this is, incidentally, and as we were also to discover, the approach of almost all 'famous Shakespeare actors'). Now, in *Coriolanus* there is the famous scene where Volumnia holds her son to account for not managing to control himself at the market where he was canvassing for the plebeians to support his election to consul (a process that had to take place in Rome in a simple shirt without pockets to prevent the candidate handing out bribes). He called them an unworthy 'rabble', so that those who had supported him now withdrew their support. Constance Cummings scolded her son with the anger of a disappointed mother and patrician who wants more than anything else to see her son on the consul's seat. We were delighted with the almost classical force of the scene, when, right in the middle of it, Constance Cummings suddenly fell into the tone of a tender mother and whispered 'Oh, Sir, Sir, Sir' to her son. We thought it was a joke and asked Constance to play the right scene. But she informed us that this was just what she was doing. When Shakespeare writes 'Oh, Sir, Sir, Sir', she argued, then he really means 'Oh, Sir, Sir, Sir'. And 'Sir' is ultimately a 'respectful form of address'. When we pointed out that the scene was 'rubbish' if this was so, she was unmoved and commented that she at least was sticking to Shakespeare. In our hour of need, we turned to 'Larry', the 'famous

Illustration 5 Coriolanus at the National Theatre, London, with Anthony Hopkins as Coriolanus and Constance Cummings as Volumnia (1971). (John Timbers/ArenaPAL.)

Shakespeare actor'. He too initially confirmed that one 'must stick to Shakespeare' and 'Sir' is a respectful form of address and not an insult. And once more old Brecht helped, who suggests turning to dialect in such situations. We asked 'Larry' if there was something similar in English slang to the Berlin habit of saying to someone who has just messed something up, 'Mein lieber Herr Gesangsverein!' or 'Großer Gott'![29] Here too neither the 'Herr Gesangsverein' nor the 'Großer Gott' are really meant, of course. So couldn't the 'Oh, Sir, Sir, Sir!' actually be an expression of serious disapproval on the part of Volumnia, to be spoken with the *Gestus* of bitter criticism? 'Larry' had to admit that there wasn't just something similar in English, but that English people even particularly like to use it in everyday speech

71

situations. Constance remained sceptical, but after this very scene was especially successful at the premiere for its 'masterly display of rage', she concluded that 'the great Shakespeare' was also 'the greatest "gestical" writer'. And here she was quite right.

The 'dominance of the *gestic*' probably also forms the basis for what people refer to as the 'magic' of theatre. I became directly acquainted with this magic once through a not uncomical series of events. The Institute for High Energy Physics, the GDR's nuclear research institute, was in Zeuthen, near Berlin. The physicists from this institute saw a performance of *Galileo* and afterwards wanted a discussion with the actor who had played Galileo, the great Ernst Busch, as was usual in the Berliner Ensemble. They were interested in how one, for example, learns roles and remembers so many lines, how he, Busch, had come to theatre in the first place, what he as an actor feels when Galileo recants, and so on. So they wanted to know things that they didn't know. After the performance everyone met in the canteen. Busch, having performed *Galileo* about a hundred times, was of the opinion that he was not just a great actor but also a great physicist and took his listeners quite by surprise when he immediately started talking about modern physics. And he did this with the passionate *Gestus* of a seasoned teacher, a veritable Galileo, for at least half an hour. Once again I wished the earth would swallow me up, for I had briefly studied physics once. But the physicists listened in fascination, the elite physicists of the GDR no less! After about thirty minutes Busch finished and the physicists applauded and thanked us warmly. The next morning Karl Lanius, the director of the Institute, rang me up. 'Manfred,' he said in his careful, scientific manner, 'something strange has just happened. Busch spoke about physics for half an hour yesterday after the performance and I didn't notice until the following morning that it was all nonsense.'

Day six

More *Gestus*. Not only individual characters take on a *Gestus* towards one another, a scene, indeed a whole production, can also have a *Gestus* by taking on a certain stance towards the third and most important partner: the audience. For example, a *Gestus* of provocation. Of encouragement. Of appeal. Of confusion. Of mockery. Of reassurance or commiseration. Or indeed a *Gestus* of shaming. One and the same play can even change its content by changing *Gestus*. In 1959 we produced *The Resistible Rise of Arturo Ui* with the *Gestus* of a market crier's street ballad that tells an incredible story. Alongside the entertaining and humorous 'gangster story' we wanted to shame those who had called Hitler a criminal but still regarded him today as a 'great criminal' whose demonic nature had seduced them. We aimed to do this not least through the fairground setting in which we placed the 'famous' story. We created a perfect travesty of Ui / Hitler as a little scoundrel (but no less dangerous for this) who creates a racket to blackmail individual vegetable stalls and thus begin his 'rise'. Today the play would probably have to be performed quite differently. With the *Gestus* of reporting a great sensation, for example, that begins with the 'great' rise of a gangster to a 'statesman'. It would emphasize the 'capital' achievement of those trust financers who enable the gangster's rise to statesman in the first place because they welcome a gangster who will keep the 'little trouble-makers' in their place, and who drop him and bedevil him as a 'terrorist' as soon as he has served his purpose. Shaming the audience by making a 'major' historical figure into a street robber is not a possible *Gestus* here, but rather shocking people with the facts that they think they know from the daily evening news, but whose immediate and bizarre 'importance', that is to say the link to important sums of money, had up until now never struck them. Such a *Gestus* would alter the content of the play and turn a historical play about Hitler into a history of the present day: the Taliban and a Saddam Hussein would be visible. As would the Pentagon, which first arms these figures with plenty of money and weapons because it needs them in its fight against the Russians and the rebellious Ayatollahs, only then to turn on them as 'terrorists' when they are no longer needed, once again using plenty of money and weapons, for now the alibi of 'terrorism' is needed in order to carry on making plenty of money out of weapons.

The composer Hanns Eisler also spoke of '*gestic*' music. Apart from songs that are sung in a particular *Gestus* in order to embolden, enrage, please or criticize people, he meant the term to refer to music that comments on events on stage by countering them with its own *Gestus*. For example, in order to tell of contradictions inherent in an event but which are not immediately visible on stage. This can increase the elements of discovery and pleasure to an astounding degree. Think, for example, of Eisler's music for Brecht's *Life of Galileo*. Here the songs that report on the respective state of science and the scientists are sung in the manner of oratorical hymns. The paradox that science and scientist must assert themselves against the dogma of the church even when the church is apparently absent is rendered astoundingly poetic and tangibly real thanks to the way the sacred *Gestus* of the music contradicts the reporting *Gestus* of the verse. Contradictions between music and text can however also create quite different paradoxes. In the case of Becher's *Winterschlacht* (*Winter Battle*), produced by the Berliner Ensemble in 1955, Brecht and Eisler almost had a terrible argument. *Winterschlacht* tells the tale of a young soldier who receives the 'Knight's Cross' in 1941 for conquering a high point one hundred kilometres before Moscow, but whose belief in the 'Führer' is destroyed by events on the Russian front. In the end, he refuses to bury partisans alive and is forced to commit an 'honourable' suicide. Not a good play, but one of the few back then that showed the conflicts experienced by young people in Hitler's war. Brecht, who co-directed the play with me, felt the end lacked an 'earned apocalypse'. He invented a pantomime of retreat that was originally not part of the play. In the deepest Russian winter a few battered figures stagger over the stage, scantily clad in rags or newspapers, guns inverted as crutches; only a helmet here and there to remind us that these are members of the 'invincible army' that once held Europe to ransom. 'Biting, vicious' recorded music was supposed to complete the debacle of these 'heroes'. The first performance of the music to the entire cast of the Ensemble however nearly became a debacle of its own: Eisler had 'smuggled in violins' (Brecht). For over the loudspeakers a magnificent 'triumphant music' sounded, played by the Große Staatskapelle Berlin. But before Brecht could loudly launch into his well-known 'Ceterum censeo' against violins in his theatre and against 'battle music of any type' (by which he unfairly understood 'symphonies, violins, Beethoven, etc.'), the music switched from the *Gestus* of triumph to one of great mourning. And all of this accompanying the needy figures sadly staggering across the stage. We were 'shattered'. Even Brecht couldn't deny the effect and 'forgot' that he had actually demanded a 'thin, vicious music'. For Eisler had curtly answered Brecht's question as to why the music should be so triumphant by saying, 'These are fascists who are being destroyed'. And in response to Brecht's question, 'So why the mourning?' he asked a question of his own, 'Are they not Germans?' The 'pantomime of retreat' became one of the most impressive closing scenes that has ever been staged at the Berliner Ensemble.

Alongside '*gestic* music', Brecht also spoke of the *Gestus* of the stage-set. This is the stance that a stage-set, whether realist or constructivist, takes towards the audience. The empty stage in the first production of *Mother Courage* in Berlin in 1949, with only Mother Courage's covered wagon, once heavily laden and then impoverished once more, rolling into war, had a real *Gestus*: it was an invitation to the audience to join in and make up for what was lacking on stage with their own experiences of the war that had just finished.

Brecht's discovery of the *gestic*, that Eisler valued as highly as Einstein's 'famous formula', goes far beyond theatre. Eisler spoke of how Brecht created a German language afresh and compared it to Luther's translation of the Bible. Luther also refreshed the written language of scholarship with spoken language. Thus the sermon was also no longer held in ritualized Latin, but in comprehensible German. Language became *gestic*. It not only described theses, but also stories that should be meaningful to the parish. And if one is looking for a way into Brecht's language, then it should be here, with Luther, and not with German Classicism. The high culture of Weimar also gave rise to a high German that, thanks to the realities of regional dialects, was not spoken anywhere. This was a 'classical' achievement for literature if one thinks of Goethe's *Iphigenia*, but this high point was also an end point, for the spoken, '*gestic*' language was once more made into a literary language that shunned the *gestic*, or real events. With Kleist, language comes back into events. Brecht too wrote by speaking. And language is for him action. Not just in his plays, but also in his lyric poetry, indeed even in his theoretical texts, which he liked to read out to us before he wrote them up. And he never denied his original dialect when writing. His Swabian-Bavarian accent can still be heard in the almost Latinized texts of the *Short Organum*. His Puntila, his Mother Courage, indeed his Galileo are unthinkable without the Bavarian 'tones' of Karl Valentin. But Brecht is not about dialect pure, as is the case with Gerhart Hauptmann – quite masterfully, by the way. For Brecht, speaking naturally is always also about speaking in a distinctive manner that is deliberate in *Gestus* and tone. Syntax and words of a dialect remain, but are formulated in the manner of 'high German'. This causes serious and comical effects alike. Puntila's language that combines simplicity with 'big opinions' is alone responsible for much of the comedy in the play. Brecht created language afresh. It is unmistakeably 'Brechtian' and at the same time universal. Likewise there is no greatness without naivety in his language, and no naivety without greatness. I believe not only linguistics still needs to discover Brecht's achievement. Even without John Fuegi's humorous claim on the occasion of Brecht's hundredth birthday that Brecht couldn't speak German properly and let cherished female colleagues write his plays, the 'centenary' would have been a good moment finally to speak about Brecht's Lutheran linguistic achievement. But back to theatre.

There is a further important criterion for '*gestic*' acting. Brecht called it the rule of 'one-thing-after-another'. In 1951 he noted under

the heading 'General tendencies that an actor should fight against':
'Instead of acting one thing after another, acting one thing out of
another.' Or, as he would say in rehearsal when actors tried to inte-
grate individual events into 'overarching curves', 'Forget the curve and
play one thing after another'. (It is interesting to note that Brecht's
supposed antithesis, Konstantin Stanislavski, came through many
detours to a similar opinion, when he told his actors to make 'physical
actions', and not feelings or personal characteristics, their starting
point.) In many theatres, and even more so in many theatre schools,
work on a role begins by determining the 'character'. There are even
specific actors for specific characters: the 'hero', the 'schemer', the
'gullible', the 'vamp', and more recently the 'raver', the 'socially integrated', the 'cop', the 'hip-hopper', etc. Once the character (or as it is
called today: the 'personality structure') has been 'fixed', it is used to
explain and justify everything that character does and thus to create
the 'overarching curve'. This procedure turns all realities on their
head. In 'real life', no 'finished' character exists before someone
develops their actions, rather it develops in line with these actions. But
the end product of 'real life' is – wrongly – the starting point of theatre: a play begins with a 'finished' character. Before a person acts in a
certain way in 'real life' he has a biography behind him and reasons
for behaving in a certain manner. In theatre, by contrast, the action is
the first thing that the actor finds in the text and he must, as it were,
retrospectively find out and make up a biography and a set of reasons
that have led to this action.

Thus for Brecht the rule of 'one-thing-after-another' was not just
something for the rehearsals. Even when first reading through a script
the actor should, as he writes in the *Short Organum*:

> [...] not understand so quickly. Even if he immediately fig-
> ures out the most natural tone for his lines, he should not
> consider what they say to be self-evident. Rather, he should
> hesitate and call upon his general opinions, allow for other
> possible messages, in short: take on the stance of someone
> who wonders. This not just to avoid defining a character too
> early, namely before he has taken on board all views, espe-
> cially those of the other characters, only then to have to cram
> a lot in later, but also – and this most importantly – in order
> to introduce the 'Not–But' into the character's construction
> [...] And along with his lines, he must remember these first
> reactions, reservations, points of criticism, surprise, so that
> they do not get lost in the final shape that character takes.

A character was for Brecht a 'blank canvas' in rehearsal, which the actor along with the other players had to write on precisely by working through the play's events 'one thing after another' and thus getting to know the character in action. Brecht belonged to those directors who were happy now and again to 'forget' their 'concept' while watching the actors (and Brecht was a thankful spectator) in order to be open to suggestions the actors may make. This often led to people who visited rehearsals at the Berliner Ensemble believing that Brecht didn't have any concept when he came to rehearsal. Brecht by contrast spoke of the 'art of forgetting'. When for example he was checking over the results of a rehearsal on the following day, he really had forgotten the work he had done the day before and saw everything 'as if for the first time', fearing that he might otherwise have something in his head that wasn't actually present on stage. A kind of 'Brechtian' materialism. Because this was how he realized his concept, which he did of course have, but in a way that was enriched by a significant element of theatre: chance.

But Brecht did, or so the story goes, strictly forbid his actors from making themselves the starting point for working through a role, and did not permit any form of 'empathy'. That is a myth, just like that 'dictator' Brecht who dictated '*Verfremdung*' in rehearsal is a myth. 'The main skill in the art of acting,' Brecht writes in his *Short Organum*, 'is observation.' Empathy, as he continues in the same place, is one of numerous observation methods, namely self-observation. Brecht deems that it can be useful in rehearsal, but it is a primitive kind of observation – if an actor only asks: How would I feel if this or that were to happen to me? How would I look if I were to say this and do that? – instead of asking: How have I already heard someone saying this and that, or doing that? So it is a case in rehearsal not just of seeking out similarities with the character but also differences. This is the only way successfully to make the leap from oneself to a new character which is however also influenced by one's own person. What Brecht did really 'forbid' in rehearsal though was the kind of 'empathy' that puts the actor in a trance:

> Not intending to put his audience in a trance, he must not put himself in a trance. His muscles must remain loose, as a turn of the head with tense neck muscles, for example, carries the viewers' gaze, sometimes even their heads too, 'magically' with it. [...] His manner of speaking must be free of priestly sing-song and those cadences that send the spectators to sleep, losing the sense of what is said. Even when he is

acting out the possessed, he must not himself appear possessed; how else could spectators find out what is 'possessing' the possessed?

Brecht finishes this passage in the *Short Organum* with the words: 'A character's wholeness is ultimately formed by the way its individual characteristics contradict one another.'

The rule of 'one-thing-after-another' is nothing other than putting into practice this dialectics behind the unity of contradictions when working through a role. There is no 'unified' character determining all ways of behaving from the outset, rather it comes about through them, that is to say out of the sequence of contradictory behaviour. That is what makes a character interesting, if one thinks of Shakespeare and his characters. 'Fixing' his Hamlet from the outset as a procrastinator – as happens time and again in numerous variations – is not only incorrect, it is above all boring. We end up expecting of him only what we already know: Hamlet the procrastinator procrastinates; or Othello the jealous is jealous; or Caesar the power-hungry is hungry for power; or Coriolanus the proud is proud, and so on. Now the 'procrastinator' Hamlet is however anything other than an undecided man of his times. When he fails to make a decision, it is not a lack of decisions but a superabundance that stops him from carrying them out. It is not a 'procrastinating character' that makes him so shy of action, but his very activity. No empty head has him hesitate, rather the multitude of thoughts that he nurtured in the humanist city of Wittenberg. When he does finally act, however, it is so completely not 'procrastinating', and so suddenly decided, that it thoroughly shocks the others in the play – and above all the spectator. Here too the rule of 'one-thing-after-another' provides the key to the reality and beauty of the character. 'Procrastination' is followed by sudden 'action', and 'action' is followed suddenly by more 'procrastination'. Neither is Mother Courage simply just courageous, as she, true to her name, is often to be encountered in many performances. For example when she falls to her knees cursing war at the end of scene six after her daughter has been disfigured by marauders, she is anything other than 'courageous'. She is at her wits' end. But already by the next scene she is back to being 'Courage', beaming as she marches along next to her trading wagon and resisting all doubts about war: 'I'm not going to let you make the war lousy. People say it destroys the weak, but they can't hack peace either. Only war feeds its people better!' She then sings her famous business song, 'You leaders lay your drums o'er there / And let your foot-folk take a rest / Mother Courage has her wares /

What for walking are the best.' Here Brecht insisted on playing 'one thing after another'. He forbade 'making an overarching curve' that would link cursing war with praising war. Like, for example, letting the one 'grow out' of the other, as Helene Weigel who played Mother Courage initially suggested: so merrily and loudly praising war, but with obvious tears in the eyes; or singing the business song loudly, but with muted pleasure. Here, according to Brecht, 'playing-one-thing-after-another' was the *sine qua non* not just for achieving the correct effect – for this is how the contradiction between the mother and the business woman becomes directly evident – but also for the play's entire effectiveness. It became one of the production's 'famous' scenes.

Such an 'unconnected' series of contradictory standpoints is by no means just a 'theatre trick' in order to facilitate surprising instances of *Verfremdung*, but corresponds to real observations. How often do people, without realizing it, take on the most contradictory of standpoints that follow directly on from each other? But also as a 'theatre trick', the rule of 'one-thing-after-another' offers actors an excellent way of 'opening up' contradictions that are interleaved in a play's *Fabel* (and thus hidden). Of course Brecht's Galileo, an astute observer of the times and a man of facts, knows that the election of a new pope who once studied Physics does not signal the beginning of a scientific age, and that this pope too will be beholden to the Inquisition. Nevertheless Brecht demanded that when Charles Laughton, the first actor to play Galileo, hears that the new pope has been elected, he should play 'one thing after another': first of all unbridled joy at seeing a scientist on the holy seat, and then the fear, that is soon to be proven right, because this pope will deliver him into the hands of the Inquisition.

Now it is time for actors to object that 'playing-one-thing-after-another' destroys every sense of closure and takes the opportunity away from the actor to create an 'overarching curve' for the character because everything is parcelled up into a rational sequence. This objection should itself be considered in the light of the motto 'one-thing-after-another', before it is made into the 'overarching curve' of the Brechtian way of acting. It is probably best to turn to concrete scenes that Brecht himself produced. I am thinking now of Swiss Cheese's death in *Mother Courage*. The mother herself is to blame for her son's death, as she haggles for too long with the firing squad over the bribe. Brecht insisted that Mother Courage really should just 'haggle' in the first instance, so do her level best to negotiate a smaller bribe in order to keep her trading wagon. The actress should not show signs of panic and fear during these negotiations. Only when the shots have been fired should her great distress set in. A piercing scream, as the actress first offered, did not satisfy Brecht; nor did having Mother Courage completely collapse bring across the 'distressing enormity' of the situation. The rehearsal was abandoned. The next day Weigel brought a photo with her that she had cut out from an illustrated magazine during the war. It showed a woman, sitting on the ruins of a house, with her mouth wide open to scream. As in the photo, Weigel now opened her mouth loud to scream when the shots fell – but no scream came. The effect was indescribable. It wasn't just the pain that impressed itself on the spectator. The scream that, in spite of the open mouth, never came, also betrayed dismay at one's own guilt. Precisely the 'unconnected' sequence of the immovable business woman and the woman frozen in pain created a 'picture of pain' that I have never since seen the equivalent of on stage. Weigel's 'silent scream' incidentally made 'theatre history'; it is found in every overview today.

The rule of 'one-thing-after-another' means that, when the character is conveyed, the breaks and rough edges remain, so that the spectator can judge the character not in one fell swoop, but changing from scene to scene, only to come to a final judgement at the end. This judgement can still remain contradictory in itself. It marks not the end, but an expectation.[30] This procedure has further advantages: after having watched for example the third scene, the first scene can appear in a different light. The vigour with which Mother Courage defended her sons from the recruiters, will be viewed differently, that is

Illustration 6 Mother Courage hears the shooting of her son (Scene 3). (Copy by R. Berlau/Hoffmann.)

Illustration 7 Image from *Life* magazine used by Weigel for 'silent scream' in Scene 3 of *Mother Courage*. (Photograph courtesy of Getty Images.)

to say more ambiguously, after the third scene, where she haggles with the same vigour over her son's life or death. Here too the shared labour of 'character construction' between actor and spectator becomes an enjoyable activity for the spectator. The character is not closed off for the spectator, like one of Leibniz's monads that has just a small window but is otherwise inaccessible from the outside; the character is delivered up to the spectator. He can make it into the object of his playing. It becomes a part of his 'objective activity' ('gegenständlichen Tätigkeit'), so part of himself.

A provisional conclusion

Brecht's theatre cannot be made without intentions, nor can it be made without opinions. But intentions and opinions do not just pertain to the great arguments of the time. Questions of the epoch are not enough for theatre. Here too Brecht's favourite saying is relevant: 'The truth is concrete.' Questions about the epoch only become concrete through questions about the everyday. For the intention of changing the world and the opinion that it can be changed do not just relate to social systems, but also to the here and now. Theatre productions need contemporary events. If Brecht took a play into his programme, there were two aspects to consider: there should be questions in it 'that will occupy us for a long time' and ones that represent 'particularly burning issues'. When we took on Shakespeare's *Coriolanus*, one of these 'big' questions for us was one which, as Brecht thought, stretched from antiquity far into the future: How can a society protect itself from great people who use their greatness to blackmail society? The general Coriolanus is elected by the plebeians as the Consul of Rome in spite of his aristocratic demeanour because he is idolized after his victory over the Volscians as the 'conquerer of Corioli'. When he tries to blackmail the city on the grounds that he is 'irreplaceable' and take back democratic achievements such as the intervention of people's tribunes, the plebeians realize their mistake, expel Coriolanus, and save the city. The question of how important it is to be able to replace 'great specialists', whether politicians, militia, doctors, scientists and so on, who try to use their services to blackmail society, struck us as also a question of survival in respect of German history. But in order for such problems of the epoch to be accessible to the audience they must also figure in the problems of our days. The historical must be complemented by the contemporary. In 1964, when we began producing *Coriolanus* we considered it not least to be our contribution to the contemporary debate about Stalin and the cult that had formed around his person which had for a long time hidden the crimes committed in his name, for Stalin was considered 'irreplaceable' until his death.

Brecht's opinion that a contemporary event is the '*sine qua non*' of theatre, from the initial act of writing through to the production, repeatedly caused bourgeois media and even more so bourgeois literary types to speak of a 'reduction in the number of purely aesthetic spaces'. One of these, who characterizes himself as the 'pope of literature', calls it 'the descent of a lyric genius into the lowlands of politics', which of course was supposed to have entailed 'the short-lived nature of his plays'. What is correct in this: Brecht did not write in a vacuum. He wrote about the great arguments of this world by describing them from his standpoint. For him, feeling moved by something was not the opposite of attaining objective knowledge about the world, but its precondition. He himself spoke of the necessity of taking a 'partisan' standpoint, which he however strictly distinguished from a 'biased' one. Only events that affect one's person could provide the impetus – at least long term – not just to see through social conditions but also to change them. And only change would lead to real knowledge. 'Driven into exile under a thatched Danish roof', for example, he hung above his bed a list of everything the Nazis had stolen from him when he fled: a library, an apartment, an entire set of furniture, coats, hats, a Steyr car in good condition, etc. When he awoke in the morning, it was the first thing he saw, and it never failed to change his knowledge of barbarity into his daily battle against the barbarians. Anger turns history into the most personal of issues. Something like this is what Brecht meant when he spoke of 'contemporary events'. But events are also just events and not the entire message of the plays. *Mother Courage*, written in 1938 as a warning against the imminent world war, also contains a far more important message: a warning against opportunism. For it is not war and devastation that destroy everything that Mother Courage owns, but her opportunism, the readiness, in order to 'cut a good deal', to fit in with everything and to accept injustice even when you have seen through it. The 'song of praise' about the curse of opportunism is the play's 'major' message. For opportunism is also a dangerous, fast-spreading bacterium in progressive societies. And Brecht's *Galileo* equally not only deals with the 'bomb' and warns against a nuclear war. *Galileo* asks the 'big' question: how does truth prevail? By itself, simply because it is true? Totally, or with compromises? But when are compromises capitulation? And when does 'recognizing necessity' amount to betrayal? Marx has given us the nice sentence that the battle for truth is mainly a battle against prejudice. Brecht's Galileo answers to those who rely on what is 'right and good' prevailing because it is right and good: 'Only as much truth will push through as we can push through; the triumph of sense can only be the triumph of the sensible.' Just how much this also applied to those who were completely sure that socialism, once it had seized power, would automatically produce only 'socialist' effects, was something we painfully had to learn.

The dialectics between the contemporary and the historical is the space where the kind of theatre that is known as 'Brechtian theatre' takes place. It should more correctly be called the theatre that Brecht suggested in order to make changing the world possible, and this it does by presenting changes in the world and by making available the necessary desires and passions to make these changes. In drawing the wonderful world of theatre into the wonders of 'man's everyday activity', this theatre allows man to take pleasure in the idea of being his own creator and thus, experiencing 'the premonition of being human', to emancipate himself as a 'more humane human'. Brecht will be present in theatre wherever theatre, showing changes, implicates itself with grace and effort, with passion and understanding in these changes and, in effecting changes, changes itself.

Illustration 8 Manfred Wekwerth in rehearsal for *Galileo* (Danish version), Berliner Ensemble, with Ekkehard Schall and Michael Gerber (1977). (Photograph courtesy of Vera Tenschert.)

Illustration 9 *Galileo* (Danish version), Berliner Ensemble, with Ekkehard Schall and Renate Richter (1978). (Photograph courtesy of Vera Tenschert.)

Day seven

Thus the heavens and the earth were finished [...] And God blessed the seventh day, and sanctified it, because that in it he had rested from all his work which God created and made.

[Genesis 2:1–3]

'The proof of the pudding is in the eating' was one of Brecht's favourite sayings. And so the question remains on the seventh day, looking at the works that he 'created and finished': where today can one find a theatre with opinions and intentions, a '*gestic* kind of theatre', that offers its audience, who share in the event, enlightenment and enjoyment? Is that not in today's muddle of theatres (some call this pluralism) a utopia?

Theatre will always be a utopia. Where utopia ends is where theatre ends. And even Brecht did not consider himself to be the last word in wisdom. He looked at his work, including what he did for the Berliner Ensemble, as the first beginnings of a new theatre that would act like a partner, accompanying, encouraging and putting into song the major process of human emancipation. His suggestions for such a kind of theatre that unites enlightenment with enjoyment, analysis with passion, high standards of professionalism with real naivety, dramatic art with the art of spectating, as he recorded them in his work *A Short Organum for the Theatre*, are science and fantasy in one. Brecht's theses, even when they sound apodictic, do not determine the future of theatre, they extend its possibilities. For in spite of rumours to the contrary, Brecht did not solely depend on planning, he also followed his gut feeling. When I asked him once how he was so sure of his dialectical thinking, he answered, to my surprise, that dialectics was a matter of feeling.

But many who intend to accompany the major process of human emancipation do not go beyond paying lip-service to theory (even when they do refer to Brecht). Immanuel Kant's famous question that underlies all philosophizing, 'What can I know?' is answered, but the second, 'What should I do?' mostly remains open, not to mention the third, 'What may I hope?' For me too there was little time left in my last conversations in 1956 to sound out for concrete solutions Brecht's unmistakeable feeling for times and their needs, precisely that 'dialec-tics-as-a-matter-of-feeling'. In his response to my question of how he imagined the theatre of the future, which, incidentally and unusually for him, Brecht shot straight back at me, he said: 'Like *The Measures Taken*.' (I mention later in this book the confusion that this answer

85

caused.) As if Brecht were only allowing the first of Kant's questions for the difficult times still to come. Suddenly leftwing theorists began talking about the 'culinary' again (which was once more confused with 'enjoyment') that people would have to do without in future 'dark times'. They referred to Georg Lukács, who in his work *The Historical Novel* deemed only the drama suitable for dramatic times. Likewise, it was argued, in 'Brechtian theatre' of the future only an appropriate sense of seriousness should be permitted for serious times, and humour was not a part of this. The consequences for theatre are well known. So let me here and for the last time make one more plea for humour, so, for Brecht.

Theatre best supports the process of emancipation that must 'continually' be undertaken in order to secure man's survival, by highlighting the unacceptable nature of contemporary social conditions to as many people as possible. It can, for example, stir up dissatisfaction where – supported by the media – satisfaction reigns, so delusion. Here it must de-delude. But de-delude so as to please the spectator. So unjust circumstances should not be shown merely to upset the audience. Or at least something that is already bleak should not be made even bleaker. For painting a gloomy picture of something that is already gloomy might provoke an emergency response, but no proper remedy. And emergency aid also always implies fear of a new emergency. Pity and fear however are neither able to awaken the ability to overcome suffering nor provide the courage to do so, never mind the desire. Indeed, an aesthetic darkening does not even allow the actual misery that dominates to be seen. Here it strikes me as better irreverently to 'blacken' untenable conditions and show how they could not possibly be imposed upon civilized people. A dark social-naturalism, by contrast, that bleakly describes how bleak everything is, only strengthens this bleakness and makes it appear unalterable. A lack of alternative, constantly invoked by politics, is thus able to mutate into a new religion and with this to a magic formula through which capital seeks to secure its 'lasting' dominance. This formula is today probably one of the most dangerous, as its danger is constantly played down and, with this, initially overlooked. The claim that everything, but above all the capitalist system, lacks any alternative is nothing other than a distraction from the real alternative, 'Socialism or barbarism', and this in favour of the latter. And Rosa Luxemburg knew the far-reaching consequences of this alternative when she formulated it.

If I have correctly understood Brecht, no gloomy lament will overcome lamentable gloom, but rather an – in the most literal

sense – overpowering sense of humour. For example when one surprises the audience by loudly agreeing with or even surpassing those
politicians who constantly use all the means and media at their dis-
posal to declare our world to be 'the best of all possible worlds'. In
this way the nonsense reveals itself. That is one way that comedy can
'bowl you over'. Brecht believed comedy to be the most suitable form
of theatre today, sufficiently serious to intervene in the apparent fate of
society, not just in theory but with real practical results. Fewer ghosts
are needed in Europe today and more Trojan horses. Long unnoticed,
they destabilize enemy bastions from the inside. The horse is initially
carried into the city as a 'great gift', and all the greater is the shock of
the city dwellers when this great horse storms 'the walls of Troy' until
they collapse amidst laughter.

Brecht also had a suitable slogan for this: 'In general it is probably
true that tragedy more frequently makes light of human suffering than
comedy.'

And whoever still doubts the truth of this should think of Chaplin.
When he shot *The Great Dictator* in 1938/39, the Second World War
broke out during filming. The film is still celebrated today as a classic
and only a few people know that Chaplin only managed to finish
the shoot with extreme civil courage. For his colleagues, including the
progressive ones, and indeed even President Roosevelt, told him to
abandon the project immediately. Some because they thought in
'dark times' one shouldn't laugh about a sinister figure like Adolf
Hitler, who is called Alois Hinkel in the film, and others because
they feared Hitler would be provoked into carrying out even more
gruesome acts in the concentration camps and conquered lands if
people joked about him. The film company stopped Chaplin's finan-
cing as a result of this. Chaplin denied he was 'joking', claiming
that he in all seriousness wanted to 'make him look ridiculous'. At a
time when all of Europe greatly feared Hitler because he was considered invincible, Chaplin considered it misguided to present him
only as a 'great fearsome presence'. That would add only to the fear
and not create any courage to fight against him. Chaplin carried on
filming out of his own pocket. He made the following observation in
his notes: 'The tragic derives from resignation, the comical from
resistance.'

Chaplin was proved right. *The Great Dictator* is rated today as
one of the most effective refutations of fascism. Hitler is incidentally
supposed to have watched the film three times because he, or so the
story goes, judged the film's ridiculous portrayal to be the greatest
danger to his 'invincibility'. Brecht's *The Resistible Rise of Arturo Ui*

had a similar effect. The play and our production of it received the Grand Prix du Théâtre des Nations and the Paris Critics' Prize in Paris in 1961 because it was judged that the fascist threat had seldom been made as clear as in this clownish travesty. And the actor who played Arturo Ui, Ekkehard Schall, was compared to Chaplin. This production, which toured through almost all European capital cities, reached the record number of 735 performances in Berlin and was only stopped, to great public protest, in 1987 because Ekkehard Schall had had enough after twenty years of repeatedly playing on stage that man of whom Karl Kraus, the great Austrian satirist, said as early as 1930: 'I can think of nothing more to say about this man.' Schall won out over the audience, who in the final performance chanted for *Arturo Ui* to remain in the programme. Sad, but understandable.

But back to the facts. Where can one find a kind of theatre today that Brecht would like? Actually only Brecht could answer this question. I can only offer my own guidance, which has the advantage of being incomplete, and so in need of additions from others. The last time I had the impression that Brecht would have enjoyed a theatrical performance was some time ago in the Cottbus Staatstheater. It was *Mother Courage and Her Children*, produced by Alejandro Quintana who, initially having come to the GDR as an immigrant from Chile, completed his traineeship at the Berliner Ensemble and is a sought-after director today.

I was warned in advance of the Cottbus production that it was 'quite different'. It really was quite different, but in my opinion all the closer to Brecht for it. Right from the moment the curtain with Picasso's dove of peace on it was raised, the spectator felt like he was in today's Baghdad: two soldiers in khaki-coloured combat gear, with cloth-covered helmets, machine guns nervously in their hands, complain that 'folk round here are so full of spite' even though they had come as liberators. That is the evening's first surprise: Quintana produced the play some time just before the Iraq war. It became prophetic. The second surprise: the costumes of today do not seduce the director into the one-dimensionality of today. He plays through the archetypal war situations on a grand scale, with sharpness, and humour, so that the contemporary costumes do not – as in so many other productions – make them 'cool'. On the contrary, the costumes make Brecht's archetypal situations even more surprising, even more alive. The third surprise: Quintana does not deny his origins. With the characters' movement and colour, coming more from Latin America than the Germany of the Thirty Years War, the story takes on a whole new dimension. This Mother Courage, reminiscent of Fernando de Rojas' gypsy Celestina, and her children full of *joie de vivre* make the family's end all the more shocking. Brecht would certainly also have accepted the ending whereby Mother Courage, who has lost her children and all her possessions to war, does not simply move on but cries out as if she wanted to wake the world from its slumber. It is as if you can hear the cry of the many millions today protesting at the wars waged by that 'empire', against whom Arundhati Roy called upon all lovers of peace at the World Social Forum in Mumbai in 2004 to wage a peaceful war.

In the case of another production that I saw a number of years ago in the Hamburg Schauspielhaus it may seem quite amazing for me to call it 'Brechtian theatre'. Above all the director would be amazed, who intended no 'politics' for his theatre and certainly no 'Brecht'. I am referring to the Swiss director Christoph Marthaler and his production *Die Stunde Null oder Die Kunst des Servierens. Ein Gedenktraining für Führungskräfte* (*The Zero Hour or The Art of Serving. Thought Training for Leaders*). Actually it isn't a play at all, rather a collage of observations, episodes, punchlines, short sketches and above all songs, fervent German folk songs. For Marthaler grew up as a musician (and there really is some heavenly, multi-vocal singing). The leaders, before they lead, have to train as feeling (singing) people with hearts. Brecht called *Fear and Misery of the Third Reich*, his sequence of scenes, a 'gestarium'. At a distance, in exile, he gathered reports, notes, pictures, jokes, phrases, standpoints, speeches and excuses from the everyday life of fascism in Germany. In other words, *gestic* things from the everyday that made fascism possible in the first place. This 'gestarium' of the everyday considered itself 'un-political' or harmless, at worst a fellow traveller and yet when seen in its totality it carried the main guilt for the terrible crime of fascism. Marthaler's *Gedenktraining für Führungskräfte* (*Thought Training for Leaders*) strikes me as such a 'gestarium'. Here the future elite of recovering capitalism practise, in an 'intensive course' and supervised by a 'trainer' acting as the barometer of the age at the 'zero hour', 1945, the things that they as future leaders will most urgently need to master: shaking hands (they practise with a plastic hand that is attached to a vaulting horse), waving to the people with the obligatory constant smile, cutting ribbons to open bridges. Above all, they repeatedly practise delivering pre-determined speeches 'without notes' from a microphone, learning to talk a lot and yet say nothing. In between they have tea breaks, drinking while standing and watching out for the little finger that must stick out from the cup in order to show culture. And over and again they rehearse phrases and songs used to train both heart and mind in the kind of patriotism that the leaders will later demand from others.

Marthaler's *Gedenktraining* is an advanced form of what Brecht calls the art of observation. The great sense of calm with which the exercises are constantly repeated gives them the *Gestus* of 'customs and traditions', in a similar manner to the way Brecht set about historicizing actions and slotting them into a system that repeatedly reproduces them. Even the way people make their beds and prepare themselves for the night follows hard and fast rules, especially when one tries to lay claim to unmistakeable individualism. Because everyone lays claim to such a thing, it becomes a stereotypical form of group behaviour that is a prerequisite for success among with the elites of Daimler-Benz or Deutsche Bank.

Merciless humour, delivered with deadly seriousness, especially when utterly ridiculous things are being carried out, makes the spectacle of thought training through song and fervent identification into a parade of losers in pinstripe suits. The very precise nature of the details and the way they are constantly repeated and juxtaposed with the style of presentation amounts to a magnificent *Verfremdung* of the everyday, the absurdity of which otherwise passes unnoticed these days. It is done in the sense of Brecht's best 'immanent criticism'. And it fulfils a further criterion of Brechtian theatre: it is incredibly entertaining.

When looking for Brecht, one cannot avoid Dario Fo. In his theatre in Milan, still a real working-class theatre, the great actor, poet and improviser links the traditions of *commedia dell'arte* with Brecht's socially critical approach and practises on a daily basis what Brecht dreamed of: philosophical folk theatre. His themes stretch from Julius Caesar to Silvio Berlusconi, from the Vatican inventing sin, to the supermarket where customers decide not to pay for anything any more. If there were proof for Brecht's assertion that not the word but the *Gestus* is the language of theatre, then this proof would be Dario Fo. In a matinée performance at the Berliner Ensemble in 1986 he improvised an English knight, who pulls out all the rhetorical stops to have a poor pickpocket put behind bars; a Swedish consultant, who praises his method of cutting stomachs open as the only valid one; a French pastor, who thunders against contraceptives. We the audience understood everything and were taken with the precise character descriptions; only later on did we find out that Dario Fo doesn't speak a word of English, Swedish, or French. He spoke 'Grammlo', a language that he invented himself and that doesn't make any sense outside of the real *Gestus*.

Before a performance begins, the actor Fo disguises himself for example as a female miracle worker who is summonsed by Queen Elizabeth I to Buckingham Palace in order to make the wrinkles disappear from her royal face. He wanders through the audience in this guise, giving his opinion on high politics, or politics of the high-ups, including the events of the day, the absurdity of which completely counters any sense of historicity and proves Fo's thesis that laughter not only opens your mouth but also your brain.

This list can certainly be continued. Brecht can be found everywhere that there are discoveries to be made, including the rediscovery of Brecht himself. May every kind of performance be welcome that opens up contradictions, makes suggestions about how to 'deal with antinomies' and develop our world by helping to 'make it inhabitable': tragedy or clownery, verse or slang, imagination or documentary, emotions or coldness, the rational or the abyss, the readily comprehensible or the absurd, building up or knocking down. In any case, Brecht's theatre is able to yield more theatrical techniques today than the most fashionable of trends, that in their attempt to do something 'never seen before' are as like as two peas in a pod.

Every generation has the right to distance itself from its predecessors. Destroying tried and tested methods is legitimate, Brecht made great use of this. But under the condition that destruction created new spaces, not scrap heaps.

Sure, there are many ways of making theatre today. The truth is, as Francis Bacon says, the daughter of time, and it seems to me that fun is its son. For jokes and games mirror their times, even if through distortion. Certainly the state theatre is often a more reliable reflection of the state of society than many a historian or even politics can offer. But if one speaks about Brecht, whether admiringly or critically, then one should know him. And one should re-read precisely those things one thinks one knows. And because I, in order to write these texts, have re-read Brecht, I can assure you his texts will not only repeatedly surprise you with their great philosophical insight, they will be above all a great source of pleasure as only great literary works can be. And you should dare to enjoy yourself – and to play.

BRECHT'S 'SIMPLICITY'
A Somewhat Deviant Contribution to a Brecht Conference[1]

1 How this somewhat deviant contribution came about

I think it was Ernst Bloch who spoke for the first time not just of 'epic theatre' but also of 'epic philosophy'. In his essay 'Revueform in der Philosophie' ('Revue Form in Philosophy') he recommends that philosophers have recourse to the 'revue form, from Piscator to *The Threepenny Opera*' to avoid the danger of 'becoming frigid'. Those on the Left must not leave fairytales and myths to the Right by allowing the 'revolution to disregard the graeculi, the lithe, dreamy, beautiful prophets, and assume a Roman coldness [...]. For far and wide the major forms of theatre have stagnated; high bourgeois culture with its court theatre and exclusive education is no longer bearing even derivative fruit. Other forms are coming to the fore from the street, the fair-ground, the circus, new forms that have been despised until now, and they are colonizing the established field.'

Brecht was of a completely different opinion. He writes in July 1935 in a reply to Bloch:[2]

I really must express my indignation at what I can only describe as your inappropriate behaviour as a philosopher. I am not demanding a frock-coat,[3] at least not on principle, but then again, why not demand a frock-coat? For also when philosophizing, my good man, I can make no exception, or where would I end up? You have to keep your feet on the ground after all. Certain basic rules remain, even when the wheels are coming off. You will laugh: one must proceed systematically. What can I rely on, Sir!! When the world is ending, it is important to be able to rely on something. Incidentally, executors in particular will have to get busy (briefly).

No displays of nonchalance from these nonentities! Those in authority are carrying out their final forgeries, everyone is getting ready for the decisive error of judgement, and you take off your frock-coat, are you drunk, Sir? You can't give your banner to the lab cleaner to hold! Believe me, the driest of tones is the correct one. No pleas of boredom!

These words hung over us like a warning when we, along with a few friends, began to plan an academic conference on Brecht's communism in the summer of 2006 at the Lake Maggiore. As this conference would also deal with, as far as Brecht and his contemporary reputation were concerned, 'decisive errors of judgement' and 'final forgeries', we of course thought of that letter to Bloch and Brecht's categorical demand for the 'frock-coat' and the 'driest of tones'. But even the extreme summer heat, albeit a little lessened by the cooling view over the Lake Maggiore, could not lead us to prioritize a search for that 'Roman coldness' that Bloch thought he could find in Brecht. Rather, we were looking for something that Brecht himself in his *Short Organum for the Theatre* once called 'the realm of the pleasing', where he planned to settle after he had returned from emigration. In short, we decided to make the conference into a meeting between academia *and* art, or better, academics and artists.

It is strange indeed: previous conferences that dealt with Brecht's philosophy of practice were often conferences about philosophy without any practice. Brecht's thought was present, but hardly any of his action. And yet this thought can only be understood as '*interventionist* thought', and therefore *as action*. Brecht's philosophy is noticeably easier to discern (and decode) in his everyday behaviour, often in tiny details, than in many of his theoretical writings, which were mostly written in response to specific theatre questions.

We decided in our conference to interrupt the scholarly papers on Brecht's thought periodically with artistic contributions that would demonstrate his action – with stories about Brecht which, when performed by actors, would present Brecht as his own best practitioner. In short, we arrived at that 'revue form' that Bloch had so warmly recommended to philosophers and that Brecht had so scornfully rejected, demanding from the philosopher a 'frock-coat'.

What's this: an anti-Brecht conference?

Then – as always – Brecht came to our rescue. Brecht who could never resist the temptation of dialectics: for changing the world includes the person who makes these changes. And so his philosopher in *The Messingkauf Dialogues* enters with quite different words and certainly not 'in a frock-coat':

> You must understand, I am consumed by an insatiable curiosity for people; I can't see or hear enough of them. How they relate to one another, make friends and enemies, sell onions, plan military campaigns, get married, make woollen suits, circulate counterfeit money, dig potatoes, observe stars, how they cheat one another, favour, teach, grill, assess, mutilate, support one another, how they carry out meetings, found clubs, plot and scheme. I'm always seeking to know how their initiatives come about and finish up, and I'm trying to discern a few rules to this that might allow me to make predictions. Because I ask myself how I should behave so that I can get on in life and be as happy as possible, and this of course depends on how others behave, so I am also interested in that and especially in the opportunities for influencing people.

2 The somewhat inappropriate contribution

Dear friends of Brecht, please excuse me for beginning our time together at an academic conference, and a very important one at that, by stepping out of line and telling stories. I plead mitigating circumstances in the first instance, as I am a man of the theatre and not a scholar (my friend Werner Mittenzwei correctly calls me just a 'lover of scholarship'). Nor do I want to attract the fury of leftwing philosophy by proceeding narratologically here – as it is called in these postmodern times. I refer, as one always does when unsure how to proceed, to Brecht. And he said in one of the last conversations I had with him in Buckow:

> We are speaking of communism as something simple that must be made difficult. But precisely those people whom communism concerns, in other words communists, are always making my theatre difficult and trying to turn it into a place purely for 'producing ideas', a 'political school', and solely measuring its value in these terms. When they talk of a 'critical stance', they are at best thinking of the 'critique of Hegel's philosophy of law', but not Villon, Rabelais or Chaplin. Ridiculous. Our style of performance is in fact all about 'naivety'. Our performances simply tell stories: the *Fabel*. Discoveries, ideas, stimuli can and indeed must emerge from

this, but our job is to tell stories about noteworthy events that will interest the audience and that are fun to watch, even when they are serious.

In this conversation Brecht inadvertently discovered in an aside, as he often did, one of the categories fundamental to his entire work. It is in fact something that he had always practised but never explicitly named: *naivety*. And I would like to describe this conversation that, like many such conversations, took place on the old landing-stage at the Schermützelsee outside his house in Buckow.

It was incidentally the same landing-stage as the one on which an actor by the name of Bierbichler, bent and unshaven like a Bavarian farmer whose cows have been stolen from his field, could recently be seen in a TV film (I think it bore the title '*Abschied von der Wahrheit*'[4]), claiming to be Brecht and pondering lost times and his imminent end. I sat in the very same place – albeit a few decades earlier – with a man of the same name, who was however clean-shaven (he incidentally didn't approve at all of his collaborators appearing 'unshaven' in the morning) and who was, even though he was recovering from a viral infection, unusually keen to get to work. He had informed us that he was intending to take a step back from theatre in the future ('Why else do I have students!') in order to dedicate himself once more entirely to his writing. While in Buckow I incidentally didn't notice any of the nymphs who had romped about the garden in the aforementioned TV film, embodying all of Brecht's lovers from the last half-century, for apart from Brecht and me there was not a single person as far as the eye could see. Besson,[5] whom we were expecting, had not yet returned from holiday and Helene Weigel only came out at weekends, in order to 'keep us alive' with smoked meats, dumplings and coffee. We were working intensively on the dramaturgical preparation for the premiere of the play *The Days of the Commune*, that great social tableau that Brecht had written in Switzerland in 1948 and had brought with him on his arrival in Berlin as a so-called 'entry present'.

During the course of this work, and almost certainly as a result of my irritating insistence on setting out the play's theoretical problems before we did anything else, Brecht became unexpectedly angry. He had, as he said, been wondering for quite some time why people who are actually his friends only ever look at his theatre from a theoretical angle and never 'quite simply' as theatre – this theatre that came about after all because he as a young man was so terribly bored by the theatre in Augsburg and wanted real theatre instead of the bourgeois surrogate. As if the world ends with theory. But that was only where it began. Theory, Brecht continued, is the beginning, and not the end, of theatre (and not only there). For that nice line by which one must progress from the abstract to the concrete also applies to theatre. Initially he blamed his own concepts for this 'obsession with the un-naive', but the more 'simply' he conceptualized things, the greater the number of misunderstandings. Clearly the real reason must lie with him. When formulating his theory he had omitted one side entirely, in the false assumption that it was self-evident: naivety. 'Without naivety no art at all is possible!'

Brecht did not mean by this the simple kind of naivety that excludes thought ('Undifferentiated naivety is primitive!') Brecht meant that kind of naivety that follows thought, one that is not the opposite of analysis, but rather its result. A genuine insight as should be conveyed by a theatre production is only really 'right' when it provokes naive attitudes from the spectator: curiosity, anger, pleasure, protest, agree-ment, rage and above all astonishment. Only these naive reactions, which are the source of enjoyment in theatre, can turn 'pure thought' into the 'interventionist thought' that Brecht so valued. It is the step from thought to action.

Even Brecht himself needed, as he said, such naive stimuli 'in order to stay awake'. And thus he described how in Denmark he had pre-vented himself from falling victim to the deceptive tranquillity of the landscape outside his window by hanging a list over his bed of every-thing the Nazis had stolen from him when he was forced to flee. Seeing this detailed inventory on waking (library, furniture, clothes, a Steyr car, manuscripts, etc.) was a huge motivation. Rage fuelled the better arguments in cases like this.

To change tack: I am surprised it is still the case today that serious leftwing research on Brecht, which can pride itself on having unearthed many new and above all useful aspects, has not recognized Brecht's final great discovery, indeed that it deliberately ignores it. While people do speak of the phenomenon of his 'simplicity' and the compelling 'comprehensibility' of his texts, they speak of these as if they were an author's skilful way of making himself more compre-hensible to 'simple' people in order to 'use simplicity to outwit' wide-spread ignorance. Even Wolfgang Fritz Haug, probably one of the most inspiring interpreters today of Brecht's thought as a 'philosophy of practice', uses the term 'tactic' in order to explain Brecht's 'simpli-city': 'Brecht makes art by using it philosophically', or 'Brecht declares his insights in a surprisingly simple manner, placing and hiding his art within this simplicity'.

This reminds me less of Brecht than Johann Christoph Gottsched, famous for banning the clown from the German stage. Gottsched saw in simple 'stories and fables' the possibility 'that the illiterate too could understand morality'.

I consider Brecht's naivety not to be a tactical approach, but rather a fundamental condition of his art. It is a constitutive aspect of his productivity, his thought, and above all his own person. His ability to unite the highest of intellects with elementary naivety strikes me as one way of explaining Brecht the 'universal puzzle'. Einstein had an even 'simpler' explanation for such contradictions: his childlike quality was what gave him his ideas, because it meant he never stopped wondering about things. Brecht did however consider 'the simple' significantly harder to create in theatre than 'the complex'. Not least because the spectator is able to scrutinize it, whereas 'complex things' defy scrutiny and can thus be shrouded in arbitrariness. The next step for the old Hegelian Brecht is to note that the concrete is always 'more complex', for it represents variety as opposed to the 'simplifications' of the abstract. Brecht's favourite saying to actors who liked to theorize during rehearsals was: 'Better to act it out, talking about it is too easy!'

But back to our conversation in autumn 1956.

By the 8th August we had made good progress on our work for *The Days of the Commune* and Brecht suggested passing the time before lunch by chatting a little. Eisler, who had arrived in Buckow that day, thought this was a great idea. For he and Brecht had previously had an argument about how music was to be used in the *Commune* play. Probably in order to provoke Brecht, as he often did, Eisler had expressed the view that with *The Days of the Commune* Brecht had succeeded in being a real classic, because in the songs he described 'culinary pleasures' for the first time without malice. This had annoyed Brecht (after all he considered himself a classic by the tender age of twenty-two!), so perhaps that was why he answered irritably that *The Days of the Commune* was his most important political play. 'And that's exactly why!' Eisler had cheerfully countered, giving as an example Père Joseph's song, in which he insists on chives in his salad for the last meal before he is hanged as a poor dog: no meal without enjoyment! 'For what is the point in achieving something if there's no reward for you?' And with this the way was clear for Brecht to become a real classic, for in order to be a classic you must not ignore the pleasures of the senses and the flesh, but rather realize their poetic potential.

Brecht was never sure whether Eisler was serious or not. That's why he answered carefully, even though he had nothing against being a 'real classic'. He responded that he really must ensure his theatre was not seen to be a place of 'teaching and learning'. Or as a melting-pot for 'thinking stuff'. To be sure, more reasoning was desperately needed on stage, but not without enjoyment! It was absolutely in the interests of reason that there should be more talk of enjoyment. Of real enjoyment. And real enjoyment must be demanded, so that no one could think that the new class is, as far as the senses are concerned, more tight-fisted than the old. Or that it exists solely and doggedly to liberate humanity; or that it has an historical mission but needs nothing to achieve it; that this is why self-sacrifice is one of the first proletarian virtues. This was all, according to Brecht, sanctimonious, and one must do the exact opposite. The class's self-esteem, which those in power had spent so long beating out of them and still beat out of them today, must be re-awakened: namely that they should make an effort only as long as making an effort is enjoyable. But how should they strive to enjoy themselves when they have no idea what enjoyment is, as it had been systematically denied them up to now and self-sacrifice praised as a virtue instead? But if they first discovered all the things they could do for themselves, others would profit enough from this. The working class must liberate itself with the 'greatest of demands', in order to liberate others in a similarly attractive manner. An ascetic working class is, Brecht said, a weakening working class.

Brecht liked the idea of an 'extravagant new class' so much that he – as was often the case when he liked something – made a great leap of imagination: in future only plays that portrayed enjoyment as a class war should be written. Demanding enjoyment as subverting a capitalism that was poor in thought and enjoyment, that constantly marketed 'human' enjoyment as 'beastly'. Insisting on chives in your salad as a class war! And here it was less important actually to have such enjoyable things straight away, than to be able to recognize them as inherently enjoyable. 'For how can you fight for something you have never known?'

Eisler, delighted with what he had triggered, suggested immediately adding a new verse to the 'Forwards and don't forget' of the Solidarity Song that would deal with enjoyment, rhyming 'enjoyment' (Genuss) with 'must' (muss). But we never got that far, Helene Weigel called us to lunch.

In the afternoon Brecht returned refreshed from his thirty-minute sleep and the conversation turned once again to 'political theatre'. Brecht was particularly unhappy that his theory was being used in order to claim that only a political theme on stage could yield political theatre. A political theme alone, Brecht countered, in no way guarantees political theatre. It could even be extremely un-political if, for example, it was boring. And plays with no politics in them could be extremely political. In his play *A Respectable Wedding* there was not a single word about politics and yet – when performed properly – it was a direct political critique of the petit-bourgeoisie. The petit-bourgeoisie were revealed, caught in their narrow little world, as dangerous enemies of the revolution, because they also have a penchant for attacking officials. For him, political theatre did not consist of a political theme but of a political stance that it takes on towards the world and provokes in others – that well-known critical stance, the doubt that brings about change. And political theatre must awaken, alongside the ability, above all the desire to effect change.

Likewise in *The Days of the Commune* the political theme was not primarily what made it into political theatre. The demand made by the young worker and communard, Jean Cabet, that after the Commune's victory he finally wanted to have some time, in spite of pressing political tasks, for his love for the seamstress Babette, was at least as political as the workers' battalion seizing the Paris Hôtel de Ville. It was changing the way people live, that was why revolutions existed in the first place. Likewise for a new production of *The Mother*, which I was to do in 1955, Brecht had, I remembered, surprised me by speaking of the 'loveable nature' of such a revolution that had been insufficiently in evidence in his first production of the play in 1951, probably because it had been 'overwhelmed by the harshness of political struggle'.

In these last conversations Brecht, when describing how he worked, hardly used the term 'epic theatre' at all any more. Coming from the 1920s, it referred 'too much to the formal'. Likewise, he only used 'dialectical theatre', a later term from the 1950s, for a short time. He deemed it 'philosophically sound', but not aesthetically accurate enough. Brecht spoke in the end – but very carefully – of 'philosophical folk theatre'. Linking the apparently irreconcilable opposites of philosophy as a high form of human thought with the naivety of real folk theatre had always appealed to Brecht. Thus he liked to answer the question about his teachers: 'They were two Karls: Marx and Valentin.'[6]

Brecht never provided us with an analysis of 'philosophical folk theatre'.

I can just remember one observation, which I made in the margins, when Brecht finished our conversation with a grin: 'Why shouldn't we make the spirit of our age into an entertainer? He should at least let himself be seen.'

I wanted to say that here so that you can see why we are 'disrupting'[7] the academic papers with art in this conference, and ask you for your understanding.

3 Stories about Brecht

'I have to discipline myself, as I'm too spontaneous'[8]

Brecht was a communicative person. He needed conversations, therefore another person, in order to think. One could also say his private life too was guided by his valued philosophy of practice. Thinking was for him taking action – speaking, discussing, criticizing, planning, drafting, rejecting, etc. A thought only existed for him if it had been spoken aloud, or, even better, written down. Brecht always needed someone with whom he could think, and therefore talk. His predilection for collective work was not – as biographies claim – the result of 'opting on moral-political grounds for the collective', but rather a basic need. Nor did it come – as biographies also claim – from the desire to exploit someone. It was his productive inability to work alone, or indeed to even want to be able to work alone. He would even call you when he was writing poems because he had to read out a poem he had written; only then did it exist for him. 'What do you think?' would always be the question. And he really did expect a (well-founded!) opinion. Indeed, as a general rule, conversing, discussing, making up stories together, laughing, speculating, 'playing around', including with the nonsensical, was his favourite way of working, thinking and living, the way he got his pleasure. (And without pleasure, he once admitted, he could not work at all.) And so it could well happen that a call would come late at night, always with the polite enquiry, 'Am I disturbing you?' – and sometimes he really was disturbing you – but of course you went along. Conversations with Brecht always had something extremely entertaining about them (not without reason did he call entertainment the noblest business of theatre). The conversations generally strayed far from the actual topic, you quickly found yourself discussing God and the world. Brecht, often suspected of being a 'mathematical logician' and rationalist, was the opposite. He actually enjoyed leaps that left him unable 'to see the wood for the trees'. And so the greatest of undertakings often came about quite by chance. This was the case one evening with the project for Shakespeare's *Coriolanus*. We had got together to find a cast for Molière's *Don Juan*, which was to be the premiere after the Berliner Ensemble had moved into the Theater am Schiffbauerdamm. On the suggestion that Ernst Busch should play Don Juan (Brecht: 'He wouldn't seduce a woman with any great speeches, he'd just pinch her arse!'), Brecht had the idea – more as a joke than anything else – that Busch the 'proletarian' absolutely must play a nobleman. After Frederick the Great had been rejected as too old, Brecht thought of Coriolanus. By the end of the evening we didn't have a cast for Molière, but the task instead of starting to translate *Coriolanus* immediately. Each of us was to have translated at least one scene by the end of the week.

Far too little has been written about Brecht the productive 'unlogician'. In actual fact he didn't only think dialectically, he even lived dialectically: 'The surprises afforded by something that develops in logical steps and great leaps, the instability of all circumstances, the humour in contradictions, and so on', he writes in 1954. In a short poem 'Vergnügungen' ('Pleasures') he places dialectics among writing, plants, the dog, travelling and new music, in seventh place on his list of pleasures. And, in a critique of Stalinism in 1956, shortly before his death, he describes Stalin's greatest crime to have been the eradication of dialectics. Once, during a conversation where he was once again making great jumps and even praising these initially rather irritating jumps as 'productivity', I asked him why he of all people had written a piece such as *The Short Organum for the Theatre* with such logical rigour and an almost Latin syntax. The answer came as a shock: 'Firstly, so that theatre people, who tend to understand everything straight away, do not initially understand it and have to read it; secondly, because I have to discipline myself, as I am too spontaneous.'

Brecht and his collaborators

In the Berliner Ensemble you were judged by how good your suggestions were, not by your 'name'. To be sure, Brecht was the 'central' authority, but we were neither afraid of Brecht nor unduly respectful towards him. And he always seemed to want things to be like this. I was after all an 'amateur' when I began in the Berliner Ensemble. And of course those who were already 'established', like Peter Palitzsch, with whom I later collaborated and was friends, were brashly self-confident, you might even say arrogant. Brecht was not like this. He never asked his collaborators what kind of status they already enjoyed in the theatre or in the public realm, but rather how they could be of use to him. You can also call this Brecht's philosophy of usability: usability not in the sense of taking advantage, as is often stupidly claimed today; rather, Brecht was interested here in 'the third thing'. Thus something that two people both used, also in order to get to know one another better as people. You were not judged by how long you had already been at the Berliner Ensemble or how many successes you had to show for yourself, you were judged by the concrete suggestions, points of criticism, and contributions that you made at the time. I had been at the Berliner Ensemble for a whole three days when I was 'thrown in at the deep end and had to swim'. I was made Brecht's assistant on his new production of *Mother Courage*. And that was where I made my first *faux-pas*. The eighth scene was being rehearsed, between the army chaplain, played by Erwin Geschonneck, and the cook, played by Ernst Busch. Brecht was called away to the telephone and casually said: 'Wekwerth, please carry on.' Of course I grabbed the unexpected opportunity. It was well known that Busch liked to rehearse with rather a loud voice, but I was unaware of this at the time. And so I interrupted him in the middle of his act and said with all the courage of the ignorant: 'Mr Busch, I think you are too loud.' The short silence that followed was deceptive. For, after just a few seconds, I heard a voice, whose metallic tones I knew well from the records and which I highly respected, but this time those metallic tones were aimed at me and my 'stupidity for saying' he was 'too loud'. Busch turned on his heel and left the rehearsal. My co-assistants, long-standing members of the Ensemble, grinned and predicted a hasty exit for me from the theatre that I had joined just days before. The following morning, however, when I went up to Busch before the rehearsal and asked him in a small voice for forgiveness he looked at me in astonishment and said – again rather loudly: 'What are you apologizing for, you idiot, I really was too loud.'

Ignorance can make you immodest, but that can also be useful. From then on I always made my suggestions, and, to my surprise, they were accepted. Nobody there knew who I was, but Brecht would say, 'Wekwerth thinks the following … ' Your suggestions could be as crazy as anything, you just had to be able to justify them. Brecht did not tolerate suggestions that were not justified. This sometimes led to outbursts of rage. And Brecht was just as much a master in accomplished outbursts of rage as ringing laughter. Both came from the heart. In actual fact, he most liked to laugh in rehearsal. And it was – also in serious scenes – mostly a sign of his agreement. He could even 'split his sides' laughing if something 'was right', that is to say had been well observed by the actor. It didn't even have to be comical. In his theoretical writings Brecht describes something like this rather more grandly as the 'art of observation', which he incidentally, like

Denis Diderot, considers to be the starting point of all art. But here too one must be careful with the myths of 'Brecht the Just' or 'Brecht the Wise'. Outbursts of rage sometimes came like lightning out of the clear blue sky. Even a harmless spotlight, switched on just a little too early, could trigger hurricanes. For this there was the well known saying, particularly among the stage technicians: 'Brecht is always right' ('Brecht geht vor Recht').

Question: Could you criticize Brecht?

Yes, according to the myth, and he is supposed to have loved criticism. That is of course rubbish. No one 'loves' criticism. Or perhaps in theory, as in the Hegelian or Marxian sense, where criticism as a pre-requisite for change is always a positive thing. Neither Brecht nor his theatre are imaginable without a 'critical stance'. But in concrete situations the love of criticism was often replaced by annoyance. If you told Brecht after a rehearsal, 'Brecht, I think what you did there was wrong' (after all, you were supposed to raise any objections), you would often get only a silent look in response. The best scenario would be a 'Write that down'. I never actually witnessed genuine enthusiasm.

It was 1952. Brecht, assisted by me, had produced the con-temporary GDR play *Katzgraben* by Erwin Strittmatter, and we were proud that we had finally found a new 'positive' ending. To be sure, it was a little 'romanticized', as reality didn't have much to offer back then by way of 'positive endings'. Palitzsch, just back from his own production in Sweden, saw the premiere. At the end Brecht went up to him expectantly: 'Palitzsch, what did you think of the new ending?' Palitzsch said in his Saxonian accent, 'dreadful'. Incredulous, Brecht turned on his heel and left Palitzsch standing. For four weeks he did not speak to him, or if he did have to say something, then addressed him as 'Mr Palitzsch', for him the most extreme form of contempt. But at some point the old Brecht won through. Three weeks later Brecht rang up Palitzsch, it was fairly late in the evening. Palitzsch could remember this well because at the time he was in bed with a female collaborator, whose 'proletarian' background he admired just as much as Brecht. Brecht asked 'Am I disturbing you?', as every tel-ephone conversation of his would begin, and without waiting for an answer he started asking all sorts of things that could equally well have waited until the following morning. When Palitzsch finally went to hang up in astonishment, the real question came – only three weeks late: 'And why dreadful?'

Brecht and the guitar

Much as been written about 'Brecht and ... ': 'Brecht and women', 'Brecht and Marx', 'Brecht and natural remedies', etc. As for as I know there is nothing on 'Brecht and the guitar'. And yet he used it daily, at least when he was still called Eugen Berthold Friedrich and lived in Augsburg. He used it for singing and making love. Even today there are reports of how his rendition of the 'Ballad of the Pirates', accompanied by the guitar in E minor, enraptured his listeners, particularly the female ones. And later on too in Berlin. Elisabeth Hauptmann reports in her memoirs: 'It was Brecht who sang and determined the rhythm, Brecht was really good in E minor. That was down to the guitar, because it suited him best, not just his voice but also his fingers, E minor, yes.'

Brecht himself has only made a few comments about his favourite instrument. In the early *Psalms* he says, 'We have bought some rum and re-strung the guitar. We have yet to earn white shirts.' And in his *Manual of Piety*:

> In the red sun on the stones
> I love the guitar, these guts come from animals
> The old girl shrieks like a beast
> She eats little songs.

There is even a slender volume by the very young Brecht with the title *Lieder zur Klampfe von Bert Brecht und seinen Freunden* (Songs for the Guitar by Bert Brecht and His Friends). Much later, in the fifties, he makes another declaration of love for the guitar. A young lyric poet who was showing Brecht his poems was allowed, and this was a great exception to the rule, to spend the night in Brecht's house in Weißensee. In order to show his interest and gratitude, he asked for the *Manual of Piety* as his bedtime reading. The following morning he bombarded Brecht with his enthusiasm for the depth of the lyric subject in the texts, the existential sense of complete helplessness behind everything, and so on. He was practically speechless as he attempted to express how moved he was. Brecht listened with interest. Then he said, 'Yes, yes, they all take up the guitar to sing.'

Brecht and Marxism

It was 1952. We were caught up in the copious spadework behind the production of Strittmatter's comedy *Katzgraben*, the first 'contemporary play' at the Berliner Ensemble and which dealt with social upheaval in a village in the GDR.

Brecht was working with great intensity. This was his attempt 'to give theatre' – as he said in the 'Katzgraben notes' – 'a literary solution for its new political tasks'. In the theatre we worked every day from 8 a.m. to 10 a.m. before the rehearsals, Brecht's favourite time for such kinds of work, and all day Sunday in Buckow, about 60 kilometres away from Berlin.

When we travelled to Buckow, where Brecht expected us in his 'gardener's lodgings' at half past ten by the latest, we noticed ploughs and harrows standing unused and rusting in the fields. We were outraged. We considered such a thing particularly anathema to self-respecting co-operative farmers. I think even the phrase 'one reactionary mass' was used, as Lassalle once termed the farmers, while we also spoke of a shocking breach of Marxism.

Brecht was horrified. But not by the farmers, by us. Our opinions were quite simply 'holier-than-thou', irreconcilable with such important historic events as the revolutionary changes in the countryside!

And just as old Cato keeps repeating his 'Ceterum censeo' in relation to the destruction of Carthage, Brecht repeated his phrase about the 'terrible lack of dialectical thought'.

For must a farmer always remain the farmer God made him? And therefore the servant of his farmstead, with the path of his life determined solely by livestock and land? To be sure, a farmer would in previous times rather have been struck dead than have something happen to his livestock; he would rather have struggled against bad weather himself and put his ploughs indoors to prevent them from rusting. But what we were referring to as 'farmers' honour' was nothing more than a dire situation where enslaving yourself was the only honour available.

If farmers wanted to become humans like everyone else, they had to step out of this God-given 'honour' like out of a shabby old suit. The very first thing they had to do was liberate themselves from their eternally bent posture and stand up straight, whatever the cost, for it had become second nature to them to be enslaved by objects that in turn objectified them. The rusted machinery in the fields was scandalous, that is to say scandalous for us, who were reliant on the farmers, and this even though there was still a general lack of provisions. But for the farmers it was a necessary act of liberation, and where was it written that acts of liberation happen without losses? Yes, perhaps the owners of those ploughs rusting in the fields had gone on holiday, previously unimaginable for a farmer! And still unthinkable for farmers today outside of the co-operatives. But shouldn't a farmer be able to do what every city dweller can do? Here we were, working on a play about the liberation of a village and at the first real act of liberation we cried out in dismay about farmer's honour and made a dear God out of economic advantage. If we were going to mention Marx, then we should mention that after a social revolution, as had happened here, the ability of each individual member of society to develop unhindered is the condition for *all* members of society to develop unhindered. And it was not just the positive results seen in this land that brought the more humane aspect to the fore compared to the old social order. Shortfalls, unthinkable elsewhere because they damage profits, also highlighted it. Including the rusted ploughs in the fields ...

It was one of those leaps of faith which we were used to witnessing whenever Brecht allowed himself to be carried away by dialectics, and I must confess that you would find yourself carried away too (and writing it all down, which Brecht liked most of all). But an element of suspicion always remained that things couldn't be quite as Brecht said, even as you were carried away by him. And when we left Buckow in the evening and travelled past the rusted monsters in the fields we found little had changed: our old outrage returned, but we were perhaps just a little more careful in respect of Marx.

For 'the user of Marx', as Brecht liked to call himself, had with a hidden grin called us 'Murxists' as he said goodbye.

And we were well acquainted with Brecht's opinion of Murxists: 'Marxism, in its widespread form of Murxism, is terrible because it makes asses unbeatable in debate.'

Brecht and Ionesco

The Berliner Ensemble's first tour, in Paris in 1954, during which *Mother Courage and Her Children* was shown, enjoyed a success the like of which Paris had never seen before. The Parisian press was in raptures. Even the rightwing *Figaro* immediately demanded that the Berliner Ensemble be given the Prix du Théâtre des Nations. Brecht was troubled by such enthusiasm, even though he did value it. The greater the applause, the happier he was to withdraw. And so one evening, as the auditorium was still filled with applause, he happily withdrew into the furthest corner of the small café in front of the Sarah Bernhardt theatre where the Berliner Ensemble was making its guest appearance. And precisely here things caught up with him. Suddenly standing before him was Eugène Ionesco, the famous representative of 'the theatre of the absurd'. After a rather overly polite greeting, Ionesco, who spoke German very well, challenged Brecht: 'I accuse you of killing feelings on stage and of unleashing the terror of reason. You are stealing people's right to despair.' And after the applause of the hangers-on he had brought with him had died down, he played his trump card: 'Don't bother, Mr Brecht, this world is unknowable!'

Brecht, as he always did when he was uneasy, moved his head from side to side, and then said in a friendly tone: 'If the world is unknowable, Mr Ionesco, then how do you know this?'

Brecht and Diderot

In the last production I did while Brecht was still alive – it was John Millington Synge's Irish comedy, *The Playboy of the Western World*, and I did it with the chief dramaturg of the Berliner Ensemble, Peter Palitzsch – we were greatly worried that those 'holier-than-thou' critics would once again take offence. The story deals with a supposed murderer, who splits his father's head open with a shovel and flees to a remote village. He is celebrated by this village as a hero because nothing much ever happens in this backward corner of Ireland. But when the father appears with a bandaged head but his skull still intact, the 'hero' is cast out as a liar. We feared the press would once again claim the Berliner Ensemble was contemptuous of 'ordinary people's' feelings. Brecht, who was still helping us to modify Peter Hacks's excellent translation, thought briefly and then dictated the theatre programme note to me: 'Tell me whom you worship as a hero, and I will tell you who you are. Diderot.' I must have looked a bit taken aback, because he immediately elaborated: 'Of course I just made that up. But whoever knows Diderot knows that he's written all sorts of things, so why not that too? And whoever doesn't know Diderot will be careful not to let on.'

Diderot was mentioned by almost all critics in an extremely positive light as the cultural-political reference point of the production.

Marxist clown shows

In 1955, busy bringing Marxist thought to those in the GDR who were trying to create a world without capitalism, Brecht along with the director Erich Engel had the idea of staging, 'as entertainment' the first chapter of Marx's *Capital*, 'The two factors of a commodity'. It is probably the most abstract part of the whole book. Because a commodity is not conditioned for personal use but only for exchange with other commodities, its value is no longer conditioned by its 'use value' (its practical use), but rather now only by its 'exchange value' (by what it can 'bring in'). It doesn't matter what you produce, as long as 'it sells'. It was supposed to be a clown show for the stage (and later for a short film), showing the 'absurd inversion' of the original exchange formula G-M-G (Goods-Money-Goods) into M-G-M (Money-Goods-More Money). The useless 'dumb clown' (exchange value) was supposed to prey constantly upon the useful 'whiteface clown' (use value), eventually swallowing him up entirely and declaring himself the dear God of commerce who was initiating new commandments. Including the first commandment: You shall only produce something that you yourself do not actually need, and this you shall do only for someone whom you do not actually know and from someone whom you are not even sure actually exists.

BRECHTIAN THEATRE

An Opportunity for the Future?[1]

My title carries a question mark. So I am asking a question here. And you certainly expect me to answer it instantly in the affirmative. I am not going to do this, and there are two reasons why.

The first reason is the times in which we live. They are more and more infected by thoughtless initiatives that are characterized by rigorous efficiency, unconditional success and cutting out all waste, such as taking the time to think or be patient. Questions are answered before they have been asked. Results are announced before research has even been begun. Something is deemed right or wrong, good or evil, not because it has been recognized as such, but because it must be slotted in to existing and anticipated paradigms of understanding. Far-reaching undertakings no longer need to be justified in any way, because they are undertaken also in order to find justifications. Impact determines reality. In science, such a mindset yields ridiculous results, in politics it produces a catastrophe, the contemporary manifestation of which is the pre-emptive strike.

Kaiser Wilhelm still had to wait for the shots in Sarajevo in 1914 before he could attack Serbia, which had been a long-standing source of annoyance to him. Even Hitler still needed the German Gleiwitz radio station to be attacked, an event that he himself staged with Germans dressed as Poles, in order to start the Second World War.

Today no such reasons are necessary. War itself is reason enough, because it too is needed to find reasons. And even if no reasons are found, that's still no reason to put an end to war, for the world has been carefully divided up in a pre-Christian, Manichaean way into good and evil, with the dividers giving themselves the role of the good, constantly under threat from the realm of evil and rogue states. And who wants to prevent an attacker, who is good, from defending himself from his victim, evil? Quite the opposite is the case. Because he who is good has the justification of being not only good, but also

109

stronger, he also has the right to declare himself his victim's protector and demand from him – as in the good old days of the prohibition in Chicago – protection money, today in the form of oil, free trade zones, military bases, goodwill, etc.

The other reason I will not immediately answer the question as to whether Brechtian theatre offers us hope for the future is Brecht himself. Brecht hated quick answers. Even if he had found an answer and liked it, he would always doubt it, precisely because he liked it. He called this a 'critical stance', and it is not just key to his thought and action, but also his theatre. He considered doubt to be a basic quality of the human species that allowed man to become human in the first place, and still does today. Brecht wrote some of his best poems in praise of doubt.

But at a point in his *Galileo* that is usually considered to be a scientific dispute, Brecht gives an unusually direct insight into his particularly personal way of thinking and acting. It is the ninth scene, in which Galileo returns to his research, even though the Inquisition has forbidden it. Pushed by his students to make a hasty statement about the recently discovered sun spots that would prove the earth's movement and the sun's stasis, Galileo answers:

> My intention is not to prove that I was right up until now, but to find out whether I was. I say: abandon all hope, ye who enter into observation. Perhaps these are mists, perhaps spots, but before we assume they are spots, which would suit us, let's assume instead that they are fish tails. Yes, we will question everything, absolutely everything, again. And we won't take giant leaps forward, but rather we will proceed at a snail's pace. And what we find out today we will strike off the board tomorrow and only write it back up once we have found it out once more. And when we find what we were hoping for, we will regard it with especial distrust. So we shall approach our observation of the sun with the implacable resolve to prove that the earth stands still. And only when we have failed, have been completely and hopelessly beaten, will we, licking our wounds and in the most wretched of states, begin to ask if perhaps we weren't right and the earth turns. […] And then, if every other assumption with the exception of this one has slipped through our fingers, then we will no longer have any mercy on those who have not done their research, yet who talk regardless. Take the cloth off the telescope and point it at the sun!

So let us begin our thoughts not by saying that Brechtian theatre is an opportunity for our time, which would suit us, but let us write on the board instead – following Galileo's advice – 'Brechtian theatre is out of date'. And let us look for the best possible arguments to prove this.

First objection

Brechtian theatre impoverishes theatre and, in its strict party-line, renders it one-sided, as it seeks to be an educational institution peddling a particular political ideology. Brecht reacted to his times with the extreme view that the audience can be educated through theatre. That is fundamentally misguided. The political role of theatre – and it is very political – is not to offer solutions and communicate ideology. Such a belief, inherent in *Lehrstücke* (*learning plays*), is arrogant and completely unacceptable. It assumes that society is made up of children who need to be taught. The *Lehrstück* is a dangerous mode of expression, it conveys Stalinism. At some point Brecht also wrote a major play justifying Stalin. Real theatre shows political situations by presenting all the contradictions. It simultaneously erects a mirror that shows the complexity of these contradictions. It trusts the audience and its ability to draw its own adult conclusions.

Because this objection comes from a big name in European theatre, Peter Brook,[2] I would like first of all to pose a question in response: What actually is 'Brechtian theatre'? Is it a theatre that only performs Brecht? Then the Berliner Ensemble, even in Brecht's day, would not have been a Brechtian theatre, because it performed more plays by others than by Brecht. Are, as the objection states, the *Lehrstücke* typical of what we call Brechtian theatre? In them Brecht cuts out what he called 'the culinary' and really does want straightforward teaching.

Apart from the fact that the *Lehrstücke* were an immediate reaction to the class wars in the 1920s and the 1930s in which nothing was more badly needed than an understanding of how capital, unemployment and fascism interrelate, they were above all conceived to teach the actors, not the audience (which is also why Brecht mainly wrote them for schools). As they played out their parts, the performers were supposed to experience contradictory situations 'first hand' in order to recognize and deal with contradictions better in real life. No 'solution was conveyed', but rather the ability to ask the right questions and find answers. But nor was this conceived as the product of an educational institution for ideology. Rather, it came from the fun in acting, from aesthetic enjoyment. I myself have been working with children on a learning play. It is called *Der Brotladen* (*The Bread Shop*), a fragment about unemployment that Brecht wrote in 1929, in which unemployed people, in an effort to understand their situation, act out both their own roles and the roles of those who made them unemployed. The children came from various schools and social classes, but they all agreed on one point: that they had never really asked what the real causes of unemployment might be. As they acted, they discovered how everything fits together: 'Rich guy and poor guy / Look each other in the eye / And the poor guy says, feeling sick: / If I weren't poor, Nor would you be rich' (Brecht). We had the idea during rehearsal to stage the premiere not in a theatre but in a job centre – to unemployed people. Having gained insights themselves, the performers – just children, remember – playing unemployed people conveyed to real unemployed people not only what they had 'discovered', but also the fun in discovering, and this in spite of the bitter theme. The 'dangerous mode of expression' that according to Brook's objection 'conveys Stalinism', conveyed in this case something quite different:

> Theatre of the scientific age is able to make dialectics enjoyable. The surprises afforded by something that develops in logical steps or great leaps, the instability of all circumstances, the humour in contradictions, and so on, these are the pleasures inherent in the vitality of humans, things and processes, and they enhance both the art and the pleasure of living.

> (Brecht)

The Generalissimo[3] would certainly have found such a thing abhorrent, for he, as Brecht writes in his obituary, got rid of dialectics. In his famous *Four Basic Qualities of Dialectics* one thing is missing: dialectics. There is no such thing as the unity of contradictions in Stalin. Likewise the 'major play that Brecht wrote justifying Stalin' would hardly have pleased Stalin. For in *The Measures Taken*, which is presumably the play meant by the 'major play justifying Stalin', a chorus checks and questions all the measures taken by the functionaries, with the result that the play was attacked by the Stalin-orientated communist press on its premiere in 1930 because of its merciless dialectics. 'a prominent communist said: if that is communism, then i am not a communist. maybe he's right' (Brecht 1930).[4] And as far as the 'party-line' is concerned, this is yet another case of confusing 'being based on the party-line' with 'being partisan towards it'.

But what is Brechtian theatre then? Before it is anything else, it is theatre. And theatre consists – at least in Brecht's view – 'of living reproductions of real or imagined happenings between people, and this for the purpose of entertainment'. If Brecht had been expected, on his return to Germany from exile in 1948, to turn once more to his learning plays in order to bring knowledge to the vanquished and confused, what he actually wrote at this time was the *Short Organum for the Theatre*, and that begins with these words:

> Let us therefore cause general dismay by retracting our intention to emigrate from the realm of the pleasing and let it be known, to even more general dismay, that we are planning to settle in this very realm. Let us treat theatre as a place of entertainment, as is only right when debating aesthetics, and examine what kind of entertainment most appeals to us.

If we are going to talk about Brechtian theatre, then we must bear in mind that no teaching takes place in this theatre that is not entertaining. No philosophy is given, nor is any politics communicated, without fun and enjoyment. Indeed, in the 1950s Brecht elaborated on his well-known thesis that theatre is all about not just interpreting the world but changing it:

> It is not asking enough when one only asks of theatre that it provide realizations, insightful reproductions of reality. Our theatre must inspire joy in the act of realization, guide people's pleasure in changing reality.

Second objection

Brecht was a Marxist and wanted to change the world. Marx is dead. The world has turned out to be unchangeable. Capitalism has won.

First: even if this were the case, it would indeed be a huge change. The world really has been the subject of some breathtaking changes in the last decades, and indeed more so than was expected by either the Right or the Left. Even if the changes are different from those planned – even by Brecht – that is no reason for calling the changes themselves into question, only the plan. Brecht would be the last person not to doubt a plan that has failed, we have only to think of his nice poem 'In Praise of Doubt'. However, Brecht did not praise doubt in order to despair, but rather to find the courage, precisely after a defeat, to start all over again by doubting and examining everything previously established.

Socialism in Europe – in as much as it ever was socialism – failed as if Lenin's forecast from 1921 were correct: 'No one can stop communism, unless the communists stop it themselves'. This can happen, for example, if they forget the basic rule, which Lenin also formulated: 'to give a concrete analysis of a concrete situation'. The loss of alternatives is a catastrophe for human emancipation. But it is maybe also an experience that can be useful in a renewed attempt 'to overthrow all relations where man is a humiliated, enslaved, abandoned, contemptible being'. For in these words of the young Marx, Heiner Müller for instance, who is otherwise a passionate sceptic, saw what Walter Benjamin once called 'the practical glowing core of Marxism', which in his opinion will never die. Thus socialism's defeat can also be a realization that without democracy, understood as a real rule of the people, there can be no socialism. Here in the GDR, after the major land owners had been expropriated, the major industries transferred into the possession of the people, and the educational privilege broken as faculties for workers and peasants were created, all 'great revolutionary events' according to Brecht, the situation was particularly favourable for a real democracy. But things only properly come into 'the possession of the people' when the industries really are taken over by the producers. Here Brecht's warning applies: 'What are states without the wisdom of the people?' Or as Heiner Müller puts it more radically: 'In the Soviet Union and the GDR a major and sustained attempt was made to disprove Marx. The attempt failed.'

But that is neither here nor there, capitalism has triumphed. Has it really? At the demonstration of 500,000 people in Berlin on the 15 February 2003 against Bush's invasion of Iraq I saw two banners. On one stood: 'Another world is possible'; on the other: 'Capitalism has not won – it has remained'.

It has remained with all its contradictions, intensified by the fact that it has lost its old enemy. The image of the enemy, communism as the 'realm of evil', more or less held the hostile brothers of capital together in their shared hour of need, slowed down the dismantling of the social and the humane, and in so doing allowed the myth of a 'social market economy' to develop – that in reality only came about under the pressure exerted by the other side's social achievements. Without an opposing force – and at least as an opposing force socialism was real – capital loses all inhibitions and sense of proportion and finds its way back to 'normality', as in Marx's *Capital*. And while I read, in response to the question in an East German 'major socialist newspaper' as to whether Marx is out of date, that he is no more out of date than stone-age cave painting, and he must just be considered in literary, rather than scientific, terms, things are presented rather differently today in the USA:

Earlier in the twentieth century some critics called fascism 'capitalism with the gloves off', meaning that fascism was pure capitalism without democratic rights and organizations. In fact, we know that fascism is vastly more complex than that. Neoliberalism, on the other hand, is indeed 'capitalism with the gloves off'. It represents an era in which business forces are stronger and more aggressive, and face less organized opposition than ever before. [...] Neoliberalism's loudest message is that there is no alternative to the status quo, and that humanity has reached its highest level. Chomsky points out that there have been several other periods designated as the 'end of history' in the past.

Thus writes Robert W. McChesney in the introduction to Noam Chomsky's book *Profit over People*. Time, or so it would seem, has caught up again with Brecht. If his plays were considered by many to be a thing of the past, today they are palpably in the present. The mass unemployment for example in *Saint Joan of the Stockyards*, written in 1930, is not (as Joan thought and as one can read again today) the result of an economic slump that will disappear again with the next boom. The 'industrial reserve army' (Marx) is an integral part of functioning capitalism. It is a product not of a slump, but success. For as share prices rise so too do unemployment figures and 'booms' produce more mass redundancies than ever before. 'Shareholder value', the unconditional run on returns, was in Brecht's view a 'social Flood'. But he would not be a dialectician if he didn't see in capital's rise also its fall. In this context, he liked to tell a story from the thirties: Henry Ford the elder proudly shows Walter Philip Reuther, the chairman of the car workers' union, a factory hall completely run by machines. 'These machines,' declared Henry Ford the elder, 'will no longer go on strike.' 'No,' answered Reuther, 'but nor will they buy any cars.' But it is not just Brecht's plays, also his way of staging them, that very technique of *Verfremdung*, that deserves our attention in a world that likes to obfuscate things. It is called 'democratization' when a country is attacked in order to reintroduce capitalism. People are told we live in a 'knowledge society' as, thanks to school closures, a shortage of teachers, and tuition fees, they are deprived of precisely that knowledge and it is instead sold on to elites for large sums of money. And that 'information society' that is supposed to have replaced capitalism continues to make every piece of information into a commodity, the value of which is not information, but the price for which it can be sold. Here *Verfremdung*, the technique that reveals the unfamiliar behind the familiar, provides not only a method suitable for today, but the chance of finding one's way in the 'jungle of cities'.

Brecht has also remained topical in more amusing ways. Recently I met a Swiss millionaire who was deeply troubled. He had a thriving business and two sons, one six years old, the other ten. His concern: how should he raise his sons? As a good Christian he wanted them to become good Christians, and on this point one must follow Moses: 'Love thy neighbour as thyself' (Leviticus 19:18). But his sons were also to take over the business at some point, and here loving your neighbour would mean certain ruin. For in such a context you must follow the mantra: down with competition!

His peace of mind was restored when I gave him Brecht's *The Good Person of Szechwan* to read. With the good Shen-te on the one hand, who does good to all, and the evil cousin, Shui-ta, on the other, who compensates with harshness all the losses caused by being good, and all this united in one person – this struck our Swiss millionaire as a feasible solution to his crisis of belief.

In spite of the Brecht renaissance, both already present and still to come, it is not the case that Brecht foresaw everything and was never wrong. His faith in the workers and their class, for example, which had almost religious dimensions, has not been rewarded. His sentence 'Wherever there is a worker, all is not lost', formulated in 1932 in *The Mother*, was already recognized back then as utopian. Many workers voted for Hitler. And how utopian it appears today. Today, where people have to fear for their jobs and see our current capitalist system, in a reversal of 150 years of the labour movement, organizing a huge army of unemployed people, and where the media insist as never before on a complete lack of alternatives, many workers have been moved not to fight against exploitation any longer, but rather for being exploited at whatever cost, so that they can at the very least secure their job (which they then only manage to do in the rarest of cases). But is the failure of *one* utopia to come to fruition a reason to abandon hope in all utopias? Losing utopias amounts to losing the will to live. But precisely strengthening the will to live is the declared aim of artistic activity, at least according to Brecht. Or as Jürgen Habermas once put it: 'When the utopian oases dry up, a desert of banality and helplessness spreads.' From Brecht's utopia of a community of free producers that achieves emancipation, equal opportunities and justice, the hope remains that today enough people can also be found who sense how intolerable circumstances have become and actively do something to change them.

'Marx is dead and Brecht is finished too.' Reconsidering this objection I am starting to have doubts. A protestant priest whom I met recently put things more plainly: 'Not even Jesus, if he were alive today and called "all that labour and are heavy laden" to come to him, would manage without Marx.'

Third objection

Brecht believed in reason. With the help of an interventionist form of thought he wanted to spread reason so that people would understand their world and change it. Reason, praised as a cure for all ills since Diderot, has turned out to be the actual illness, belief in science a fatal mistake. The world cannot be understood.

I can still remember when Brecht himself was confronted with this last objection. It was 1954, the Berliner Ensemble was on its first Parisian tour with *Mother Courage* [...].Eugène Ionesco met Brecht. [See 'Brecht's Simplicity' earlier.] After he had accused him of the terror of reason, his speech culminated in the impassioned exclamation: 'Don't bother, Mr Brecht, this world is unknowable.' Brecht politely listened to him and, when he had finished, said in a friendly tone: 'If the world is unknowable, Mr Ionesco, then how do you know this?' An anecdote, certainly, and this is not the place to solve whether the world is knowable or set about destroying the concept of reason, an approach postmodernism has recently introduced. We are talking here about Brecht's understanding of reason, whether we share it or not. When Brecht talks of reason, he does not mean faith in science. He was not interested in a dreary rationalism that allows no mysteries. Or in expressing how humans live together in mathematical terms. On the contrary, Brecht's concept of reason actively takes issue with such a mathematical approach when he has his Galileo say:

A few experiences were able to give you a completely false view of what we have always called the future of reason. But a single man can neither promote reason nor bring it into disrepute. It is too great a thing. Reason is something all people share. It is the self-interest of humanity as a whole.

In spite of all rumours that Brecht reduces man's existence to logical causality, Brecht's reason is actually a basic stance for mankind, even when it is breached. 'It is' – as the philosopher Wolfgang Heise once put it – 'man's ability ultimately to represent his own interests.' And history, if we can believe the old man from Trier,[5] is not a planned sequence of laws, but rather nothing other than people following their goals.

Thus this form of reason also contains 'unreasonable' elements. I am sure it seems surprising when I claim that Brecht accorded at least as much importance to hunches as to planning. When Galileo developed his laws of gravity in the leaning tower of Pisa, he was already working with gravity, even though the term 'gravity' must have seemed highly suspect to him. According to contemporary knowledge, the earth did not exert any force on bodies, rather bodies possessed an inner force that attracted them towards the centre of the earth. But there was also reason in Galileo's mistake.

Brecht's admiration of Kafka is well known. He even once called him a 'Bolshevik writer'. That is certainly one of his 'unreasonable' exaggerations, but it surely helped to have Kafka's reasonableness recognized as that of one of the greatest realists of our time. Kafka did not know of the fascists' death camps, indeed his hyper-real description of the death machine in *In the Penal Colony* was considered in his time to be the nightmare of an outsider. History retrospectively made it into a reasoned warning.

This form of reason also has no problem with emotions. People's ability to represent their own interests, that is to say act reasonably, relies above all on a desire to succeed, and this entails passion. 'The triumph of reason can only be the triumph of those who are reasonable.' Another sentence of Brecht's Galileo enrages the anti-Brecht camp, it is well known from school books: 'No one is able to resist the temptation of a proof.' This is held up as the unforgivable error that comes from misplaced conviction. People overlook the fact that Brecht presents this sentence precisely as Galileo's hasty error of judgement. In the very next scene the monks certainly do resist the temptation of a proof. They simply do not look through the telescope with which Galileo wants to show them Jupiter's newly discovered moon. The church does not like these moons, so they don't exist. The church turns out to be stronger than a proof.

Brecht's concept of reason does not destroy, as is claimed, all spontaneity in favour of conscious action. On the contrary, it does not entail any irreconcilable opposition between spontaneity and consciousness. I can consciously behave spontaneously. Brecht practised this in every rehearsal, when he deliberately reckoned that coincidences would provide solutions and demanded that actors forget their concepts. Concepts were always good if you could think of nothing else. Or: 'Results are generated in close proximity to mistakes.' Those were favourite lines during rehearsal.

Theatre today likes to labour away at the so-called 'subconscious', which is also seen as the opposite of reason. Brecht is accused of ignoring man's subconscious, because he supposedly only gave credence to what can be known for certain.

When dealing with Brecht, a certain prejudice against the subconscious really should be overcome, even though this prejudice probably comes from Brecht himself, when he made fun of how Sigmund Freud's couch was supposed to coax the famous 'id', 'ego' and 'superego' out from the depths of repression. Whatever about the couch, the subconscious – or habits that are no longer reflected upon – guides the majority of human behaviour. Why should this be taboo for Brecht, whose theatre aims at representing precisely the highs and lows of human behaviour? Even if his writings should tell a different tale (and Brecht specialists will be quick to find this out), Brecht's 'subconscious' behaviour was by no means actively hostile towards the subconscious. I once jotted down a sentence during rehearsal that backs up my thesis: 'Actually I think dialectics are a matter of feeling.' And that too is Brecht.

Couldn't such considerations also help enrich theatre today – and not just the Brechtian kind – with a cheerfulness that would keep alive people's desire to live, also, or indeed even especially, during difficult times, and even when the stories being shown on stage are anything but cheerful? Doesn't the scope offered by this conception of reason allow us to uncover its universal possibilities: it is people's elementary desire to survive and to live? Is not this reason, that is in some places ridiculed for pretensions to enlightenment, precisely theatre's chance to escape the threat of being left completely high and dry by a lack of planning, thought and moral rigour?

Theatre, if it does not want to be deaf and dumb, needs a message, both good and bad. And if it has always been the case that it is not the bad message but the messenger who is shot, theatre should nevertheless not be afraid of being this messenger.

Fourth objection

Brecht wants political theatre.

[…] It seems to be self-evident that political theatre is antiquated today, out of date, laughable even. The latter cannot be entirely dismissed, if one understands politics as what the so-called 'political class'; today's troop of politicians, present us with, for this really is shoddy farce. But theatre practitioners' distrust, if not outright avoidance of, political theatre usually stems not from rejection on principle, but rather resignation. [...][6]

Yes, Brecht does want political theatre. Even with his *Lehrstücke* he makes a direct contribution to the class wars of the 1930s. *The Measures Taken*, a discourse about morality and class warfare, was not just performed for workers, but by workers. Likewise, *Senora Carrar's Rifles*, written during the Spanish Civil War, makes a direct contribution to the political struggle by making the succinct observation that in this war there is no such thing as neutrality. But it is incorrect to limit Brecht's political theatre to political themes. Of course a play such as *Senora Carrar's Rifles* is eminently political. But not because it deals with political topics, rather because it takes on a political standpoint: the pleasure in changing things, both in the political and the private realm. Communard Jean's love for Babette, which he insists upon even though there is no place for it in a future without hope, is at least as political as the storming of the Parisian Hôtel de Ville. Conversely, a play like *A Respectable Wedding*, where not a single political word is uttered, can be more political than many a political pamphlet, dismantling as it does in a Chaplinesque or Valentinesque manner the greatest obstacle to all revolutions: the self-satisfied and self-contented petit-bourgeois.

Plays with political subjects do not have to be political, for example if they are boring, and plays dealing with the most private of realms can further revolutionary causes, just like Beaumarchais's *The Marriage of Figaro*. Rejecting politics, as is currently fashionable in theatres, is not an apolitical stance, rather a questionable one. It is 'the state of self-inflicted immaturity', which Kant has already warned us about. Brecht goes one step further:

> Without opinions and intentions it is not possible to make representations. Without knowledge, nothing can be shown; how are you supposed to know what is worth knowing? If the actor doesn't want to be a parrot or a monkey, he has to take on history's lesson about how humans live together by taking part in the class wars.

Fifth objection

Brechtian style. Brecht wants to use his theatre to enlighten the audience. The time of enlightenment is past. Today the world is disintegrating into individual details, wider contexts are disappearing. The struggle, as the well known representative of postmodernism, Jean-François Lyotard, says, is 'against the white terror of truth with and for the red cruelty of singularities'.

But how should an actor present the abysmal depths of today's world, when Brecht only allows for the rational? And how should the spectator experience these depths, when Brecht uses *Verfremdung* to create distance and prevent any participation on the part of this spectator?

First, the dark abyss is not a recent invention. Perhaps we are more aware of it today, because we talk about it more these days. But even Brecht's *In the Jungle of Cities*, written in 1923, shows the abysmal fight between two men who do not know why they are fighting, rendering the fight even more acute. It is just that Brecht – as an old Hegelian – calls the abyss by its bourgeois name: 'contradictions'. And if Brecht wants to 'enlighten' his audience – and he really does want to do this – then it is with the fact that contradictions (or the abyss) not only exist in the world, but determine it. But where others start to believe in the eternal abyss, Brecht starts to doubt it: what grounds underlie this abyss? So Brecht not only allows for the rational, but also the irrational. But the irrational does have to allow itself to be questioned. Not in order to belittle it, quite the opposite, the abyss (or contradictions) becomes all the deeper the less one allows it to be 'eternal', that is to say God-given, or a law of nature (an 'ever-thus', as Brecht would say) and one regards it instead as something that has come about, and is thus transient. Precisely as earthly, man made.

Brecht does not deny that there are some things that cannot be changed in this world. For 'what has not been changed for a long time [...] seems unchangeable. Everywhere we come across things that are too self-evident for us to need to bother understanding them' (Brecht). Against this sense of the self-evident that sets in through familiarity and is thus able to go unnoticed, and against the 'cruelty of singularities', that is to say those individual details that deny their wider context, in short, against a world that is standing still, Brecht developed his theatre, which he termed 'non-Aristotelian'. It is well known that in his *Poetics* Aristotle saw tragedy's effect residing in the way it aroused pity and fear in the spectator by imitation of an action, which then purged the spectator of pity and fear. In order for this to happen, the actor identifies completely with the character being portrayed and causes the spectator to do the same and experience the hero's fate as his own. 'This purging is the result of a peculiar psychic act, of the empathy experienced by the spectator towards individuals, acting in a certain situation, represented by actors' (Brecht). In this context

Brecht also points to Cicero who tells of the Roman actor Polus. In order to evoke more empathy in the audience when he was playing Elektra mourning her brother, he carried the urn containing the ashes of his own recently deceased child.

As early as 1773 Denis Diderot wrote his famous *Paradox of the Actor* against a theatre of simple empathy. In the spirit of the Enlightenment, Diderot too felt that simply imitating nature and its feelings on stage was not enough in order – as he writes – to progress from the 'feeling to the thinking person'. For Diderot, it is not the personal suffering of the actor on stage that leads to great feelings, but rather the extent to which he is able to represent 'with a cool head and excellent powers of judgement' great feelings that he has observed in other people. And the less he shares them on stage, the more effective they will appear. Indeed, Diderot even recommends developing the opposite emotions in order to retain 'a cool head and excellent powers of judgement': so in a love scene also fostering a possible sense of dislike, in a scene of pathos nurturing its prosaic opposite. The high point of empathetic theatre was almost certainly the 'system' developed by the great Russian theatre reformer Stanislavski, who in calling for 'truthful feelings' on stage rebelled against the clichés of the kitsch theatre of his day and achieved great realistic effects. But after the revolutionary upheavals in Russia he too had to concede that empathy alone was no longer sufficient to present the social contradictions inherent in the new order. In his later productions he demanded the actor show alongside empathy with the character also criticism of that character, and he demanded 'physical actions' before empathy, so that the character's feelings could first actually be tested.

Uncritical empathy carries a greater risk of deception in theatre than in other art forms, with the result that the audience can be seduced. Brecht also saw this danger in 'the theatricalization of politics'. Thus he called the Nazis' mass dramatization of the Nuremberg party rallies 'a theatre of making-believe'. A contemporary equivalent of this kind of theatre is the so-called show-business 'events' that are the empty experience par excellence of something that masquerades as reality. 'Theatricalization of politics' also regularly takes place during election campaigns, where real battles are feigned as if between real alternatives. Brecht also developed his 'non-Aristotelian' theatre against the misuse of 'empathetic theatre', creating a new relationship to the hero on stage. The spectator should no longer follow the hero's fate 'as if on a leash', but should 'be able to intervene with his judgement'. With the aid of specific artistic measures, called *Verfremdung*, simple empathy on the part of the spectator is prevented so that he, from a conscious distance, can go beyond the subjective horizon of the stage character to discover relationships and contradictions unknown to the character himself but which actually make his behaviour and personality recognizable (and accessible). In this, what is 'entirely self-evident' and 'the most natural thing in the world' is presented in such a way as to provoke astonishment on the part of the spectator, the most important step towards attaining knowledge, but also a good source of entertainment.

'Aristotelian' theatre, by contrast, uses the 'magic' inherent in theatre to make it appear completely unalterable. This is precisely that art of deception that confers on the action and the hero's character and behaviour the sense of being 'the only thing possible', 'eternally-determined-by-nature'. 'Non-Aristotelian' theatre, on the other hand, through its very style of performance causes the spectator not to accept the hero and his behaviour as 'fate', but rather to add other possible courses of action to those shown on stage for the duration of the play. In his additions to the *Short Organum for the Theatre*, Brecht puts it thus:

> In order for something particular to emerge playfully from among the reactions and situations presented in theatre and invite a critical response, the audience writes other reactions and situations in its head, and as it follows the action it compares them with those shown on stage. With this, the audience turns itself into a narrator.

Consequently the events on stage lose the sense of being 'ever-thus'. They are 'historicized'.

Incidentally, 'historicizing' is one of the key techniques in Brechtian theatre. Brecht did not just 'historicize' historical plays, but also contemporary plays and themes in particular. The contemporary easily loses its historicity by virtue of being well known and familiar, that is to say, it is considered 'ever-thus'. People do not ask how it came about, or reflect upon its transience. As a result – whether consciously or not – it becomes impossible for man, in this case the audience, to understand it. 'Historicization' means uncovering the human activity in everything that history presents, regardless of whether one is talking of human achievements or those powers that are alien or even supernatural to man, for they too are the 'congealed labour' of man. Strictly speaking 'historicization' is the application of Marx's first Thesis on Feuerbach to theatre: 'The main flaw in all materialism up to now [...] is that the object, reality, sensuousness is conceived only in the form of an *object* or of *contemplation*, not however as *human sensory activity* or as *practice*; not subjectively.'

Brecht at no point underplays the dark abysses, sharp corners, and rough edges of this world in order to teach the spectator from a safe distance. On the contrary, Brechtian theatre is about opening up contradictions and getting the spectator actively involved, not just as an observer but as a co-narrator. Its aim is not to solve contradictions quickly on stage so that the spectator enjoys a quick release. On the contrary, Brechtian theatre is about increasing the number of contradictions to the very limits of what can be tolerated, in order to have the spectator question his readiness patiently to put up with things, a readiness that prevents change. So it is the attempt to bring movement to everything that has become entrenched, whether through familiarity, the everyday, routine, or ideology. Yes, the principle of *motion* – at the end Brecht liked to speak of 'dialecticizing' – is actually where all his efforts in and for theatre begin and end. That look of astonishment with which the actor approaches his role and the look of astonishment with which the spectator regards the stage are able to set everything that is shown on stage in motion, stasis itself included.

Thus Brecht valued that 'hymn' to total stasis, Samuel Beckett's *Waiting for Godot*, as 'greatly attractive to the dialectician'. He was even planning a production of the play at the Berliner Ensemble shortly before his death, but it was not to be. A world's complete stasis, the subject of this play that can easily lead in conventional theatre to boredom or a pessimistic mythologization of the world, was, thanks to Brecht's style of acting, set to become a breathtaking process whereby the spectator does not join in the waiting on stage, but instead, astonished at such behaviour, opposes it with his impatience and thus historicizes (criticizes) stasis. Estragon and Vladimir, who are waiting for Godot, were in Brecht's version not supposed to be mere layabouts, rather they were unemployed. That unemployed people are waiting not for work but for Godot makes the scenario all the more absurd, it becomes a clown-show. Brecht was often reproached for the fact that in his anti-war play *Mother Courage and Her Children*, Mother Courage, who has lost everything in the war, does not learn anything and in the end carries on participating in this war. But if played correctly, Mother Courage does not need to learn anything for the spectator to be able to learn. Her very unteachability, taken to the limits of the plausible, provokes the spectator's incomprehension. And it is not only his reason that criticizes Mother Courage's unteachability, it is also his feelings, including the most important one of all when new discoveries are at stake: horror.

'Epic theatre' was what Brecht called his way of making theatre in the 1920s, and it relies on stories being told on stage, through the actor's acting, that turn the spectator himself into a narrator. And that the *Fabel*, the very story being told, is at the heart of theatre (here Brecht agreed with Aristotle). Later, in the 1950s, busy trying to find a poetic form for the socialist revolutions that were taking place in East Germany, Brecht spoke of a 'dialectical theatre'. But when he tried to link philosophical insights with elementary enjoyment (the result precisely of naivety), as he attempted in the final years of his theatrical work, this term too was no longer sufficient. In the end Brecht spoke – still very carefully – of 'philosophical folk theatre'. Linking a high form of human thought, philosophy, with the 'lowly' pleasures of mass entertainment, whether in the circus or at the Oktoberfest (where the young Brecht played an active part alongside Karl Valentin) must have greatly appealed to Brecht in his final years.

Brecht never saw himself as a philosopher. He has a philosopher appear in *The Messingkauf Dialogues* who gets into a terrible argument with the theatre people, but he avoided setting up a systematic philosophy himself. Indeed, in an article in *Der Spiegel* on Brecht's hundredth birthday it was even claimed that Brecht was a passable dramatist, a brilliant lyricist, and absolutely not a theoretician. The proof: that there is nothing systematic in his work. I believe that Bertolt Brecht the philosopher is still to be discovered, even if he himself never wanted to be one. His philosophical statements, scattered across plays, poems, texts, and songs strike whoever puts them all together as an amazingly consistent philosophical structure that draws on Socrates, Descartes, Bacon, Hegel and Marx. His later teacher Karl Korsch probably introduced him to a kind of philosophizing that he himself, grinning gently, called 'a philosophy of all trades':

> You must understand, I am consumed by an insatiable curiosity for people; I can't see or hear enough of them. How they relate to one another, make friends and enemies, sell onions, plan military campaigns, get married, make woollen suits, circulate counterfeit money, dig potatoes, observe stars, how they cheat one another, favour, teach, grill, assess, mutilate, support one another, how they carry out meetings, found clubs, plot and scheme. I'm always looking to know how their initiatives come about and finish up, and I'm trying to discern a few rules to this that might allow me to make predictions.[7]

125

Here Brecht meets Antonio Gramsci and his thoughts concerning a philosophy 'from below', a new everyman's philosophy. This equates to the knowledge evident in the behaviour of many people who act philosophically without realizing it: 'The old woman who, the night before a journey, unceremoniously gives the mule an extra bundle of hay, the seaman who, when buying his provisions, thinks of both the storm and the calm, the child who puts on his cap when he learns that it might rain, all of these are my hope, they all listen to reason,' says Brecht's Galileo.

It may well be that Brecht's meeting with Gramsci (which strangely enough he never wrote about) was the reason that Brecht, who actually never wanted to be a philosopher, came to the concept of 'philosophical folk theatre', which towards the end appealed to him greatly, although he never explained it. 'That's for you to do,' he said to us back then.

That's all very well, I hear you say, that's the theory. But where is the practice? Where can you find this 'philosophical folk theatre' today that, if we listen to Brecht, is the 'hope' for the future? And even if you can't find it as a whole theatre, where at least can we see the beginnings of such a theatre? So where can Brecht still be found today? Is Brecht present wherever Brecht is performed? But just as Brecht plays are once again being performed even in Germany, it is striking how absent Brecht can be – even in his own plays. If, for example, they are performed 'without opinions and intentions', and just in order to improve upon low ticket sales, because Brecht is 'in' again. In the Deutsches Theater in Berlin I recently saw a production of *Mother Courage and Her Children*, and this by a famous director, that with all the skilled one-dimensionality of popular TV shows managed to flatten even the exciting story of the trading woman and her children to such an extent that one is ultimately forced to ask – plagued with boredom – whether Brecht was a dramatist at all. Or *Baal* in the Weimar Nationaltheater, which the director so butchered with that old cudgel of symbolism that even the play's eroticism was beaten out of it as everything drowned in symbols. Interpretation runs amok before Baal's licentiousness has even been discussed.

There are however also examples, at least in Berlin today, of Brecht plays being produced 'without opinions and intentions', and thus without Brecht, that have enjoyed great success with the audience. This concerns – as a Berlin theatre manager and artistic director puts it – the 'dangerous plays', that is to say Brecht's plays with a revolutionary content. When *The Mother*, for example, is performed, one can be sure, regardless of the quality of the production, that there will be a sense of solidarity among leftwing spectators who are happy under the present circumstances to have heard Brecht's political texts at all on stage. And that is absolutely a victory for them. But it is also 'attractive' for the 'rightwing camp'. For they definitely partake in an exotic event when, in officially anti-Communist times, they get to hear 'In Praise of Communism' on stage. This is known as the 'pleasurable shiver of horror'.

In *Mother Courage*, by contrast, this kind of thing doesn't work because the play only reveals its 'danger' in the way it is acted and the action *gestically* interpreted (which was a real 'trickery of reason' when it was written). This Brechtian play cannot be performed without Brecht, unless it is to produce, as described above, extreme boredom.

For Brechtian plays whose effect does not reside in an external tension are, when performed 'without Brecht', considerably more boring than plays by any other author. That is, as it were, a built-in self-defence on the part of Brecht. But in today's commodity-based society boredom too can become a value. Thus the applause at least is guaranteed at the end of such a performance, for in a commodity-based society a theatrical performance as a commodity is worth as much as it has cost. And here inflated ticket prices increase the value of a

Illustration 10 Manfred Wekwerth with Gisela May in rehearsal for *Mother Courage*, Berliner Ensemble (1980). (Photograph courtesy of Vera Tenschert.)

theatrical performance, for the spectator buys along with the theatre ticket the right to believe that what he has invested his money in is valuable.

However, I have also recently seen productions in Berlin where Brecht seemed to me to be present, even though the producers certainly didn't intend this to be the case. At the Deutsches Theater, *Wartesaal Deutschland* (*Germany the Waiting Room*) by Klaus Pohl, directed by the author, and at the Volksbühne *Murx den Europäer* (*Murx the European*) by Christoph Marthaler. Both cases represented a genuine mastery of reality through observing reality. The absurd that today rages all across the world is in this case not the product of an absurd messing-about on stage, but of extreme *gestic* precision. *Germany the Waiting Room* consists of different lives at the time of the upheaval in Germany in 1989. These are reports delivered in an almost statuesque manner. A wealth of precise details, set against one another in contradictory fashion, lead to an incredibly fluid kind of action, with the most varied of individuals literally entrusting themselves to the spectators and challenging them to make parallels, assumptions, associations, and criticisms. In Marthaler's *Murx the European* at the Berliner Volksbühne (and even more so in his Hamburg production *Die Stunde Null oder Die Kunst des Servierens. Ein Gedenktraining für Führungskräfte* [*Zero Hour or The Art of Serving. Thought Training for Leaders*]) the word 'politics' is never mentioned, as indeed are very few words at all. Nevertheless the starkly precise dismantling of petit-bourgeois behaviour yields a genuinely political theatre that is wickedly humorous. And another refreshing thing: caricatures (so beloved of directors) are not necessary here, quite the opposite, the play's bite is a result of its deep and serious affection for the characters. As Hegel says of 'irony', nothing 'inconsequential is annihilated'; rather, monuments are toppled that were previously carefully constructed. And despite the fact that the techno-age is represented, techno-time does not have the upper hand on stage. On the contrary. These human case-studies can be pleasurably contemplated in epic calm. And as the audience's reactions show, people will gladly forego the usual drive for action and breathlessness that characterizes contemporary theatre if actions, serenely repeated over and again, etch themselves onto one's memory as 'traditions and customs'. Pictures stick in one's mind like 'The Three Men in the Fiery Furnace' or 'The Feeding of the Five Thousand'. This is no absurdly excessive stage business on the part of the actors. Rather, the 'strict' logic of stupidity and the precise manner in which absurdity is observed remind us of the comedy of Karl Valentin.

When looking for Brecht you cannot avoid Dario Fo. The mixture of commedia dell'arte and Brecht's theatre techniques attracts an audience to his Milan theatre every evening which clearly enjoys his insolent treatment of history and fiction. His style is marked by clowning around and criticism, and its popularity proves Dario Fo's claim that laughter opens not just your mouth but also your brain. The list could go on. Certainly it should include a theatre that is also located in Berlin but is generally not included in theoretical discussions, even though it is called Grips-Theatre, because it is officially a children's theatre. In reality, great theatre happens here and it proves that the reality 'outside' can be reworked into exciting theatre, as long as you possess the right abilities. And another thing about it stands out: Its *Linie 1* (*Line 1*) means it is well travelled in all the fashions. And its 'faithfulness' to reason tells us something else: even 'modernity' can be shown in a far more varied, and above all far more humorous manner than 'modernism' has managed. Brecht can be found everywhere that an emancipatory stance towards reality is taken that is based on discovering things and making changes, and that discovers, invents and changes its formal techniques accordingly. Every kind of performance that helps to open up contradictions and leads to discoveries that allow us to, as Brecht calls it, 'deal with antinomies', is welcome: tragedy or clownery, verse or slang, imagination or documentary, emotions or coldness, the readily comprehensible or the absurd, building up or knocking down. In any case, Brecht's theatre is also able to yield more theatrical techniques in the future, even 'absurd' ones, than can fashionable trends, which are often as like as two peas in a pod. Adorno seems to be right when he speaks of the 'jargon of particularity'. If somebody just wants to be different from others he will end up, because others have exactly the same notion, becoming ever more like everyone else. That Brecht supposedly only allows for rational sources and prevents actors from showing the irrational is something that theatre people often claim who themselves only know of one source: namely themselves. A view of theatre that considers itself to be the last word is in my opinion a terrible step backwards. It only allows for 'perceptions' and no 'truths'. To be sure, we know of times where supposed truths covered over real perceptions, where the wood could no longer be seen for the trees. But allowing only what you can see, hear, smell, feel, taste is making a leap back into the naturalism of the last century, where something by the name of 'positivism' was honoured as philosophy and the inventor of the 'merely-mundane', Karl Popper, was elevated outright into the universal spirit of the age. But the opposite as well, the claim that the stage now only consists of interpretations and ideas and has no place for proper stories, is naturalism, albeit one with 'its feet in the sky'.

Five objections to Brecht: there are certainly many more. They shouldn't be dismissed out of hand simply because they are wrong. For they too demand that one reconsiders and considers afresh. 'Results are generated in close proximity to mistakes' was after all one of Brecht's favourite thoughts.

So what then? Does Brechtian theatre represent an opportunity for the future? We shouldn't ask Brecht this question, rather ourselves. And Brecht's 'categorical imperative' might give us some inspiration: 'The proof of the pudding is in the eating.'

2

POLITICAL PERSPECTIVES

In these recent pieces Manfred Wekwerth reflects on two key issues for the political Left. In the first, 'The Left's Difficulties with Culture', he criticizes the tendency of those on the Left to separate cultural activity from politics – as if self-realization through education, culture and the arts were not integral parts of economic, political and social life. Drawing on Brecht, Wolfgang Harich, István Hermann and Georg Lukács, he develops his own definition of cultural activity as the constant production of the relations that are generated by the people themselves in the process of their daily lives.

In 'The Uncertain Thing about Certainty' (dedicated to Uwe-Jens Heuer, a leading academic lawyer and later member of the German Bundestag) he responds to the challenge facing Marxists when the GDR collapsed in 1989; in particular, the confusing issues of legitimacy and democratic accountability that faced many Marxists with their misplaced faith in historical inevitability. Drawing support from Heuer and other traditions of Marxism represented by Lenin, Rosa Luxemburg, Gramsci, Bloch and Benjamin, he proposes the alternative view that the stability of a socialist society rests in its ability to change. Rather than 'certainty', Wekwerth values uncertainty and quotes Brecht's poem 'In Praise of Doubt'.

AH

THE LEFT'S DIFFICULTIES WITH CULTURE, OR THE PRACTICAL USE OF BRECHTIAN SLOGANS

Polemical Thoughts[1]

The occasion giving rise to my critical comments is actually a pleasant one: almost 400 people came to the Milbertshofen cultural centre in Munich on the 9th November 2007, making its celebration of the 90th anniversary of the October revolution a sell-out. Under the heading 'Witnesses of the next Red October', a young woman and a young man charmingly and humorously presented a programme, the first part of which consisted of a refreshing talk by the philosopher Hans Heinz Holz[2] on the topic of 'October today'. In the second part we performed Brecht's verse rendition of *The Communist Manifesto* to an enthusiastic audience. The music was by Syman, who also played the piano, Renate Richter and Hendrik Duryn were the speakers, Torsten Adrian was on the percussion. *Rotfuchs* magazine spoke of a 'magnificent October celebration', and the CSU confirmed the event's success by taking the DKP[3] to court. They wanted to ban them from using the 'Milbertshofen Community Centre' in future on the grounds of 'leftwing extremism', for this event apparently proved that the DKP was advocating a 'nationalization of the means of production'. The charges had to be dropped, as the DKP turned out to have a better grasp of the constitution than the CSU. Article 15 of the Federal Republic of Germany reads: 'Land, natural resources, and means of production may for the purpose of nationalization be transferred to public ownership or other forms of public enterprise by a law that determines the nature and extent of compensation.'

In view of this this pleasing result, it is almost inappropriate to take a small event during the presentation as the starting point for critical reflection on a concept of culture commonly found amongst the Left and also evident here. For when the young people, those 'witnesses of the next Red October', announced the Brechtian *Manifesto* after the break, they did so by speaking of the 'cultural part' that would now follow the presentation. Ignoring the fact that this meant Hans Heinz Holz no longer belonged to 'culture', reducing culture to a 'cultural part' or a 'cultural framework' amounts to something that Franz Mehring[4] already lamented as 'a bad habit of the labour movement' back in 1897.

Culture is actually an unquestioned part of the Left's political work; this really should not be a matter for debate. But precisely because it seems so self-evident, old Hegel's words on the self-evident apply: 'What is well-known is, because it is well known, not known.' That is why I would like to reconsider the definition of culture (or should I say: our definition of culture).

Revolutionaries – and here I also include Marxists in non-revolutionary times, provided they really are Marxists – actually have always had a very good understanding of culture. Not just because they brought about great cultural achievements in the course of their history, thinking only of literature, films, and music, but because Marxism itself is a noteworthy part of human culture. For it is, in my view, the most sustained attempt by man to create a humane way of life. This necessitates replacing 'ordered disorder and planned arbitrariness', long used by capital to secure and extend its rule, with a 'Great Order', as Brecht says in his *Me-Ti: Book of Changes*. 'But,' so Brecht elaborates,

> beware of people who preach to you that your purpose is to put into practice the Great Order that already exists as a finished theory and just needs to be put into practice. They are Holy Joes. Once again they read something in the stars that you should carry out. Up until now, you existed for the Great Disorder, now you are supposed to exist for the Great Order. But the truth of the matter is you need to take your affairs into your own hands and order them; if you do this, *you* will create the Great Order.

And one could carry on with Marx:

> For we do not regard communism as a state that should be produced, an ideal that reality will have to follow. We call communism a real movement that will supersede the current state of affairs. The conditions for this movement are a result of what is available here and now.

In 1871 the Paris Communards, for example, did not wait for more favourable times in order to improve people's way of life. In the first days of their people's rule that lasted a mere seventy-two days, even as they were still embroiled in fighting and constantly battling with hunger caused by the Prussian blockade, the Council of the Commune issued its first decrees: on 'respecting human dignity'; 'postponing all debt obligations and abolishing all interest accrued', 'linking government salaries to workers' wages', 'abolishing night shifts at the bakeries', 'remitting rental payments', 'reorganizing medical faculties', 'reopening theatres' and 'creating a commission for women's rights'. For seventy-two days it represented an unprecedented culture of political thought and action.

In 1945, before the battles against the fascists were over, the Red Army distributed both much-needed bread to the starving population and works of literature (this was how I came across, for example, Chekhov, Gorky, Sholokhov, Gladkov, for the very first time). In the midst of ruins they put on concerts with works by Tchaikovsky and Shostakovich; one of Marshal Zhukov's first commands was to reopen the theatres. Those who today dismiss this as 'Communist propaganda' neglect to mention that the Deutsches Theater in Berlin opened with Lessing's *Nathan the Wise*. The Red Army made the production possible by providing the necessary material for the stage scenery.

In 1949, that difficult first year of the GDR's existence, when clearing all the rubble of war and rebuilding society was taking up all the energies and resources available, the GDR opened a 'Workers and Peasants Faculty', open to all those who up until then had been excluded from further education because of their social background (and many of whom would later become world-famous scientists).

In 1959, while the struggles against the pro-USA Batista regime were still raging, the Cuban revolutionaries started a literacy campaign among the rural population, the like of which had never been seen before in Latin America. Later, under the continuing stranglehold of US imperialism, Cuba developed a health system in that was unique even outside Latin America. In spite of the most difficult economic circumstances caused by the US embargo, Havana University was established. It trained doctors for other Latin American countries, while its German Studies department is highly regarded worldwide.

And it was revolutionaries who – having come to power in the socialist countries – immediately enshrined one of the most significant demands of human culture in the constitution and put it into practice: the right to work.

You may wonder why I am listing here what we already know, especially given the way it has been so discredited by the bourgeois media and individuals in recent times.

That is what I find strange. Why have those who, as the Senior Representative of the Council of the Paris Commune said at their final meeting in May 1871, 'have achieved more for people's dignity in just a few days than other governments in centuries' – why do revolutionaries, who in the history of the labour movement have achieved so much for human culture in terms of knowledge, experience, art, thought and way of life, often have difficulties with the 'idea of culture' on an everyday level? For example, when in their political work culture just becomes a 'cultural framework'? Or when to be 'cultured' one simply makes political gatherings 'more attractive' by including a few songs? Or when a string quartet honouring some worthy person's birthday is considered proof enough of 'support for culture'?

Let me make myself clear: I am not asking whether it is right to utilize 'culture' in politics. Quite the opposite. Artistic contributions make meetings all the more political, because they make them more effective. And in this way one can perhaps also reach people who would otherwise not be interested in politics. Great names such as Ernst Toller, Ernst Busch, Hanns Eisler, Erich Mühsam,[5] John Heartfield and George Grosz are associated with the Agitprop movement of the 1920s and 1930s, in which art was a direct political weapon. And it was Brecht who, shortly before his death, convened a meeting with the aim of bringing the Agitprop movement back to life in the GDR because, as he said, 'in the GDR too even the best of us do not turn up our noses at Agitprop as proletarian culture'.

My question is different: why does the everyday work of leftist politics reduce culture to something along the lines of 'a cultural framework'? Why do Marxists in their actual practice of politics regard culture – a fundamental part of man's daily activity after all – as an aid for achieving political aims and not as a political aim in itself? And in any case: why don't they regard politics as an important part of culture?

Hanns Eisler, who was not just a great musician but also a philosopher of considerable standing and wit, once said that this was the way to trace Karl Marx back to Saint Augustine. For Saint Augustine in response to the question as to why music exists gave the simple answer: 'So the congregation is better able to remember the psalms.'

But perhaps precisely the awareness 'that', as Franz Mehring also said, 'the proletariat's struggle is humanity's most cultured achievement', perhaps precisely this 'historical certainty' is the deeper reason why people no longer reflect on culture in the daily business of politics? In 1921 Lenin surprised his audience at a communist youth congress, who were expecting rallying cries about overcoming the economic crisis caused by the civil war, when he claimed that the revolution could only be continued if they managed to raise the cultural level of the masses. Lenin's observation that socialism reigns wherever the kitchen maid too could rule the state is popularly cited. But the quotation continues: 'And that is exactly what she has to learn.'

Likewise Che Guevara, when asked how the revolution's continued existence was best ensured, answered: 'In the first instance through extensive education. José Marti said that only an educated people can be a genuinely free people. They must know what they want and how to achieve their goals, then they cannot be manipulated and deceived any more' (quoted by his daughter Aleida Guevara).

My attempt to reconsider the idea of culture reminds me of an initial conversation I had with Brecht as a newcomer to the Berliner Ensemble in 1951. I was enthusiastically telling him of the great impression his production of Lenz's *The Tutor* had made on me as a 'new teacher' when I saw it at the Berliner Ensemble at the first Germany-wide meeting of the FDJ.[6] I was particularly impressed by the epilogue, and recited it to him by heart: 'Teachers and pupils of today / Learn from this man's servility / That it should help to set you free.' Expecting a few words of praise for my 'art of observation' and a lesson on the 'causal nexus' that creates such impressions in the first place, I was rather taken aback by his explanation: 'Brecht's slogans are the best.'

So let's assume that this is right and ask ourselves if his slogans have always had such a 'cultural' impact. Recently I found a letter in the Brecht Archive. It dates from 1952 and was addressed to the GDR government. It contains seven proposals for improving the educational curriculum in GDR primary schools.

Brecht made – something that few know today, or want to know – many such proposals. It was his way of playing a practical role in the 'societal revolution', for this was how he saw the GDR, in a manner that went beyond his literary work. For he believed:

> These great revolutions in the countryside, expelling the landed gentry, destroying the monopoly of education for a small ruling class, taking over the industries, guidelines, plans, new schooling – these are all things that have not been properly brought to people's attention.

And here, Brecht believed, art could do a great deal. But 'great achievements', for this was how he considered the 'revolution', must be reflected in everyday activity. It was not enough to be 'well conceived', tangible improvements had to follow. Because, for Brecht, thinking meant intervening, or, as he liked to call it, 'interventionist thinking'. And his 'interventions' actually related to everything: improving the training at theatre schools as much as improving the work of parliament, the people's chamber, from which he demanded greater public accountability; securing sufficient payment for writers, in particular lyric poets, so that they could live from their work, but also introducing an employees' council that would have a say in publicly owned companies. He made concrete suggestions for orthographical reform, and he communicated words of encouragement to work collectives that if their views were not taken into account they should be prepared to resort to strike action. He made suggestions concerning a selection of fairytales for kindergartens and suggested to the finance ministry that they should not deny their own standpoint in discussions with capitalist partners in order to curry favour with them. And he put forward a suggestion for a new national anthem (which has unfortunately to this day not been accepted). He suggested that theatre managers and artistic directors appointed by the ministry of culture should first be subject to vetting by the Academy of Arts, and he repeatedly protested against the daily papers' 'standardized-opinions' and their 'language of the prayer-wheel', linking this to a suggestion to establish a representative weekly paper that would feature the independent contributions and opinions of well known writers and scientists. As well as demanding that the incessant music be turned off at the Baltic coast, because it was ruining the resort for those seeking relaxation there, he also offered to become a cultural guardian of the publicly owned Siemens-Plania company along with Hanns Eisler. With his *Thesen zu Barlach* (*Theses on Barlach*), provoked by a Barlach exhibition that was discredited as 'late bourgeois decadence', he undermined the false cultural politics of the party leadership and offered his services to the same party leadership to rewrite the 'miserable German' in which their slogans for the 4th Party Congress were expressed – which he then did, although his suggestions were rejected as 'entirely unnecessary'. And there were those suggestions, already mentioned, for improvements to the educational curriculum in GDR primary schools. In the letter to the people's minister for education, I read under point 8:

Possibly introduce the pedagogical subject 'Kitsch' from as early as Class 5.

The current curriculum lacks any off-putting examples. Neither political nor aesthetic judgements can be formed solely on the basis of what is good. It is easier to recognize the greatness of Tolstoy's prose when it is contrasted with that of Ganghofer.[7] It can only help form a deeper insight and a more discerning sense of taste if the bad example always precedes the good. For this is the only way that the quality of what is good can really be measured. Only those who have seen how low you can go will properly appreciate the highpoints of art.

(Bertolt Brecht, Berlin, 31 January 1952)

This is almost certainly also the source of my never-ending search for a definition of culture that is as inclusive as possible, and which is also suited to the kind of everyday cultural work that Brecht carried out.

What might such a definition of culture look like today?

First of all I consulted people who can still speak Latin. And they told me the word 'culture' comes from the Latin verb 'colere', meaning 'to cultivate'. I think that's not bad at all. It immediately prevents the belief (also common on the Left) that culture is a matter for the head (writing, thinking, cleaning your teeth, etc.). 'To cultivate' means to create an environment that is suited to mankind. So it refers to human activity involving change. Man as an 'objective entity' ('gegenständliches Wesen': Marx), puts himself into his works and can enjoy these works as he recognizes himself within them. But this is of course still not a definition.

I appear to have inherited Brecht's dislike of quick definitions. But it speaks in Brecht's favour that he also claimed the opposite: 'What cannot be said in one sentence does not say enough.'

So I'd like to try a definition with two philosophers who have really helped me arrive at a handy 'definition of culture' for my work.

Because he believed ignorance among his collaborators to be 'immoral', Brecht sent us assistants in the early hours of the morning, before rehearsals started, to Wolfgang Harich's twice-weekly lectures. Harich, who was just twenty-two years old at the time, was the youngest and probably also most idiosyncratic philosophy lecturer at the Humboldt University. To this day I refer to these lectures as 'Pentecost for atheists', for we really did find ourselves filled with great insights. The flames were not on our heads, as in the Bible, but inside them.

Harich spoke about culture and I still like his idea of culture today, because he boldly went beyond the limits of the 'purely intellectual'. On 13 September 1951 I wrote in my lecture notes:

Man is not only biologically but above all historically conditioned. As a result of production he increasingly loses his direct link to his surroundings, and, with this, his natural ability to adapt to his surroundings, diminishes accordingly. He is, in biological terms, a 'flawed creature' and is forced to create a 'cultural' environment for himself where, however, satisfying his needs always results also in the creation of new needs. That is why Marx defines the creation rather than satisfaction of new needs to be man's 'first historical step'. Producing himself through the act of production, man becomes a 'cultural' creature who constantly reproduces himself and must reproduce himself, because man's alternative in society is to develop or to perish.

Culture as the constant production of relations which are produced by man himself – even in class-based societies where people are first and foremost 'abject, enslaved, abandoned, despicable entities' and 'overturning social relations' itself is their greatest cultural concern – this concept of culture was extremely well suited to us and our work at the Berliner Ensemble, the 'Brecht Theatre'.

István Hermann, the second philosopher I consulted, was a student of Georg Lukács and one of the most important in my opinion. And he is one of the most important Marxist cultural theorists of recent times. His works *Probleme der sozialistischen Kultur* (*Problems of Socialist Culture*) and *Probleme der heutigen Kultur* (*Problems of Contemporary Culture*) had the misfortune of appearing around the period [of German reunification], a time that is known as the *Wende* ('turn') but which ought more accurately to be rendered as the *Rück-Wende* ('backwards-turn'). István Hermann died before even leftwing philosophy could take note of him. But this is something that, particularly in the current phase of re-evaluation, is overdue.

István Hermann on the concept of culture:

Man constantly reproduces himself, and the only question is whether he, while reproducing production in a more developed form, is also capable of reproducing himself in a more developed form. In other words, the question, also for Marx, is whether the subject can succeed, in his free time, in fashioning himself into another subject and in this manner re-insert himself back into production as a newly developed subject. If he manages this, if the unity of social foresight and individual foresight is achieved in man's free time, then a key moment in human culture and its developmental process will emerge. This very concept of foresight plays an important role in Marx. For foresight means constantly redesigning man with regard to man's self-worth; with this, man not only secures his existence but also constantly develops it and enjoys this development.

Coming back once more to the initial question of how politics relates to culture, Wolfgang Harich and István Hermann also strike me as helpful in this respect. If I understand them correctly, culture cannot be rendered subordinate to politics, because there is, for example, also a culture of politics, or more precisely: there should be. Or a culture of thinking. Indeed, even a culture of arguing.

I see a particular need for the latter among the Left, when I think of how much collective knowledge we are losing because of the increasing tendency on the part of bitterly entrenched leftwing theoreticians to measure the success of their arguments by the failure of their opponents. That the internal battles of the Left – and this not even face-to-face, but rather through publications in newspapers – are characterized by a 'who-whom?' approach, which Lenin actually intended for the class war, strikes me as not just intellectually fruitless but also lacking in culture.

Likewise, we should repeatedly re-examine the culture of thinking, for here 'holy rituals' and 'icy wastelands of abstraction' (Walter Benjamin) can insidiously creep in, or, in layman's terms, mere status-games.

Lenin's much-quoted sentence, 'Marxism is omnipotent because it is true', can be extremely misleading if it is taken as a confirmation that by being a Marxist you are always personally in possession of such omnipotence. And, so the misguided logic goes: because Marxism is right as a matter of principle, the individual Marxist is always right. Because you are in possession of 'the great truth', all the little things you do are also 'true'.

Even Saint Augustine warned against this kind of 'flight into certainty', because he believed that people must repeatedly search for God. And what applies to heaven almost certainly applies to its secularized version, known as Marxism. In any case, Lenin gave some very practical advice with regards to Marxism's 'omnipotence': make a concrete analysis of a concrete situation. This strikes me as something of a 'categorical imperative'.

As a suggestion for a 'culture of arguing', here is another text[8] by Brecht. It comes from his *Life of Galileo* and in it Galileo tells his students how he is planning to take part in the heated argument about the existence of sun spots. A text, therefore, that deserves to be read out at the beginning of discussions and conferences every once in a while:

> My intention is not to prove that I was right up until now, but to find out whether I was. I say: abandon all hope, ye who enter into observation. Perhaps these are mists, perhaps spots, but before we assume they are spots, which would suit us, let's assume instead that they are fish tails. Yes, we will question everything, absolutely everything, again. And we won't take giant leaps forward, but rather we will proceed at a snail's pace. And what we find out today we will strike off the board tomorrow and only write it back up once we have found it out once more. And when we find what we were hoping for, we will regard it with especial distrust. So we shall approach our observation of the sun with the implacable resolve to prove that the earth stands still. And only when we have failed, have been completely and hopelessly beaten, will we, licking our wounds and in the most wretched of states, begin to ask if perhaps we weren't right and the earth turns. […] And then, if every other assumption with the exception of this one has slipped through our fingers, then we will no longer have any mercy on those who have not done their research, yet who talk regardless. Take the cloth off the telescope and point it at the sun!

THE UNCERTAIN THING ABOUT CERTAINTY

A Dubious Eulogy[1]

Uwe-Jens Heuer surely won't mind if I – inspired by his latest book *Marxismus und Glauben* (*Marxism and Faith*), but without intending to deliver a sermon – place a proverb at the centre of my remarks: 'There is nothing less certain than certainty.'

But first let's turn to the man we are celebrating. We know that Brecht was not particularly fond of lawyers. Whenever they appear in his plays, they share one particular characteristic: they are not interested in justice. They are interested in other things. Thus for example the judge in the play *Round Heads and Pointed Heads* sings the famous 'Song of the Stimulating Effect of Cash'. In another play, *The Good Person of Szechwan*, the gods themselves slip on the judges' robes only to disappear quickly into heaven when a good person asks them for justice. In *The Caucasian Chalk Circle* Brecht even decorated the lawyers' hats with large snails in order to indicate that they were professionally inclined to draw out every case for as long as possible. But there is one instance in Brecht where a judge dispenses justice. This is Azdak in *The Caucasian Chalk Circle*, the 'poor people's judge', as Brecht calls him. Ending up in the judge's chair by chance while the palace is in the grip of a revolution, he makes just rulings because he is ignorant of the existing laws. And when the lawyers make great vocal and theatrical efforts to present their pleas to him, they are amazed that he asks them not for their arguments but their fee. And, when asked why: 'I listen to you quite differently if I know you are good.'

Why am I starting my eulogy for such a just person as Uwe-Jens Heuer with Brecht's view of justice as prescribed injustice? There is a simple logic to this. The fact that none other than a Professor of Law proved to be a good adviser in bad times to Brecht's theatre, at that time the Berliner Ensemble, is a real example of the

143

Verfremdungseffekt in the Brechtian sense. And this was not just in relation to his own area of expertise, jurisprudence, but in all areas of politics, philosophy and aesthetics, all of which were directly linked to a theatre's survival back then. I am speaking of 1989, the year of great changes. Actually things should have worked out the way Brecht once wrote about change: 'Oh changing times, you give hope to the people.' But the cry 'We are the people' very quickly changed to its final form of 'We are *one* people.' Capitalism on the other side of the border was prepared to pay a pretty price for this change, about 50 million Deutschmarks according to a reliable estimate. For capitalism was pushing with all its might to return to the point where it had lost control forty years previously. And most people who had taken to the streets back then actually wanted a better socialism, not a triumphant capitalism. However, this country's government, which really should have seen in these changes the kind of hope that Brecht praised as 'the people's hope', retreated to 'the Big House', as the central committee was popularly known, and surrounded themselves in 'class-conscious' silence, stabilizing the situation by removing the word 'change' from all publications. So it was a time that more urgently than ever required independent initiatives.

We had already invited Uwe-Jens Heuer to meetings at the Berliner Ensemble, following a recommendation from friends. The meetings were a concept that dated back to Brecht. They were intended to enable us to address and discuss topical issues of the day in politics and society with the relevant experts. At the time Uwe-Jens Heuer had just finished his book *Marxismus und Demokratie* (*Marxism and Democracy*), a topic that many of our plays had repeatedly addressed. Beginning with the idea that a socialist country can only be stable by constantly changing, and that our reality is nothing more than the daily activities of those who populate it, we tried to communicate to the audience in our theatre both the ability to make these changes and above all the desire to make them. In one of the last productions at the time, Heiner Müller's *Germania. Tod in Berlin* (*Germania. Death in Berlin*), we had just come across the text by Brecht that he had written in his *Me-Ti: Book of Changes* as a kind of address to the working population:

> But beware of people who preach to you that your purpose is
> to put into practice the Great Order that already exists as a
> finished theory and just needs to be put into practice. [...]
> But the truth of the matter is you need to take your affairs
> into your own hands and order them; if you do this, *you* will
> create the Great Order.[2]

In our meetings at the time with Uwe-Jens Heuer we discussed many things, including of course juridical aspects. For back then we couldn't understand why the GDR government was not enacting a government resolution that was based on Brecht's last wish. According to this resolution, Brecht's estate should pass into the hands of the Academy of Arts on Helene Weigel's death, but with the heirs retaining their financial claims. Uwe-Jens Heuer, a jurist with great experience of this country, immediately told us why no such thing would happen. Notwithstanding the legal framework they themselves had created, socialist politicians would not be brave enough to put a socialist decision into practice for fear that the bourgeois press might speak of an 'infringement of civil law'. A pity, it would have saved us a lot of trouble. But this only as an aside. At that time Uwe-Jens Heuer helped us above all with one critical question – how the failure of the GDR could have come about.

And now I come back to the proverb upon which I have based my remarks: 'There is nothing less certain than certainty.'

In 1989 we theatre people felt that the confusion that had gripped state and society was a direct consequence of the increasing uncertainty displayed by leading politicians in the country, which we believed could be traced back to their chronic deficiency in theory. Uwe-Jens Heuer showed us the error of our ways. In the middle of a heated debate, one of the many that were constantly raging in those days, he made a discovery that surprised us all. Seen from today it was hardly new, but for us back then it was in the truest sense a 'revolutionary practice'. With recourse once more to theology, I should like to call it 'the flight into certainty'.

For in Heuer's opinion it was not the fact that the politicians were unsure of themselves that was causing increasing confusion (and their inability to deal with conflicts); on the contrary, they were too sure of themselves. It was that fatal certainty that they, as Marxists, always knew the truth and acted in accordance with the law. They backed this up by appealing to Lenin, who once said, 'Marxism is omnipotent because it is true', and in so doing forgot the rest of the sentence that actually validates the first part. For there Lenin insists on 'a concrete analysis of a concrete situation'.

This certainty of always being right and, thanks to Marxism, of always being in the right (known as 'the flight into certainty' in theology), is an old sticking point for Marxists, one that was at odds above all with Marx himself, who called 'doubt' his favourite virtue.

Uwe-Jens Heuer writes on this:

> The events of 1989 must have made the last Marxist question that historical thinking that equates history with an inevitable natural process that knows no alternatives and yet guarantees victory. This approach was not invented by Stalin, it is manifest in the work of Kautsky, but also in Engels. However, it probably reaches its highpoint in orthodox Marxist-Leninism and its school book versions. Not only Rosa Luxemburg, also the work of Lenin, Gramsci, Ernst Bloch, Walter Benjamin and many others repeatedly fought against this understanding of Marxism. It may have served the 'march of the column', but not the self-led, independent battle … Hans Heinz Holz made this very clear in his appreciation of the *Communist Manifesto*. Each sound prognosis also embraces the effects it will have, 'which is why it is always a prognosis concerning real possibilities – and cannot be compared with the degree of certainty with which a solar eclipse or the appearance of Halley's Comet is predicted'.

Thus writes Uwe-Jens Heuer in his book *Marxismus und Politik* (*Marxism and Politics*).

Today there is a very different kind of 'flight into certainty', carried out by very different people and to very different ends. Today the certainty is to be created worldwide that outside of the existing capitalist system and its leap of faith called 'neo-liberalism' there is no other possible way for humans to live together. Intensively studying Marx and guided by McKinsey, managers too have come to hold the opinion that a theory can only become a material force when it is taken up by the masses. And so the pulpit, the lectern and the TV screen repeatedly announce a new religion. It bears a female name and actually even comes from a lady, albeit one who was called 'the Iron Lady'. For TINA, and that is the name, stands for There Is No Alternative, and the 'Iron Lady' intended to use this to halt the march of history on the grounds that with neo-liberalism history had reached the greatest freedom possible. The stereotypical claim that, although this world might not be the best of all worlds, it is the only one possible today should, according to this world view, subconsciously inform people's general everyday behaviour, for, even more so than violence, it reliably ensures the rule of 'ordered disorder and planned arbitrariness'.

Uwe-Jens Heuer probably wrote the following text as a result of his great fear that this religious belief in a lack of alternatives might spread to the Left:

The Marxist-Leninist orthodoxy subjugated theory to politics (and politically formed ideology) and largely suspended its autonomy. Today, however, a leftist party is faced with a very different danger, namely that politics has completely emancipated itself from theory in order to succeed in bourgeois political circles. Here many practice pure pragmatism, while others use quotations from Marx, or even Lenin, offering good analyses and interesting constructions for the future, but lacking any actual consequences for practical politics. But without Marxist theory there will be no socialist politics in the long term.

Thus his text from the early 1990s.

Finally, allow me to mention another of Uwe-Jens Heuer's personal qualities that makes a Professor of Law into a philosopher, also in the Brechtian sense: humour. And I can still hear the splutters of laughter today from another important Marxist philosopher when he declared: 'Revolution is too serious a thing to undertake without humour.' Hanns Eisler said this, and it is well known that he was first and foremost a musician. And I can also see in Uwe-Jens Heuer a further quality that I was able to observe in Hanns Eisler and that made him into a real philosopher. I would like to call it a 'philosophical stance'. It consists of knowing when to stop philosophizing. For example, when sitting with friends over a glass of wine. Before I first did this with Uwe-Jens Heuer I was informed that he was a 'Savonarola of dialectical materialism'. This was probably supposed to be a warning. However, I saw and still see today something quite different in Uwe-Jens Heuer when we are relaxing in private: he is – to stick with literature – an entertainer of Rabelaisian wit.

And Uwe-Jens Heuer's humour will allow me here at the end of my eulogy to speak of a rather different quality that appears to haunt leftwing philosophers. And I don't want to pretend that it isn't also frequently present in theatre people. Behaviourist studies speak of 'authentic self-assurance'. This, in common parlance, is 'status-games'. For example, when two leftwing philosophers meet one another, regardless whether for an internal exchange of opinions, at a conference, or for a private chat, you can be sure that those who come together as indivisible soul-mates will part as irreconcilable adversaries. Or at least until the next meeting, where the process will be repeated. Marx is not supposed to have been any different on this point, one has only to think of how he attacked his 'favourite enemy' Bakunin. A simple difference in matters of 'ideology', for example whether one talks of 'false' or 'interested' consciousness, can cause those on the Left of today to refuse to greet one another. Consequently, after the kind of defeat we have had, the sensible suggestion of examining one's own knowledge and starting afresh with Marx is rejected in excommunicatory fashion as 'attempting to liquidate Marxism' or 'revisionism', or 'counter-revolutionary', and so on.

So that is why, as I come to a close, I should like to return to the proverb that I placed at the beginning of my remarks: 'There is nothing less certain than certainty.' Of course we need certainties, even if all they tell us is that nothing is eternally certain. And knowing how to attain knowledge that permits certainty is always going to be an important question for Marxists.

So reliable knowledge, or, as Uwe-Jens Heuer suggests in his book *Marxismus und Glauben* (*Marxism and Faith*), knowledge that can be believed in. But the question remains: how can one be certain of something? And, as ever when good advice is hard to come by, Brecht can help out. And he himself did not at all dislike being used to help people put their thoughts more eloquently:

Whenever we thought
We had found the answer to a question
One of us would loosen the tie on the wall of an old
Rolled-up Chinese screen, so that it would open out to
Reveal the man on a bench who
Doubted so much.
I, he told us,
Am the doubter. I doubt whether
The work that ate up your days was successful.
Whether what you said, said even worse, will still mean anything to anyone.
Whether you did even say it well and didn't for example
Rely on the truth of what you said.
Whether it can have many meanings, for every possible mistake
You will be blamed. It might also be too clear-cut
Depriving things of their contradictions; is it too clear-cut?
Then what you say is unusable. Your thing is lifeless.
Are you really in the thick of events? In tune with
Everything that's going to happen. Will *you* still be? Who are you?
To whom
Are you speaking? Who is helped by what you say?
And by the way:
Is it also sobering? Can it be read in the morning?

Does it also link up to existing ideas? Do you use sentences that
Have already been said, at least counter them? Can everything be
proved?
Through experience? What kind?
But above all
Again and again, above all else: how should one behave
If what you say is to be believed? How should one behave?

Thoughtfully we considered the doubting
Blue man on the screen, looked at each other and
Started again.

3

THEATRE MAKING
The *Fabel*

The main article in this section, 'Keyword – *Fabel*', dates in part from Manfred Wekwerth's doctoral thesis, and first appeared in the book, *Theater und Wissenschaft* (*Theatre and Science*) in 1974. Wekwerth acknowledges that in retrospect its view might seem 'utopian'. One of his more important theoretical pieces, it appears here substantially revised and augmented. For Brecht, 'Everything depends on the *Fabel*; it is the heart of the theatrical performance.' As noted earlier, *Fabel* has been left untranslated in this book as no English word – 'story', 'fable', 'plot', 'narrative' – is an adequate equivalent for Brecht's concept. Wekwerth provides different models for construction of the *Fabel* and analyses with examples the ways in which the *Fabel* engages the spectators through a dialectical process in parallel analogy with their own imaginary worlds. (His consideration of Brecht's 'parable' form, clownery and the participatory, community-based 'model' play are of particular interest.) The artistic development of the *Fabel* for any production therefore depends on an analysis of contemporary realities. Wekwerth concludes with a consideration of the challenge that theatre faces in a world of predatory neo-liberal economics and global capitalism.

In the following piece, Wekwerth provides an account of four play-texts that he has adapted and directed. He does this through an analysis of the ways in which they provide opportunities for spectators to engage with the values and ideas of their own historical moment. In each case they demonstrate how to take a 'critical attitude' ('kritische Haltung') from a contemporary point of view is the basis for preparatory work on the *Fabel*.

AH

KEYWORD – *FABEL*

1978 in Utopian Retrospective[1]

> The interpretation of the *Fabel* and its communication through suitable means of *Verfremdung* is the principal business of theatre. And the actor does not have to do it alone, even if nothing can be done without reference to him. The *Fabel* is interpreted, developed, and presented by the theatre in its entirety, by actors, stage designers, make-up artists, costume designers, musicians and choreographers. They all pool their artistry in this common enterprise, always without relinquishing their independence.
>
> (Brecht, *A Short Organum for the Theatre*, section 70)

The very search for plays, material, stories, observations will become an important part of collective theatrical work, so that *Fabeln* dealing with our times can emerge. Everybody engaged in theatre will be involved in this search, and that includes the spectators. The resulting programme will no longer be just a programme detailing the individual plays to be shown, but rather one that sets out the development of the theatre itself and how new plays and projects are to be developed. The running order should be dialectically organized, the plays and projects should be arranged in line with specific points of view, so that the performances illuminate one another, complement and contradict each other. New approaches to programme planning will not just be applied to new plays (although it is also to be hoped that they will result in many new plays). The major plays of world literature should also be considered from new points of view. Not so much epochs like the classical drama, Spanish theatre, the Elizabethans, German classicism, naturalism, Brecht etc., but rather areas from which *Fabeln* can be constructed with themes that matter to *us*.

For constructing a *Fabel* to be 'interpreted, teased out, and put on display' in a performance, is first of all the search for a theme.

One of the greatest themes of the immediate future will be man in his productive daily activity that allows him, in a contradictory manner, to develop into a universal, emancipated, conscious, socially effective personality, into what Marx would call a 'social individual'.

It will be useful to investigate the extent to which particular periods encouraged the development of individuals. In this way, contemporary man can regard himself as an historical process, whereby he is at one and the same time its result and its creator. When searching for such themes, we should apply Brecht's criterion that a theme should have both historical and contemporary political dimensions, as daily politics is not the opposite of history, but rather the field upon which it draws.

But searching for a *Fabel* is not just a search for themes, at least not when one takes *'Fabel'* to represent not just the literary concept of 'plot', but one of the fundamental communicating elements of theatre. A significant part of this communication does not reside in the written text, indeed the text is not even the main element in it. Rather, *the on stage performance itself* is the key.

The conventional work of theatre up to now consisted primarily of looking for themes when looking for plays. Once they had been found, the directors were left to take care of the performance. The different 'signature styles' of the individual plays ensured they came across differently on stage. Performance technique, the style of performance, was more a matter of chance.

Now, 'systems theory' has told us that a 'system' becomes all the more 'capable of variation' the more it is 'organized'. Even what appears 'accidental' on stage must be organized, as indeed what is to be communicated in theatre – the play – must be sufficiently 'organized' in order for it to be 'variable' enough to carry different intentions and messages. That is to say, 'hard and fast' rules and established conventions do not limit theatre, but actually give it scope and variety.

Theatre deprived itself of much of its effectiveness when it was looking only for specific themes without paying equal attention to the specifics of their mediation. Thus searching for themes in future will also be a search for the ways of communicating these themes. And the different ways these themes are mediated need to be sufficiently 'established', that is to say, familiar to the audience. For the spectator can only take part when he knows the rules of the game. His point of orientation should specifically not be limited to the themes of the plays and how he can use what is shown on the stage 'thematically' in his own life. Rather, it should also include the play itself, for it is even more the case in theatre than in other art forms that form is also content. The spectator's independence in theatre will increase as not only what is shown but also the way it is shown, the way it is mediated through the actors and the director, *becomes a conscious experience.*

The way something is mediated (the play), which does not have to be identical with what is mediated (the theme), enables – as we have seen – an additional capacity for discovery and enjoyment. The spectator is not presented with a story that is eternally valid, but rather with one possible version that he can 'play' with, that is to say, treat as he sees fit. The theatre will deploy certain techniques that stimulate the spectator to think up other kinds of action, different from those shown on stage. For this, the style of communication (the actor's and director's 'technique') must be developed beyond the purely 'intuitive', the anarchical, the arbitrary. Just as tragedy, comedy, the morality play, commedia dell'arte and so on developed historically as 'fixed' agreements between the stage and the audience, new agreements must be made, meaning that new forms of mediation must be found. For this, not only the art of acting but also the art of spectating need to be developed – now with reference to the different ways things can be mediated, a kind of art of observation not just of 'what' but also of 'how', in order then to proceed towards strengthening political insights as well – and above all towards helping the spectator become an emancipated, active creature who is able to enjoy himself.

Mediation is not used here to refer to dramaturgical interpretation, but rather to the direct, *gestic* performance of the play on stage by the actors and director. I shall attempt to draw up two models. The first concerns possible themes, the second possible basic types of mediation that would allow these themes to be realized on stage.

Model I

Possible themes

A *The public figure as a prism for viewing social revolutions and contradictions.* The increase and reduction of individual character traits as a reflection of social processes and contradictions. Repercussion on society as an engine or a brake. These people are the revolutionaries, pacemakers, advocates of the new. But also those advocates of the new who were ahead of their time, who could not yet be used by their society, and failed. However, they could also be public figures who, carried along by their society, are capable of productive achievements but later fall short of their own achievements because they do not keep up with society's pace of development.

B *The public figure who is not a prism for viewing great social processes but who claims to be one; his substance is destroyed by his own insubstantiality.* This is the basis of comedy.

> The comical on the other hand (as opposed to the ridiculous) entails endless cheer and confidence, most serene in its self-contradiction and not for example bitter and unhappy about it; the bliss and pleasure of a subjectivity that, sure of itself, is not unduly perturbed to see its purpose and realization dissolved.
>
> (Hegel, *Aesthetics*)

C *The exaggerated public figure.* The self-server or blackmailer, who blackmails his surroundings with services or talents and must be destroyed.

D *Destruction of individual relations* as a result of outdated social formations. These kinds of circumstances no longer produce real individuals because they directly objectify relations. In the extreme, they 'objectify' human existence as a run on profits and income. Meaningful daily activity becomes meaningless management.

Note: This model primarily provides viewpoints on world literature. It does not mean to suggest that so-called world literature will be better represented than new plays. This model could also determine the parameters of a search for new material from the immediate present. The viewpoints A to C are also valid for socialist conditions.

Model II

Mediating forms (structures for possible Fabeln)

A The history play

This does not refer to 'the history play' as a literary type, but to a mediating form in theatre. It consists of discovering and reporting on noteworthy events and people. It does not primarily follow a logical (dramaturgical) structure, but rather an historical one ('how it happened!'). The heightened focus on the individual by the actors and by the production as a whole forces the spectator constantly to complement the historical (apparently random) unfolding of events with his own logical sequence if he is to understand how the *Fabel* hangs together and to apply it to the needs of his own life. This he does by ordering, comparing, mentally flicking back through the pages, constructing theories, generalizing, etc. The history play as a mediating form can be applied to the classic history plays (*King Richard III, King Henry IV, King John, Titus Andronicus,* etc.), but the technique is above all useful for writing and performing contemporary plays. Constructed as this kind of history play, a play about the day in the life of a manager for example could be rendered 'dramatic' without any need for great catastrophes, creating tension in the audience instead by placing a special emphasis on the manager's individualism, for example highlighting the differences between his words and his deeds. In order to avoid naturalism, the selection and montage of the scenes must allow a range of individual characteristics and contradictions to emerge, including traits that are not so easily explained, in which social circumstances are separated into their constituent parts, as light is refracted by a prism. The history play is a suitable way of confronting the individual in the audience with the individual on stage. Its technique resides in highlighting the individual.

B The parable

If the history play contributes to the construction of ideologies by encouraging activity on the part of the spectator, the parable makes ideology itself into its subject. It critiques ideology. It is not primarily concerned with discovering people or processes, but rather discovering discovery itself. Its effect is similar to that of a catalyst. Without actually being integrated in a system, its presence is enough to trigger actions and processes which, although present without it, are not otherwise visible. It also speeds up slow processes and slows down fast ones.

Ideological processes usually elude consciousness; through repetition they are disguised as self-evident. They appear to be fixed once and for all and escape our conscious grasp. Here the parable, by placing the familiar in unfamiliar surroundings, is able not only to bring the subject back to our attention, but above all to clarify the methods that serve to mystify something as 'unchangeable'.

The technique of the parable rests on a lack of identity between meaning and content, and on general incongruity. The meaning is deliberately pitched against the content. Thus the stockyards of Chicago at the turn of the twentieth century are the least appropriate place to find Saint Joan.[2] Christian naivety and the brutality of a capitalist system that itself actually appeals to this Christianity combine to destroy common opinions and views that no longer stand out simply because people have adapted to them. The parable plays a trick. It does not represent its allegory of capitalism's immorality as a moral lesson, instead it endows the parabolic equivalence – here Saint Joan – with her own concrete life, so that she can indeed be imagined in her current form as a girl from the Salvation Army at the turn of the twentieth century. It requires the spectator actively to compare ideology and reality throughout the performance.

The parable does not have to destroy the familiar in order to make it visible. It takes it on in its familiar, concrete manifestation and renders it transparent through the power of analogy. In *Saint Joan of the Stockyards* is shown the process of concealment with which capitalism tries to disguise itself. Capitalism creates its own ideology whereby its ways, like those of the dear Lord himself, are unfathomable. But the parable does not have to destroy the veil in order to make it visible as a veil (this would be unrealistic and lead to the false view that it is easy for individuals to see through things); it can retain it in all its density. It can even make the veil denser still for the spectator, until it becomes unbearable. If it is unbearable, then it can be perceived and thus torn apart (dialectically: accumulating ignorance until it tips over into knowledge). Such immanent criticism is possible because the spectator is not fully integrated into the actual story. The analogy with the historical Saint Joan causes him constantly to draw comparisons, generalizing from individual details and as a result discovering the means by which individual events are arranged. This enables him to apply it to the needs of his own, individual life. If in the capitalist context concealment and adaptation have an objective quality, for us in the socialist context they are primarily subjective distortions, as they are not the result of a socially determined system. And yet concealment and adaptation acting in this way can have particularly damaging consequences, for they obstruct the *sine qua non* of our own society – constant change.

The parable can also reveal false ideologies in the socialist context, such as those that can occur through blind routine, conservatism and everyday consciousness as a whole. Thus a GDR factory for agricultural machinery[3] is in the first instance not an 'appropriate' place for a 'Saint Joan', who thinks and acts naively and spontaneously. The complex nature of the technological revolution has no place for the 'simple' judgements of this girl, who only defines things as good or bad depending on how useful they are for people. On the contrary, her judgements seem to be an obstacle. But precisely this unusual meeting of the naive with the high-tech makes visible things that in their simplicity (because they seemed to have been established 'once and for all') were no longer even perceived by many: how technological development often takes place with absolutely no regard for people's needs and health. Again, the parable endows the key figure of its analogy with enough real, independent life so that this Joan of Döbeln can be conceived as a normal girl of our times, but also of course as Joan of Arc. Such a doubling effect constantly places the spectator in the position of an evaluator, a judge, a discoverer. As such, the facts narrated in the play are not in themselves complete. Only the way they are told makes them into real events, because they coincide with the spectators' interests. The play's purpose is only fulfilled when, inspired by the narration on stage, the spectator becomes a narrator in his own right.

If the history play discovers a noteworthy individual on stage, the parable uses the spectator to give a noteworthy discovery an individual note. The parable as a mediating form, as I have been describing it here, is not identical to the parable as a literary technique, which always needs metaphorical fables in order to achieve a parabolic effect. Here, we are more concerned with the stance taken by the actors and the stage production as a whole. So this is a technique that through the style and stance of the performance also allows real events on the stage to be presented as if they were allegories, that is to say as if they represented more than just a specific event in the play's *Fabel*. This performance method can be applied to almost all plays. It uses theatre's general parabolic nature, but takes it to an extreme.

C Clownery

This is not identical to the literary genre of the comedy, although much of its material can be found here. My model in general is guided by an attempt to define theatre's different mediating forms less from a literary aspect than a theatrical one. Clownery is first and foremost an acting technique. It consists of a disjunction between the content and the effort employed. If an actor whispers something into his partner's ear and does this louder than he would normally speak, it creates a clownish effect. The same applies to a *gestic* inversion, if I for example express dissent while physically taking on a stance of agreement, or vice versa. But it does not just produce humorous effects. For example a tissue held at face level is enough to indicate tears.

The technique of clownery has to a large extent already become a matter of convention. The spectator is familiar with a series of fixed agreements. This concerns first and foremost the characters themselves: (a) the dumb clown, (b) the harlequin, (c) 'Mr. Loyal' (ring master). They have fixed character traits: a = stupid, b = cunning, c = humourless. The types themselves cannot be so easily transferred to contemporary theatre, but the type-casting of the acting can.

Clownery is an excellent way of presenting individuals. Its criticism is individually tailored. It brings out the contradictions in the character itself, without any reference to external circumstances. It is, as it were, an inherent variant on the character. This doubling effect immediately places the spectator in the position of the evaluator and exploiter. He sees the character only in accordance with its individual use value: he knows it has been created for him. If it is intended to be humorous, laughter is its use value. Because laughter decides on the quality of the character shown and of the actor doing the showing, the clownery offers a high degree of objectivization, as it can be directly controlled following fixed criteria. The mismatch between content and effort forces the spectator to think of the exact opposite as an action is carried out, because this is the only way he can laugh. When the great clown Grock laboriously pushes the piano towards the stool so that his fingers can reach the keys, the spectator of course mentally pushes the stool towards the piano. This yields the tension that provokes laughter. But the tension need not only be dispelled by laughter. A serious variant of the clownery would be possible in Shakespeare's play *Timon of Athens*. In times of heightened money–commodities–money relations (original accumulation) that turn every human relationship into one based around money, a rich Athenian wants to secure human relations that are rooted not in his wealth but in his person. If the play is produced in sympathy with Timon's view of his rejected public person (Model I, B) and encourages pity, it loses its edge. But if the technique of clownery is used, so a disjunction is made between the effort and the content, the play displays a social dimension as soon as the character comes on stage. Timon must not be, as he considers himself, handsome and clever in order to be 'loved', rather particularly ugly, tasteless and stupid. Then when the painters eulogize his great taste and the philosophers praise his wit, the real relationship is clear. And when they of course abandon him after he has lost his wealth, this angry clown will go to ridiculous lengths to burn down a whole city simply because it no longer finds him handsome, tasteful and clever. The clownery, here not only comical, gives the character strong individual contours but nevertheless positively provokes social criticism, and this at the point of performance itself.

Clownery does not leave anything unexpected in the character for the spectator to discover. On the contrary, the spectator quickly picks up on the inverted logic and expects specific instances of this false logic colliding with reality. His activity, or better his fun, resides in countering the obvious illogical elements with a 'logical' (real) series of events. Clownery as a mediating form is in this way able to base even the 'ontological' irrationality of many plays in recognizable realities, and this to the pleasure of the audience.[4]

D *The model play*

Of all the theatrical mediating forms described here, this is the least tested and probably has the greatest potential. It could be a real product of our participatory democracy as this too is now applied to the way a theatre event is run. The model play often has a direct social sponsor (a company, university, co-operative, military services, etc.). The most important individual is the spectator himself. His initiative has brought about the event and his practical activity will be its consequence. In line with the classic 'reafference principle',[5] the spectator's reactions influence the stage. The most important reactions from the spectator are 'effectory performances' (suspicions, other variants, curiosity, agreement, rejection), that are communicated from the respective 'effectors' via corresponding 'receptors' and in this manner provide continuous control over all reactions that aim to have an effect. The play is, as it were, under the direct control of the spectator, who can use his reactions to determine what happens.[6]

Brecht's *Caucasian Chalk Circle* is a classic example of a model play, if we understand the prologue in Kolchos to represent reality. A famous storyteller is invited to adjudicate in an argument between two Kolchos peasants about how a valley should be used (to raise goats or grow fruit). He describes an old model, according to which motherhood is defined not biologically but socially. Applied to the actual case of the peasants' argument, the message is: it is not the natural law of property that decides what should happen with the valley, but the social law of productivity. If we consider once more the objections raised by the old goatherd who, in order to keep the valley, invents the variant of an additional stud farm, we arrive at the model of 'effectory performances' described above.

The model play relies on an important assumption about the audience if their reactions are not to be blurred by the naturalistic tendencies in each individual's everyday consciousness. Because the spectator is the prime productive individual in the model play, he must be integrated into the stage's artistic system. A chance spontaneous encounter between so-called unbiased spectators and the rules of play on stage is not very useful. It would yield unpredictable reactions, roughly equivalent to a happening or a quiz. If the spectator is to become an effective partner in the play, he must be initiated into the play's system following the laws of game theory, in order to proceed to sensible 'strategies of play' with 'strong winning functions'. So alongside showing stories, observations, negotiations and plays, theatre must above all deliver the social systems that will give the spectator the key to dealing with these systems, criticizing and changing them, i.e. producing them himself. (It is the same with language: language is not meaningful when I 'spontaneously' confront someone with the sounds, it only becomes meaningful when he has mastered the syntactical and semantic system that enables him to understand it. For even someone who listens does not simply listen passively, but rather, in listening to noises and recognizing their grammatical order, he actively forms the sentences in his head in order to understand them.)

The model play could be used in newly written plays and texts to treat questions concerning individual institutions, companies, social groups, etc., but it could also turn old plays into models for specific questions. The performance itself can be as flexible as possible. It could take place in companies' club houses, in schools, in car parks, but of course above all in the theatre.

An example

Shakespeare's *Troilus and Cressida*[7] is usually mishandled as a piece of cabaret. It is not credible that the heroes of the Trojan War should have been so degenerate that they each change their opinions many times during the play, whenever it suits them. Because such a sudden change of opinion is usually a matter for comedians, the story appears comical by default. In reality it is one of Shakespeare's cruellest stories. The warriors' boredom, the pleasure they take in sex and in changing their minds, the depravity of their interrelations are not signs of frivolous people but rather very serious people who are engaged in a bizarre war. A war that has become unwinnable, where everyone has forgotten why it is being fought. It brings out the horror in 'famous' trench humour, where senseless killing overrides one's conscience and thus makes it possible to kill. Those who indulge in homosexual and heterosexual activity in front of the gates of Troy have been waging one of the longest, cruellest wars – but no one any longer knows why. Because the war is already more than a generation old, very few still know how Paris abducted Helen, the reason behind the war, indeed many have never even heard of the names. This is the dangerous absurdity displayed by the third variant in Kafka's interpretation of the Prometheus myth: the eagle pecking out Prometheus's liver as it grows back every day does not do so from a position of knowledge but out of habit. He has forgotten the reason why, but the system works. If this play were staged as a model play, the audience would have to be given the system of an unwinnable war of destruction, the original reason for it, and how this was forgotten and the war became an end in itself. Then every opinion, especially when it is quickly revised, can be acted out in complete seriousness, i.e., appropriate to the seriousness of this terrible war.[8] In a war without opinions, a lack of opinions is the appropriate 'normal' approach to life. This above all concerns Cressida. The scenes in Troy between her and Troilus need the seriousness and beauty of the love scenes in *Romeo and Juliet*. The spectator must be made to speculate as to the whereabouts of this beautiful soul. Then when things take a different turn – when Cressida defects to the Greek camp and in just a few hours becomes a camp whore – the spectator will understand much about the system of an unwinnable war of destruction. The model play, a communicative form still to be discovered, not only exhibits a variant of an event in order to make the spectator come up with alternatives, it keeps everything open so that these alternatives can also influence the events on stage.

Note: The mediating forms described here (structures for the *Fabel*) try for once to structure the possibilities offered by the stage in line not with literary genres but with the possibilities instead posed by the producers themselves: the actor *and* the spectator. They have been chosen from among other possible types with a view to the greatest likelihood that their performances will illuminate the subject matter performed. In the theatre's planning, the plays must be arranged into a matrix of models I and II in order to develop the programme.

Other models can also be drawn up. The models are not mutually exclusive, they condition one another. When examining a play they should figure twice: first thematically and then as a mediative possibility. In this way, for example, a comedy (*Troilus and Cressida*) can be mediated as a serious model play without losing its humour. Or a tragedy as a clownery, without damaging its seriousness.

More – on *Fabel*

The concept of the *Fabel* and the *events* within it not only allows us to present reality on stage in all its variety, but also genuinely to bring together the various kinds of theatrical work, artistic as well as organizational.

All work in theatre is aimed at narrating the *Fabel*. Aristotle already knew that the *Fabel* is the 'soul of the play'. Let us add to Aristotle: it is not the soul of the play but its 'body', its actual existence. There is nothing internal about it, it is an expression: the performance on stage. For only in this manner can it be separated from the actor's 'inner life' (although it cannot survive without his art of observing and giving shape to human beings), and becomes instead a matter for *everyone* in theatre. Because the *Fabel* is expressed through visible interactions between people on stage, everyone involved in it can treat it with ease. It becomes tangible, visible, something to be discussed, experienced, contradicted, changed, in short: it becomes *playable*.

This definition of the *Fabel* maintains the unity of the theatre process. And in this very unity lies theatre's ability to be disparate, that is to say varied, able to invite many art forms and sister art forms to contribute. For they are given the opportunity to unite their most contradictory contributions in the *Fabel* as a unified whole. But they do not carry on existing as individual, discrete contributions, rather they *co-operate* in the *Fabel* to yield a new, contradictory unity, which is of course theatre.

The playwright sketches out the artistic possibilities of the *Fabel*, which he notes down in his play. The stage designer draws up the scenery within which the *Fabel*'s possibilities will be brought to life. The musician further challenges the *Fabel*, as it must also support his interpretation. The director, in charge of the performance and 'the audience's delegate', co-ordinates the various art forms and sister art forms as they contradict one another, communicating their different intentions and ensuring 'that everything can be easily seen' (Brecht). But the stage technician also comments on the *Fabel* in his own way. Only if the stage scenery can be easily constructed and changed will it be possible to make 'flowing' transitions that will in turn allow the play 'to flow'. And at all times during the performance the actor makes the *Fabel gestically* apparent as a series of interactions between people, allowing the spectator to follow them and 'intervene with his judgement' (Brecht).

This double function of the *Fabel*, that is to say narrating a story and at the same time inspiring co-operative activities, leads to something completely new: the 'play' in which theatre incorporates the reality of the spectator by becoming a *source of enjoyment for the spectator*. This enjoyment feeds into the spectator's real lived experience in many ways: as immediate pleasure taken in the play, as enjoyable information and satisfied curiosity, as a surprise, as the metaphorical application of information to the needs in his life, as a short-term, light-hearted self-affirmation (laughter, applause, amazement), but also as an 'attitude', meaning a lasting, unconscious kind of behaviour inspired by the performance. Only as a result of these various and very different effects is theatre really *useful* for society because it *enriches* people in so many ways.

Thus the *Fabel*, the sum of all processes within a theatre production, is not just the elementary unity in which all the work of a theatre comes together; as a co-operative form, it itself expresses theatre's disparate and contradictory nature. For it allows many art forms and sister art forms to contribute to a theatrical production by making their contributions themselves into part of the *Fabel*'s action. In this unified whole, art forms and sister art forms are suspended in the dialectical sense: they disappear, they persist within the whole, they are elevated into part of a grander process.

However, the *Fabel* is not just a constitutive element of a theatrical production, it also gives expression to theatre's own elementary dialectics. Everything that theatre can present as 'established' the *Fabel* must show as an action, that is to say, unfolding in all its contradictions. The action not only allows dialectics to be shown on stage, as a term itself it represents a dialectical (contradictory) act. It is by no means simply the activity, or physical action, or information on a certain theme, although it does contain all these elements. As action on stage, it is the 'language of theatre' that allows theatre to model different subject matters, relationships and connections underpinning reality in order to understand and present reality as a fluid process.[9]

Translating something into the 'language' of theatre amounts to *dialecticizing* it, rendering it fluid as *action*. This can be both beneficial and damaging to society. For in times of decline and stagnation, theatre is able to create the impression of movement for its audience, where in actual fact things are stagnating or going backwards. The best example of this is the plays of the Jesuits. Ignatius of Loyola's religious exercises, which stigmatized thought in an extremely dogmatic fashion, were complemented by the Jesuits' theatre. The sacred stasis of dogma was 'put in motion' by the secularized art of theatre. The Jesuits' odd thesis, that the quietude of pure faith can only thrive among the hustle and bustle of the world, gained full expression in the theatre of the Societas Jesu, which was as fascinating as it was reactionary.

Dialecticizing (a term that Brecht suggested in his final years) represents an opportunity for socialist theatre to make dialectics itself enjoyable. Everything that this theatre shows is shown as an action, with the result that the 'eternal' is rendered transient, the 'harmonious' contradictory, the 'unchangeable' is revealed as merely not having been changed for a long time, and the 'established' as something that has been 'fixed' by common convention. In short, it 'sets things in motion' and shows the world as it is – changing and changeable. And it does this for the purpose of entertainment.

Thus narrating the *Fabel* and showing action is not a possible performance style for theatre, it is theatre itself.

Of course *in rehearsal* action is first initiated by the simple question: What is happening? And the simpler the answer, the more varied and lively the possible 'interpretations'. This was why Brecht invented scene titles. For example:

'Mr Puntila finds a person', or 'Mother Courage as last seen', or 'The young worker Pavel Vlassov receives his first visit from revolutionary comrades who want to print illegal pamphlets against his mother's wish', etc.[10]

The scene titles are 'signs' of the action, by no means the action itself. They are aids in rehearsal, not the message communicated in the actual performance. For what the actor must do first in rehearsal comes last in real life. In real life, what you do is the result of a process of considering, planning, deciding, etc. In rehearsal, the first thing the actor comes across when working on a role is the result noted in the text (actions, characters, opinions, habits, etc.). The director must make him 'dialecticize', meaning once more to seek the factors behind the fact, the processes behind the results and a character's origin behind his existence in the text.[11] The titles that Brecht gave to individual scenes are useful here, because they identify the simplest action. They are supposed not only to communicate information about the content of a scene but above all to bring out a certain stance from the actor (and later the spectator): the epic (narrative) stance. Like a narrator, he should not be satisfied with what the character thinks or says about himself, he should look for the connections behind what is said and thought that make him talk and think in this way. In short: he should know more than the character.

With this, the *Fabel* as a compendium of all action on the stage as well as in the auditorium does not just provide a point of orientation for the 'action' (although this is also important), it is also a fundamental element of theatre, namely the opportunity to 'dialecticize' through the play and 'to make reality dance to its own tune'.

A digression

What does reality on stage actually mean? or Theatre's significatory practice

When people talk of 'reality' on stage or 'realism', what is often meant is a direct reproduction of real life, which is why many, mostly young, theatre makers reject realism for the stage today. It strikes them as too 'narrow', limiting them to just what is present in real life anyway. Realism prevents any sort of 'transgression' ('Überschreitung') and in transgression they see – quite rightly – the true purpose of art. With this, realism would also contradict Brecht's aims, as he purportedly wanted to change reality. For change always also entails transgression.

Apart from the fact that here we can see the 'classical' tendency to confuse realism with naturalism, it strikes me as important at this stage in our considerations to pose once more the question as to what reality on stage actually is. And how it is produced. Above all, how it is different to realities on, for example, the cinema or TV screen.

Not to beat about the bush: we are dealing with the general 'significatory practice' of theatre. 'Sign' here refers to something that is 'doubly' present. First as a real object, for example a round metal sign with a white horizontal line at the side of the road, a dot with a line on a piece of notepaper, a fully loaded trading wagon on stage, or a charred wooden beam. But, second, a 'sign' is an object that 'signifies' something. The metal sign at the side of the road, for example, means 'one-way street', the dot with a line is a note in a musical score, the fully loaded trading wagon is an 'illustration' of how well Mother Courage is doing, and a charred wooden beam can 'signify' a house marked by war. It is clear that the 'signification' does not necessarily naturally reside in the object, which is in itself only a piece of metal or printer's ink on music-paper. It only gains its signification through people, who bring knowledge of the relevant 'agreement' to the object: for example, the traffic regulations that allow one to recognize a one-way street, or an ability to read music that ensures you hit the right note. And in a performance of *Mother Courage* you have to have 'latched on' to the fact that the fully loaded or empty trading wagon 'signifies' in each case how Mother Courage's business is doing, while in the stage scenery for *Mother Courage* a charred beam 'signifies' a ruined house. The general significatory practice of theatre allows this and is as old as theatre itself. It subtly has the spectator enter into these agreements and 'decode' the signs' signification. And this contributes to the spectator's enjoyment.

Because this is to be a 'companion' to Brecht, I do not want to go into greater detail on 'semiotics', as the study of signs is known, but refer interested readers instead to the work of Charles William Morris and Georg Klaus, as well as to my own work, *Theater und Wissenschaft* (*Theatre and Science*), which deals with theatre's 'significatory practice'. Here I would just like to tell a story of how I myself fell victim to that 'classic' tendency to confuse naturalism with realism, in short, how I tried in vain to apply stage solutions directly to a film. For unlike the stage's 'significatory practice', film (and sometimes even television) reproduces real 'realities'. Or, as Brecht put it, 'Film is a montage of documents, real or invented'.

One of the lasting impressions made by the stage production of *Mother Courage and Her Children* was the ending. Mother Courage has lost everything to war and, still unable to learn anything, she follows the ragged army to try and carry on taking her cut in the twenty-fifth year of this murderous war. She awkwardly places the empty wagon's straps around her shoulders to the raucous, tired singing of the troops starting off on their way, and exits pulling her wagon after the soldiers with gritty determination. Brecht wanted to show her – unteachable – losing her way in the endlessness of an unwinnable war.

Illustration 11 Courage sets off to follow the army (Scene 13). (Copy by R. Berlau/Hoffmann.)

He entitled the scene 'Mother Courage as last seen'. It made sense to have Mother Courage and her wagon travel to the back of the stage. The wagon could then have disappeared backstage, so that Mother Courage really does get lost on stage. But this didn't make much of an impact: it was a normal exit. We came across the solution by chance. After we had tried to have the wagon disappear at the back, Weigel came to the front with her wagon to hear what the directors were saying. It was tremendously effective. Because she didn't really appear to be coming forward, rather it looked as if she was continuing on her never-ending journey. This was because the circle marked out by the stage revolve had been established throughout the performance as her 'long journey' through the war. Throughout the entire performance, whenever Courage's wagon criss-crossed Europe it always circled round the perimeter of the revolve. The spectator had entered into this agreement throughout the play. He did not take the travelling wagon to be unmediated reality, but rather a 'sign'. So now, even when the wagon was rolling towards him, he perceived it to be travelling away from him as long as it travelled around the edge of the revolve. We realized that when presenting the 'wagon's disappearance on a never-ending journey', we couldn't really have the wagon disappear; rather we had to stick to the signs we had agreed on during the course of the play: so Brecht had the wagon, pulled by the dishevelled Mother Courage, travel once more around the perimeter of the revolve, first towards the back of the stage, then around the curved horizon, until it came back round to the front, heading straight for the spectator. As it turned towards the back again, the curtain closed. I have rarely seen the difference between 'reality' on stage and its 'signification' more clearly illustrated than here! Although the 'reality' contradicted the 'signification' (because, after all, the wagon came back round to the front), the spectator understood it as a sign of the never-ending journey.

In 1960/61 we filmed this production with DEFA.[12] And here the process was inverted. Of course we wanted to keep the ending, which was now world famous, in the film. Indeed, we had high hopes for an even stronger impact as we had inserted a number of additional close-ups of Mother Courage. But we were soon to learn about the difference between theatre and film. For the film shots of Courage's journey that was supposed to lose itself in nothingness were dreadful. There could be no talk of 'entering into war's never-ending journey'. In front of a white cyclorama, the studio's curving horizon, a covered wagon circled undecidedly, only to travel out towards the camera at the end, making it look as if Courage had changed her mind in the end and turned back. In spite of all our cameraman's tricks and artistry, the filmic genre asserted its essence here: it documents 'reality'. Or as Brecht formulated it, highlighting the difference with theatre: 'Film is a montage of documents, real or invented.'

The film took the 'sign' to be a 'document', therefore direct reality. The wagon really did turn round and come back. In theatre, on the other hand, it 'signified' something else 'real': when the wagon travelled around the perimeter of the revolve on stage towards the spectator, the spectator perceived it to be getting further away. For the 'agreement' (the title of the scene) was 'Mother Courage loses her way in the never-ending war'. In order to achieve the same effect in our *Courage* film we had to 'really' show Courage losing her way in the never-ending war.

We had the wagon travel off into the depths of the large film studio and strengthened the 'expanse' by using a black masking frame from silent film. In a reduced, narrow picture format we showed the wagon from behind, gradually getting further away from the camera. As it moved away, we very slowly opened out the frame, so that at the end it opened up to the whole studio, showing now in full scale cinemascope format. Thus we were able to show the never-ending expanse in which Mother Courage gets lost.

Supplement: The context in 2009

Today it is much doubted whether theatre is still of any practical use or is not just a cosy end in itself. These doubts are however less the result of placing too high an expectation on theatre, as was for example the case in the years around 1968, as not expecting anything from anything at all these days, least of all theatre. At least, not in relation to society. Seeing that the end of history has been officially declared and human progress is believed to have reached its final stage in 'neoliberalism', the move now is to eternalize this situation – whether in praise or disgust – and work with those affected to produce a state, as Noam Chomsky puts it, of 'consent without consent'. The new religion, declared from the pulpit, lectern and TV screen, is called 'the unavoidable'. What was previously known as 'fate' is nowadays 'material constraints'; the 'categorical imperative' is now to increase the quota, and the 'moral code in me' regulates how competition is swept aside. If theatre is expected to do anything, then it is to be like TV: provide 'events' such as 'Who wants to be a millionaire?' or 'America's next top model'. 'Events' are reality shows in which the 'what' disappears behind the 'how', where artificiality suffices to convince people that art is no longer needed. Culture is more profitable if it becomes a cult. Against a background of such elaborate productions, theatre's 'limitedness' is of course considered deficient, and so theatre is either increasingly replaced by the 'limitless opportunities' of the media cult, or it becomes a cult itself.

The age of great mystifications or, as it is known by many, the age of 'constitutional irrationalism' has begun. And this to an unprecedented extent. Merciless wars for oil and gas, markets and trade zones, sales and demand, profits and bumper profits, returns and resources are once again the order of the day. But these battles are 'embedded' in mysticism and irrationalism, accompanied by a very different war: the war on truth. Incessantly spreading untruths is intended to make people accept the unacceptable. Wars are like natural events, they come and go like changes in the weather or seasons. One might regret this, but it cannot be changed. That is why wars today are no longer call wars, but 'sanctions for restoring the peace' or 'pre-emptive strikes to safeguard Western values' or, quite simply, 'a war on terror'. Attacking other countries, once known as a war of aggression, is now called 'targeted military interventions against the infringement of human rights', because the UN Charter and the Basic Law of the Federal Republic of Germany ban wars of aggression. Occupying regimes are established merely to support the 'introduction of democracy' or drilling for oil. And everything always revolves around freedom, that so-called 'enduring freedom' that really means 'freedom to attack at any time'. For terrorism is present everywhere and at all times. But because we do not know who the terrorists are or where they are hiding, we have to look for them everywhere. For example in Afghanistan, where the German parliament, against the wishes of 77 per cent of the German population, sent German fighter planes, but only in order to 'reconnoitre the terrain' of the embattled south of the country. If US bombs are subsequently dropped on the reconnoitred countryside, our planes have long since safely returned to their airbase in the 'quieter' north and have nothing to do with this 'collateral damage'. They are only 'development agents', after all. True, civilians do also get killed in this (in Iraq the figures have meanwhile exceeded a million), but that is as unavoidable as breaking eggs when making an omelette. How are the bombers supposed to know whether terrorists are not also hiding among the civilians? The Middle Ages have returned. But what was called torture then and used to force confessions out of people is today known in the industry as 'manipulating the conditions of interrogation', including 'simulated drowning' which, invoking a spa treatment, is called 'water boarding'. And it was 'material constraints' that led German entrepreneurs to provide poisonous gas to a despot by the name of Saddam Hussein, whom of course they abhor today, because in a global market naturally their competitors would have otherwise supplied the gas. If today German companies are world leaders in the sale of arms to war-torn areas, then this is only in order to 'secure jobs in Germany', even if they are below the minimum wage. But everyone is only doing their bit for 'Standort Deutschland' (the economical and political well-being of Germany), which is only another way of saying 'the German homeland'. If in the time of the Kaisers we sang about the 'guard at the Rhine' standing strong and true so that the fatherland could sleep soundly, today it is 'our boys' defending Germany in the Hindu Kush who are letting the country continue its slumber.

This 'real fog', as Ernst Bloch called it, that day in, day out settles over people's brains as 'constitutional irrationalism' has a very rational purpose: it is supposed to get people used to barbarity. They may regret this barbarity, they may protest against it, indeed they may even demonstrate against it, but it cannot be changed. If you do try nevertheless, then you are trying to 'change the system' and that only leads, as past experience tells us, to a deterioration. Because even the lack of unemployment in the failed GDR state was – as can be read in a highly regarded financial magazine – nothing less than the prescribed enslavement of an entire people, as the Stasi[13] mercilessly prevented redundancies and forced full employment on society. That's why everyone should stop meddling and repeatedly remind themselves: whether you like it or not – There Is No Alternative!

No matter if, even as the economy is yet again supposedly 'bouncing back', Volkswagen make 5,000, Deutsche Bank 6,000, the German Post Office 8,000, Daimler-Chrysler 13,000, Siemens 17,000, Airbus 20,000 and Deutsche Telekom 50,000 people redundant; no matter if Deutsche Bahn prepares to float on the stock exchange by raising the number of high speed trains and consequently 'slimming down' its regional services, leaving entire regions cut off; no matter if the parliament, against the wishes of two thirds of the population, increases the retirement age from 65 to 67, and this even though there is no longer any work for people over 50 – in all of these measures you will always find that little word, 'unavoidable'. Its very harmlessness, as if this were a game of bridge, disguises the fact that it is being used to reverse whole eras of human progress. For man only became human by realizing and using to his advantage all the alternatives that constantly surround him. Declaring the 'end of all ideologies' is itself the greatest ideological move of all, as it claims nothing less than the end of history. It would have us believe that progress has reached its highest point with contemporary society and has thus come to a 'natural' standstill.

People declare this standstill unavoidable so that their own businesses will be made all the more buoyant. And while they talk of the end of the class war, they actually intend to continue it with renewed vigour. Under the positive-sounding word of 'reforms' the greatest dismantling of society has taken place of the last hundred years. Equally, wars for raw materials and markets are carried out with far fewer scruples once they have been declared a natural part of creation, for there have been wars for as long as there have been people. And if wars cause misery for many people, then misery itself is unavoidable. And so on.

This is actually an incredible opportunity for theatre. Like no other instrument, theatre is suitable for dissipating the 'real fog'. It is able to de-mystify the mystified, revealing it for what it really is: 'Nothing but people pursuing their aims'. In so doing, it also entertains the audience. That fateful 'material constraints' turn out to be people's skill in appropriating 'material' for themselves (financial gains, property, hedge funds, and so on). And unfathomable irrationalism quickly reveals its rational basis: it is the successful activity of consultancies like McKinsey, who are always at the ready to turn mass redundancies into 'providing for a more humane existence', as people are 'freed from the oppression of a work-based society in order to act in a self-determined manner', etc.

The very 'limitedness' of theatre that can 'only' show things as a form of action between people might here turn out to be particularly suited to showing the worldly and the other-worldly, the physical and the metaphysical, and those despicable and heroic acts as nothing other than 'the results of people pursuing their aims'. In so doing it would ultimately show that man 'has everything in his hands', if he can only be brought to appreciate this fact. The 'simplicity' of theatre can help man 'to recognize his situation' and conceive of himself, in spite of the 'fog', as his own creator. In this way, he makes hope into his principle, above all where depressing darkness reigns. For theatre can reveal 'a premonition of the human condition' in everything, even the apparently most hopeless of situations. Or at least this is what Ernst Bloch suggests in his *Principle of Hope*, bravely calling it 'the ontology of not-yet-being'.

TRANSLATION, ADAPTATION, DRAMATIZATION

Everyman by Hugo von Hofmannsthal[1]

Remscheid version: Manfred Wekwerth

At the end of the sixteenth century, when Hans Sachs wrote his 'comedy of rich, dying people', which provided both the inspiration and many of the rhyming couplets for Hofmannsthal's *Everyman*, so-called 'dances of death' were not solemn religious plays but rather carnival performances. Clearly the audience greatly enjoyed the contrast between their own wild exuberance and the play's message about human mortality.[2]

In Vienna – at the end of the nineteenth century – people had a very different relationship to death. Freud's 'uneasiness in culture' and his 'thanatos', also known as the death-drive, made death into a sombre partner for the overly sated bourgeoisie. It justly struck people down because they were worshipping a new god: money. Hofmannsthal's interest in contemporary theories of money convinced him that money, 'through a demonic inversion, became the aim of all aims'. Man could only be saved from this tragic entanglement, or so Hofmannsthal thought, by being reminded of the Middle Ages, where the Almighty was still feared and believed. Thus *Everyman* became a rousing example of how man can only save himself from his corruption by stepping before the highest judge in order to face the judgement on his earthly works.[3]

In 1948 Bertolt Brecht also wrote a *Salzburg Dance of Death*. He too sees man's corruption in 'Mammon', but does not locate the blame for this so much in the individual person as in the social circumstances that allow one man's wealth to lead to another man's poverty. It is not a lack of belief that corrupts man, but rather a wealth of possessions, for the owner does not own his money, instead money owns the owner. But Brecht uses this 'demonic inversion', as Hofmannsthal calls it, as a source not of solemn reflection but of humour. He shows not how low man has sunk, but how inverted the world has become. And he believes this can be changed.

I have a very personal relationship to Hugo von Hofmannsthal. Having escaped the war, at the age of fifteen we found ourselves in 1945 surrounded by physical and mental ruin, facing oblivion. What was actually a liberation was for us a complete collapse. In order to escape the looming sense of apathy and resignation, a few people in our small town founded an amateur acting society. Looking for a play that dealt with inner turmoil, fear for one's life, but also possible hope, we came across Hofmannsthal's *Tor und Tod* (*Death and the Fool*). Claudio's fate and his dialogues with death that we now performed on stage helped not only the audience but above all us, the performers, to a new hunger for life. Later on we performed *Tod des Meisters* (*The Death of Titian*), where Hofmannsthal has the dying Titian's students search for the confidence to carry on their work without the great master.

I always had a rather different relationship to *Everyman*, which I have seen on a few sets of cathedral steps. The 'heavy bells', the trembling cries of Everyman, the religious solemnity of the setting always made me believe that I was not attending a stage performance but a sermon, albeit a very poetic one.

Siegfried Jacobsohn, the famous editor of *Schaubühne*, had a similar sense at the premiere in 1911. Max Reinhardt, on whose insistence Hofmannsthal had quickly written his *Everyman* as 'Everyman' fever, originating in England, took hold of the theatres, chose Schumann's circus in Berlin for the premiere, with no fewer than five thousand seats. Jacobsohn wrote after the premiere that *Everyman* 'belongs in a church or a literary man's pub, performed to either highly emotional or highly critical minds, to heady believers or clear-minded rationalists – but certainly not to everyman'.

Reinhardt repeated the performance in 1920 on the steps of Salzburg Cathedral, and since then it has been an 'indispensable folk-loristic attraction' (Friedrich Torberg) and a 'modern-day immortal' (Joachim Kaiser).

Today, confronted once more with *Everyman*, I was reminded of a story: someone who works on the stock exchange had recently said to me that capitalism would have long since dispensed with itself if it were profitable. In our times, where not money but profit has become the only god, prepared to market joy and suffering, death and devil, thinking and feeling in order to achieve ever higher profits, it seemed a good idea to perform the 'play about the rich man's death' not as the solemn religious play it had been performed up to now, but instead – as Hans Sachs had done – once more as a 'comedy' that in its day was played on carnival nights. For never had the proximity of pleasure to downfall, profit to death, and celebration to bankruptcy been greater than today. But the consequences of this 'demonic inversion' are far more painful today than in Fugger's time. War and catastrophes on an unimagined scale have been the direct result. But, as Chaplin observes in his biography, 'comedy is a far more appropriate form than tragedy for fighting back'.

I consider my reworking of *Everyman*, which in many areas of the text and *Fabel* draws on Hans Sachs, to be a variation on a well-known theme. And, just as in music 'Bach variations' do not imply disregard for Bach, but rather the opposite, admiration for the master, my *Everyman* variation is also a homage to Hofmannsthal.

Dangerous Liaisons (*Les liaisons dangereuses*)[4]

Scenes adapted from Choderlos de Laclos by Manfred Wekwerth

Preface to the 2000 dramatization[5]

The epistolary novel *Dangerous Liaisons* (*Les liaisons dangereuses*) became a 'bestseller' as soon as it appeared in 1782. It entailed numerous scandals, as it became the favourite reading primarily of those who were directly involved in it. Queen Marie-Antoinette is said to have read it, albeit in secret and with a different dust jacket. The novel very quickly had the same fate as *The Threepenny Opera*, published one and a half centuries later, that was written against the rich but enjoyed 'bestseller' status among them. That may be why for a long time the novel was first and foremost deemed erotic fiction and not literature.

Choderlos de Laclos, the author, himself an aristocrat who later became a general of the revolutionary troops, was surprised by the success he enjoyed among those he had mercilessly criticized. But precisely the merciless attention to detail with which he described the downfall of the aristocracy of the *Ancien Régime* was the actual secret to his success. Never before had the aristocracy's social and sexual affairs been observed with such precision and detail. Where once whole areas of the globe had been conquered now it was the opposite sex, and here too fame was measured by the number of victims taken. Plans and strategies tested in the art of war were now used, including the art of love, in order to destroy one's opponent, in this case the opposite sex.

Choderlos de Laclos describes all this not with the ferocity of an aristocracy-hater, which he doubtless was, but in the 'grand style' of the epoch that is able to make the lowliest of acts and the pettiest of motives into affairs of state. In this deadly seriousness lies the humour of Choderlos de Laclos, who had personal experience of the great art of letter writing and elevated language, using these skills to make baseness appear even baser by dressing it up in fine materials. The inappropriateness of the form punctures its own content, but without distorting it like a caricature. The author delegates judgement to the reader, who does for his part need a great deal of patience and love of detail. If he possesses these qualities, however, gruesome pleasure will follow. Lies, right into the minutiae of their telling, become the one universally valid truth, crime a valid moral code, pointlessness the whole point of life. In this interplay are revealed the emptiness and stupidity of an age that called itself 'great'.

Herein also lies the difficulty of staging *Dangerous Liaisons* for theatre. The attempts of which I am aware – I exclude Heiner Müller's *Quartett*, because this is a play in its own right – either reduce the 'high' epistolary art form of the original to everyday dialogues, or they have the characters simply speak the letters, as if they were dialogues and not letters. This version, by contrast, attempts to stage the action *and* the letters in such a manner that they comment upon, add to, and contradict one another. Perhaps this will allow the spectator to see something beyond the exciting detective plot (that is already well known from the film versions), to experience something of the tragic and comic presumption of an age that, as a direct result of its particular crudity, repeatedly allows itself to be carried away by polished rhetoric and is in this respect not dissimilar to our own.

The *Scenes Adapted from Choderlos de Laclos* are conceived as a play in their own right that, employing motifs from the wonderful novel, also makes use of analyses and views expressed by Heinrich Mann and Heiner Müller. In as much as passages from the French original are used, they largely draw on the first translation into German by Christian von Bonin in 1783, or were translated afresh.

Celestina[6]

Tragicomedy about the famous procuress from the Spanish original by Fernando de Rojas (original title of 1499) by Manfred Wekwerth

Reflections on the 2002 Theatre Version[7]

1

Celestina is certainly not one of those brave types who throws down the gauntlet to the age in which he or she lives. By any measure of heroism, one can only conclude that she is nobody's hero. She has found her way in her world, a world she knows like no other. Beatings, maltreatment, empty pockets and 'a perpetual surplus of appetite matched only by a perpetual absence of bread in the cupboard' have taught her well from a tender age. They endowed her with that 'plebeian outlook' that is not easily fooled. Celestina views the age in which she lives, the famous 'golden age of the Catholic kings', as it really was: a universal trading-place for material and immaterial values. She knows that when morals are frequently mentioned, morals are not what is meant, but rather Mammon. Honesty is most passionately invoked when cheating is the aim. And piety is the willingness to accept this as the will of God. By this definition, Celestina is moral, honest, and pious. Thus, as a successful procuress, fortune-teller, quack-doctor, in short a witch, Celestina is untouchable, even for the Inquisition that at the time was at its height. She does what the authorities demand: 'The best way to deal with morals is to obey them.' Her opinions, which she likes to share at length, preferably over a bottle of wine, with all who will listen, and which are littered with quotations from Aristotle through to Saint Augustine, are difficult even for practised ears to denounce as heresy. Policemen, priests, notables know that she is pulling the wool over their eyes, but because they can't or don't want to prove anything, they prefer to be her customers than her judges.

Celestina seems irrepressible, and exactly this is to be her downfall. Her enemies pose her no danger, for she expects danger from this quarter. It is her friends who are dangerous, for they are her best pupils. And because she ceaselessly proves to them in all manners possible that great times are also great because everything, friendship included, can be taken to market, they eventually come to ask themselves why they shouldn't take their friendship with Celestina to market. For she offers not only advice, but also money: they kill her. Celestina's misfortune is her success. She has to reap what she has sown.

2

In 1499, one hundred years before Cervantes's *Don Quixote*, a text bearing the title *Comedia de Calisto y Melibea* appeared in Spain that went on to achieve world renown under the name of *Celestina*. It was a sequence of dialogues between confidence tricksters, whores, crooks and this very procuress Celestina, to whose wheelings and dealings the two lovers Calisto and Melibea fall victim. The story has a surprisingly banal ending. Attempting to climb the wall of the garden where Melibea awaits him every night, Calisto falls from the ladder and dies.

It cannot be the story alone that quickly turned *Celestina* into a 'handbook' for the Spanish (later, too, the eighty-six-year-old Picasso dedicated 300 sketches to Celestina). Nor can the author be responsible; he was not only completely unknown at the time of publication but also refused, probably out of fear of the Inquisition, to reveal his name. His name can only be discerned in a poem that was placed at the beginning of the first edition and in which he apologized for the 'failings' of his work. When the first letter of every line is read from bottom to top, 'the student Fernando de Rojas' emerges. But even this unknown author denies authorship, claiming that he has only reworked a text by a certain Juan de Mena. What was so shocking about *Celestina* that the author felt such a need to hide from the Inquisition? The concept of the Inquisition does not even figure once in the whole novel. What strikes us today as trivialization or disguise must have appeared in a very different light to the text's contemporaries. It was a provocation. The omission indicated danger. If a novel that is set in a time marked by the horrific omnipresence of the Inquisition completely neglects to mention this feared instrument of power, then the intention was clear to all. Especially given that the text by the student of law Fernando de Rojas is crammed with characters whom the Inquisition would consider criminals: witches, whores, confidence tricksters, poisoners, procuresses, devil worshippers, blasphemers, all presented in their unmistakeable jargon and endowed with outlandish views, subversive humour, sneaky philosophy and a lust for life that is as loveable as it is cunning. But they are only behaving like the refined nobility, just without their heavenly transfiguration. Their behaviour is marked by a shocking directness: they call cheating cheating and do not make any claim to the will of God, while love is for them desiring the opposite sex far more than fulfilling any holy sacraments.

Never before had the 'lowly rabble' snatched so much attention for itself in European literature. This could be seen as a 'Copernican revolution': the ascent or descent from heaven to earth. The dominant pathos of the tales of chivalry and the colourful mists of the romances were swapped for a prose that was based in reality. (In fact, *Celestina* is the first novel that was not written in verse but rather in prose, until then reserved for history and account books).

In any case, Fernando de Rojas's dialogue novel is one of the few examples in literature of how 'it's not what you say but the way you say it' that counts. The reader back then was moved less by the events in the story about Calisto and Melibea (they are actually, and not only for the reader of today, really rather simple) than by the way they were narrated. The 'prosaic' language and the unusual cast alone undermine the official picture of the age that was being promulgated by church and crown at the time. In the midst of Spain's glorious rise to a world power as it had been 'reunified' by the 'Catholic kings' Ferdinand and Isabella, in the midst of celebrations for conquering Islamic Granada and expelling 'foreigners' (Jews and Moors), in the midst of hymns of praise to the morality and purity of the rulers Isabella and Ferdinand (whom the Catholic Bishops' Conference of Spain still wanted to beatify in 2002), and in the midst of unceasing reference to the patience of the 'simple folk', a troop of figures march onto the scene who, coming from the lower depths of a reality that officially did not even exist, seem almost spectral. But these procurers and crooks behave exactly like the 'better people': they assume that everything can be taken to market, including one's own skin if needs must. And God too is allowed to exist: as a business partner. But another god rises up even more powerfully: money. And whether you are a hero or a shark decides how much of it you own. This god by the name of Mammon works the real miracles: he turns the criminal into a saint, the thief into a legislator, the confidence trickster into an apostle, the freak into Adonis.

One hundred years before Shakespeare, we can already see Shakespearean figures taking shape here, the almost absurd contradictions in their characters boldly developed by a young student by the name of Rojas. And five hundred years before our time we can witness concrete awareness of what is today known as 'total marketing'.

In the novel nothing and no one is safe from this. Even the two lovers Calisto and Melibea who fall victim to immorality do not offer a moral counter. They do not desire one another because they want to enter into the eternal bond of marriage, but because they desire the opposite sex: they want to sleep with each other. They pay for Celestina's procurement with their lives, but first they have to pay the procuress with their money. The depravity seems complete. And no one in the novel is bothered by this.

'*Celestina* is a great, pessimistically knowing book of life', writes Hans Martin Gauger in the *Badische Zeitung*, 'the world doesn't have to be as it is, but this is quite simply how it is.' The student Rojas is unfairly, five hundred years later, brought into the proximity of the modern 'postmodernists' who, however much they complain, fit into the world quite simply as it is. Or as the famous Jean-François Lyotard says: 'The question is no longer: Is something true?, but rather: What is its purpose?' In the context of the marketization of knowledge, this final question means: 'Can it be sold?'

To my mind, the blanket acceptance of everything that Fernando de Rojas and all his characters display, as well as the fact that the general depravity does not bother anyone in the novel, are not signs of the author's 'postmodern' resignation, but rather a form of criticism that is particularly radical because it is subversive. Precisely because the social circumstances do not bother anyone in the novel, they bother someone else all the more: the reader. And the fact that we are dealing here not with a tragedy but a 'tragicomedy' that is given over to biting humour shows a thoroughly optimistic (interventionist) approach to the world on the part of the author, and this is also indirectly communicated to the reader. That is to say, if one believes criticism to be the optimal activity of man.

3

It is a matter of contention to this day whether *Celestina*, designated a tragicomedy by the author, is really a novel or wasn't actually written for the theatre. A number of aspects speak in theatre's favour. Not only is the text divided into acts, it is above all in dialogue form. And so it is not just in Spain that numerous attempts to stage *Celestina* have found a grateful audience. The character of Celestina is the main focus of narration. But because the text had to be significantly shortened (it consists of twenty-one acts, after all, which would amount to over ten hours of theatre), the theatrical performances often left out what makes the novel so unusual and aesthetically pleasing: the unswerving rigour with which it shows the characters, above all Celestina, mutually fooling one another. Meandering off the point, with the aid of a fantastic imagination, nonsensical conversations and a tendency towards splitting hairs are part of the renaissance novel's incomparable humour. Reducing everything down to the pure 'story' does shorten the text, but it also shortens the author's method – his provocative claim that the 'lowly' characters are the actual 'poets and philosophers'.

On closer inspection, the dialogue form too rather counts against theatre, for dialogues do not allow situations to develop, but rather describe them, albeit in a compelling manner. Theatre however lives off direct situations where characters confront one another with their different standpoints and in so doing make surprising leaps. Here, however – in contrast to the novel – what is unexpected is most effective. Theatre is not primarily communicated through the spoken text (as every pause in the text proves), but through attitudes, which underlie the text as well. The language of theatre is its *gestic* material'. Thus even a meandering digression can generate extreme tension, for example when the situation necessitates speed. (Another example of this is the 'long' story about the jug told by Marthe Rull in Kleist's *The Broken Jug*). The dialogues in the *Celestina* novel are rather more like Platonic dialogues, in which opinions, views, characteristics are set out one after the other and the situation barely plays a part at all.

In order to warn his master about Celestina's curious ways, the servant Parmeno describes her infamous character traits in lurid detail. One of these is the way she is proud, not insulted, when called a whore. In a theatre version it makes sense to turn this description into *gestic* material', that is to say, to show it as action in a scene. But the spoken, 'epic' parts can also be turned into action by converting them into *gestic* material'. For example when Parmeno, in an attempt to scare his master away from the procuress Celestina, lists the ingredients of the love potion in quasi-absurd detail (donkey's brain, snakes' heads, ropes from recently hanged bodies, and so on), and his master is not put off, but rather receives the witch waiting at the door all the more warmly. This unexpected turn can then trigger the kind of tension in the spectator that is called theatre. This version of *Celestina* tries to retain the novel's uniqueness on stage even when it occasionally parts company from the novel's 'story'. It also tries to use the wealth of descriptions as *gestic* material', without ever seeking to replicate the novel's prodigality.

Optimistic Tragedy[8]

TV film adaptation of the revolutionary play by Vsevolod Vishnevskiy

On the 2007 re-screening

In 1956 Brecht proposed including a 'revolutionary cycle' in the Berliner Ensemble's programme. He wanted to use the techniques of theatre to counter 'the shocking ignorance of revolutionary processes that has come to light in East Germany too', especially seeing as back then slogans were appearing – also from political leaders – declaring the aim no longer first and foremost to abolish capitalism but rather to overtake it. The West's incessant attempts to defame every revolutionary movement, beginning with Spartacus's slave revolt, did one last thing. They inspired Brecht to suggest the Berliner Ensemble should regularly perform plays that counted as world literature and that 'both showed social revolutions and made such a thing possible'. Under consideration were, alongside Brecht's plays *The Days of the Commune* and *The Mother*, Georg Büchner's *Danton's Death* and Vsevolod Vishnevskiy's *Optimistic Tragedy*. This play deals with the disputes that set in immediately after the October revolution, and it particularly caught Brecht's attention, because 'with unusual boldness it does not shy away from contradictions, including those inherent in the revolution, but rather opens them up for all to see'. And as is always the case with Brecht, quite practical reasons also lay behind his grand designs. Angelika Hurwicz was to play the female commissar, the play's lead role, because she wanted to have this 'fantastic role' after her successes as the mute Katrin in *Mother Courage* and Grusha in *The Caucasian Chalk Circle*.

The [stage] premiere of *Optimistic Tragedy* on 1 April 1958 came too late for Brecht. Elisabeth Hauptmann, Peter Palitzsch and I had, with the help of Sonja Vishnevetskaya, Vishnevskiy's wife, created a version that was based on the original 1930 version of the play. I can still remember how surprised Palitzsch and I were when we were greeted in the doorway of the Moscow apartment where we were to meet Sonja by a *grande dame* exquisitely dressed entirely in purple, who introduced herself with the words, 'Sonja Vishnevetskaya, Colonel of the Baltic Fleet'. We owed our gratitude to this clever lady, originally a set designer, for scenes that up until then had never before been performed. For example, the great argument between the female commissar and Alexej the anarchist, who considers the greatest danger for the revolution to be the bourgeois mentality that threatens to take over as a regressive desire for property and authority.

Sonja Vishnevetskaya also familiarized us with Larissa Reissner, the real-life source for the commissar. Larissa Reissner was assigned to the ships of the red Volga fleet as a political commissar in 1920. Vishnevskiy, himself a red sailor at the time, had got to know her as they fought against the Whites and their foreign allies who were threatening to close in around them. She, a St Petersburg intellectual from a patrician background, was not only accepted by the sailors but virtually revered for her courage, her empathy, her modesty, and her rigour. In the harshest of conditions of civil war she placed an unwavering value on her femininity; even in battle she is said always to have worn a fresh white blouse. She was also a very beautiful woman. In 1926 she died from tuberculosis. She left a whole series of books behind, of which the best known is *October*.

An ARTE TV documentary that was recently broadcast as part of the preparations for the 90th anniversary of the October revolutions was also dedicated to the person of Larissa Reissner. Played by an average but unusually ugly actress, a fanatical woman was presented to the TV viewer. Wearing men's leather clothing, she forces sailors at gunpoint to board the yacht left behind on the Volga by the Tsar's family as they fled, insisting they search the ship for the Tsarina's jewellery. When she finally finds the jewellery, she immediately puts it round her neck and triumphantly looks at herself, 'the red Tsarina', in the mirror, where, for good measure, she cynically etches in the date of her successful conquest with a diamond ring fresh from her booty. The voice of a commentator helps us understand what is going on by explaining that all this happened by the order of Lenin, who carried out a coup on 7th October 1917 with a few accomplices in St Petersburg, so that injustice could spread from here to engulf the whole country.

Reviewing the *Optimistic Tragedy* today is quite simply an imperative to restore the truth.

The film was shot in 1971. It is based on the Berliner Ensemble's stage production, but engages with the play in a completely new manner on both an artistic and a political level. First, it attempts to synthesize cinema and theatre. Two halls were made permanently available to us in the DEFA feature film studio in Babelsberg for the entirety of our six months' shooting, something that is unimaginable today. The large central hall, today known as the Marlene-Dietrich hall, was the endless expanse that the sailors had to cross on their march from Kronstadt to the Black Sea; the slightly smaller Hall 5 contained a constructivist structure, boldly designed by the set designer and painter Karl von Appen, symbolizing a ship of the Baltic Fleet. This made it possible to direct a great variety of crowd scenes in mass choreographed sequences. We only filmed at night, because when the hall was fully lit we used as much electricity as a middle-sized town – so much electricity was not available during the day. Working at night had an advantage: we managed to get together an ensemble of actors who had many other commitments during the day. Like Renate Richter as the commissar, Hilmar Thate as Alexej, Rolf Ludwig as an officer of the old school, as well as Günter Naumann, Bruno Carstens, Norbert Christian, Peter Kalisch, Hermann Hiesgen, Stefan Lisewski and others. We used clips from great revolutionary films for our battle scenes such as *Chapaev*, *Arsenal*, *We are from Kronstadt*, which we then inserted as black-and-white sequences between the colour feature scenes. The composer Hans-Dieter Hosalla turned the score from the theatrical production into an extended film sound-track that provided an impressive commentary on the action.

As far as our intentions were concerned, we took the changed political situation as our starting point for filming. The 1968 student movement had rebelled against an increasing reactionary trend in West Germany and put the topic of 'revolution' back on the table for discussion. In the East too, young people in particular began to ask what form revolutionary behaviour might take under the new circumstances. Almost certainly out of fear that the West German students' largely anarchistic behaviour might spread to the East, we began presenting the negative aspect of anarchism as an absolute in the GDR. Anarchy, which when accurately translated means 'lack of rule', was now discussed in Eastern newspapers only in terms of arbitrariness, destruction, chaos. And yet precisely in Russia anarchism had played a significant part in revolutionizing the masses, one has only to think of the writings of Kropotkin. Or of Durutti and the great backing he had from the people when seeking to mobilize resistance against the fascists during the Spanish Civil War. The Berliner Ensemble certainly supported the student movement even when there were differences on certain specific issues. When Rudi Dutschke[9] suggested to us in 1967 that we should jointly organize a protest against the coup recently carried out by the Greek colonels, we put together a literary-musical programme, our actors managed to cross the border under the pretence of a theatre visit, and the event, at which Dutschke also spoke, was able to take place the very next day, performed to a packed Auditorium Maximum in West Berlin's Freie Universität. The programme, entitled 'Pattakos hält die Uhren an' (Pattakos stops the clocks) – it is the first line of a poem that Heiner Müller wrote overnight – was so effective that the participants at our event went straight to the Greek embassy afterwards and smashed its windows to renditions of Brecht's 'Solidarity Song'. On our return to the East this earned us harsh reproaches for anarchism, as our foreign policy consisted of strict 'non-involvement' in the affairs of West Berlin. But because we were of the opinion that, particularly given the 'ordered' circumstances of our state, a little productive disobedience would do no harm and that socialism too should not do without the mobilizing effect of anarchism, we suggested that anarchism should not be fought in the media and above all in the theatre in every possible way, but rather complemented in every possible way. Our film was conceived as just such a 'complement'.

When we returned to our work on the *Optimistic Tragedy*, we reconsidered the anarchists, those counterparts to the female commissar, and found their critical observation that too much belief in authority and too much obedience must unavoidably lead to, as Lenin had called it, a 'barracks communism', questionable, even at the point in the play where it is invoked specifically in order to cause offence. Consequently, we wanted to return to the question that young people in particular kept on asking: what, among the peaceful circumstances of orderly daily work and secure existences, is left to inspire revolution? For one thing seemed clear to us: even in times of peace, the revolution cannot survive without revolution. 'Ordered' circumstances and 'the dictates of discipline' more than ever demand individualism, personal initiative, readiness to take on risk, courage, and – we hoped to show this with our film – also the 'adventure of revolution'. In this respect, a telegram that Konrad Wolf[10] sent us after the film had aired on television certainly gave us hope: 'After the *Optimistic Tragedy* the world has become more optimistic.'

4

TWO SPEECHES
Two Moments of Change

Manfred Wekwerth includes two occasional speeches. The first and more important, prefaced by a poem by Volker Braun, was given for the re-opening of the Berliner Ensemble after reconstruction work in 1989, the year that was the fortieth anniversary of the foundation of both the Berliner Ensemble and the GDR itself. The speech was made in September. Two months later the Berlin Wall came down. Wekwerth balances regret at the disintegration of the GDR and the eclipse of its positive achievements with recognition that socialism cannot endure without responding to criticism and the need for change. That recognition in turn determines the role of art. To that end he announces – at a watershed moment – an impressive new season of progressive and challenging political theatre for the Berliner Ensemble.

The second, more personal, speech was given by Wekwerth for the recent opening of a new theatre school at Delitzsch. When, following re-unification, theatres are closing all over Germany, this is a cause for celebration. As new students begin their training, Wekwerth takes the opportunity to recall his own beginnings in the theatre – and meeting with Brecht.

AH

ON THE RE-OPENING OF THE BERLINER ENSEMBLE AFTER SIX MONTHS OF RECONSTRUCTION WORK IN SEPTEMBER 1989

Prologue by Volker Braun

How unclear is the stuff
Of this world. To the storms and floods
The inevitable earthquakes
Come the quakes of the people and
The landslides of thought.
For ages it seemed as if the times were standing
Still. In the clocks
The sand, the blood, the stale remains of the
Day. Now it is starting
The youngest once again and unexpected.
Where do things go from here or, put more modestly
Who knows what's front and what's back?
The strategies are going mouldy
Like damp dismantled tents
After the refugees.
States, built future! and sunk
Into the grass that they eat. Rock-solid
Alliances staggering in the blood marsh, and
The unbreakable friendship
Suspiciously surveys
Its effluent.

1

Over there they have passed over the hunger for communism and
demand

Bourgeois fare; and there
They have turned the tables on history and sit at an empty one.
But remember
That there too hunger reigns
With the mandate of the masses, hunger
For justice.

2

Our state announces its successes as if we had salvaged the
GDR from the sea. Really, it was a sea of rubble. But the
rubble women stand humbled into a monument, and at their
plinth a flattened landscape seems to be turning to sand.
From afar it maybe looks like a large dune: a quiet holiday
during the revolution. The inhabitants, all picking and sorting
the same with such strained expressions, as if they were waiting for a miracle, holding out while the purpose fades, in the
dark of their own shadow thrown by the floodlight of the
western misleaders. They see themselves transported to an
island, washed round by a tearing current, or is it a strong
spring tide, and they ram wave-breakers into the meadows or
blindly take their places in the last Icarus.

3

OWN SHOTS, SHOCKINGLY CLEAR THE WORDS
FIRE IN THE LETTERBOX
UNDER THE CARPET THE CRACKS
IN THE CONSTRUCTION
TOUCH ME!
THE ROCK'S VEINS ARE BREATHING

4

Our stage, offering room
For the great contradictions
Is being re-opened.
The trader's covered wagon
And the comrade's engine
Collide. What funny old
Vehicles, unable to turn!

Their obvious difficulty gives us courage
For a different action. Let us too
Start a conversation
About the turn in this land.

5

It is imperative that we are completely honest with history, keep nothing silent, admit to every error as soon as it has been seen, face up to the full extent of events, even when the debris of our vanity threatens to obscure them. If we do not live with history, it will live against us. Instead of correcting history retrospectively, we should put the effort into correcting the future. Whoever does not dare to say the whole truth about everything has no right to be a comrade. For his cowardice shows only his distrust of history, that is to say, his distrust of the people.

Dear colleagues, welcome to the start of our new theatre season and to the fortieth anniversary of the Berliner Ensemble, which by no coincidence is also the fortieth year of the GDR. Our theatre was founded by the same people who helped found this German state. They stayed by our side in bad times as well as good, productively agreeing and productively disagreeing in equal measure. They did much to define this state in a way hitherto unknown in Germany that included avoiding war, fighting fascism, and promoting social justice and friendliness. This little state has – sticking to the area we know best – done much for world culture. Every now and again we should remind ourselves that it is not only – as our newspapers would have us believe – swimmers, canoeists and ice-skaters who rank among the world's best, but also dramatists, novelists, composers, sculptors, yes, people from the arts in general. Why am I saying this here when we, who have not been uninvolved in it all, are surely already well aware of it? I think the time will come – perhaps it already has – where we should not only celebrate our artistic achievements but also defend them. To those, for example, who have been using all means available to them over the last sixty days to rubbish on an hourly basis just about everything this country has to offer, including what they still considered valid sixty days ago. But above all to that enemy who is hard to notice because he is the product of our own minds: that crippling sense of self-evidence. This sense makes us lose sight of the amazing things that have been achieved here by turning them into an uninterrupted statistical success story. It no longer asks any questions, but rather gives the impression of having all the answers. It makes a format into a formula, friendliness into a simple service. Indeed, it incorporates changes, of which we have had many (and which could still be inspirational today), into an 'unshakeable stability', so that it never even occurs to anyone today that something might be in need of change. This is how self-evidence gives rise to self-satisfaction.

This was going through my head when, listening to the radio and television during the holidays, I was forced to observe how a clever journalistic style from over there was constantly skilfully stoking the hysteria over here, while on our side a sense of self-satisfaction with its ritualistic linguistic conventions pretty much left one speechless. And yet we find ourselves in – this has to be said – a very serious situation, reminiscent of times when repeated efforts were made to eradicate this state from history. This time the fortieth anniversary is practically demanding it. This fortieth year, which is also the fortieth year of the Berliner Ensemble, should however be a source of courage and confidence, even in difficult times. One has only to think of the enormous difficulties we have repeatedly had to surmount. When it was founded, this state was given not forty years but four weeks. But above all it should give us cause for reflection and re-consideration. In politics and poetics, working consensually as well as critically, and showing both solidarity and resolve, we need to discuss at much greater length what we intend to do with this state and we must publicly include as many as possible in these reflections. For a state cannot be made without the multitude.

Setting to one side the spectacular TV reporting on ARD and ZDF, which this week had all the trappings of a new series of 'Spiel ohne Grenzen'[1] (when for example long streams of cars fleeing the GDR were welcomed at the Austrian border with a stall offering bananas and oranges), we really must ask ourselves what we have failed to do that so many people are letting themselves be seduced. This state is after all rich in social and cultural achievements, why are people turning their backs on it? Certainly, as Günter Gaus[2] once put it, the rich cousin's open arms next door, living in the same house and speaking the same language, play a part (as well as the anachronistic claim of a 'common nationality', made even as real asylum seekers from Turkey, Iran and Pakistan sit awaiting deportation). And I am referring to the embarrassing arguments forwarded by many who have relocated, which shock me at least as much as the numbers of emigrants. I am referring to the question of how such a mood could develop in the first place, how could it take hold to such an extent? Above all, what can we as a theatre do about it?

I suspect our plan of opening the forty-first season at the Berliner Ensemble in the fortieth year of the GDR with a 'repertoire of political theatre' has in this respect become all the more topical. For one thing seems certain: moods are not dispelled by opposing moods but by arguments. The five plays in our 'repertoire of political theatre', Heiner Müller's *Germania. Death in Berlin,* Brecht's *Untergang des Egoisten Fatzer* (*Downfall of the Egotist Johann Fatzer*), Volker Braun's *Lenins Tod* (*Lenin's Death*), Nikolai Erdman's *The Suicide,* Mikhail Shatrov's *Blue Horses on Red Grass,* contain much by way of an analysis of our times, offering critical reflection and possible suggestions. Political theatre of the kind we are attempting does not stop at political themes. Quite the opposite, these days it is primarily about individual areas, because that is where decisions are made. Political theatre today is above all a stance that in spite, or because, of difficulties that have arisen does not shun a single theatrical technique, from farce through to tragedy, in its assumption that the world can be changed. And changed by mankind. Better: by people. To Brecht's belief that people's will to live can be strengthened by enjoyment we must add today: theatre must help the individual live his life. Help him overcome the difficulties that this country, with its relative lack of experience, of course repeatedly poses for the individual. We should not leave the inner mission to the church. This is life-counselling not as a therapy that presumes illness, but as help for everyone who wants to take his life in his hands and make it something he can actively experience. In this manner help him to hope and towards a future. Here – or so I believe – making all conversations and discussions as public as possible is one of our most important working hypotheses. It is the call for truth and for information.

Eleven years ago, a one-day plenary session at the Academy of Arts was dedicated to the topic 'The Public' that unfortunately reached far too few members of the actual public. Back then we were discussing – formulated by Robert Weimann with incredible foresight – the necessity of extensively informing a large number of people about a large number of things in order to satisfy a fundamental human need. This is a prerequisite for social cohesion. The conference raised many significant issues, and many are still open. But major changes, triggered by unprecedented problems encountered in changing society, also changed our approach to the issue of the public. Today we are no longer concerned just with satisfying needs but with the absolute priority of productivity in the material as well as the intellectual realm. Only the informed, that is to say involved, individual will display the kind of interest in his community that yields the wakefulness and creativity on which socialism simply must draw if it is to progress. It has no other option. The individual person, whom we must reach, win over and win back, is our only and significant chance, but he is also our greatest problem. Administrative procedures can compel. But even when such compulsion might help fulfil an aim more quickly, it certainly doesn't produce that gentle force of good sense which helps man motivate himself to do useful and humane things. Intensification always also entails intensifying human motivation.

Likewise, in order not to lose ourselves in theory at this point, where much might be more easily explained but not resolved, I should like to share in these last few minutes an observation from the everyday business of art. It is a story that could be entitled: 'The Possibilities for Art in Difficult Times'.

It is set on a Sunday afternoon in the Capitol, a suburban cinema in Adlershof. I specify 'suburban cinema', because, as the film was showing, one of the projectors kept cutting out, resulting in a long break after each reel. But a 'suburban cinema' also because it attracts an audience that would rarely be seen at the premieres. At some point I had missed Heike Misselwitz's film *Winter Ade* (*Farewell to Winter*), with the result that on this Sunday afternoon I went to the cinema. The sun was shining and we were sure we would get tickets before the film started. Wrong. The cinema was sold out. We had to dig for our tickets. The audience went from the very young, through the middle aged, to myself. Likewise, all sorts of professions were represented. The chief script editor of GDR television, for example, was also among us. The film began and – as I said – was very quickly mercilessly truncated by the defective projector. But surprisingly: nobody complained. That had to have something to do with the film. For seeing as this wasn't the first time that the projector wasn't working in this cinema, I knew what kind of a row usually broke out. And equally surprisingly: at the end of a documentary film on a Sunday afternoon in a suburban cinema, virtually the whole theatre broke into applause. I wanted to know why and spoke to a number of attendees, both young and old.

The film has, to use that nice little phrase, some 'tough bits'. It touches areas that everyone knows exist in our country but that are missing in official portrayals. Probably because it is assumed that difficult problems would be too difficult for our spectators. Critical elements depress them. Acknowledging the problems – or so the theory goes – would simply make our situation, itself not easy, even worse. And showing the mistakes in life's small details might raise doubts about the bigger picture. But if the spectator sees one person working well on stage, then this spectator, so it is claimed, will also work well the next day. If you like something in a film, you like it in life as well. Things that are problematic, on the other hand, negativity in art and journalism, only highlight the negative and problematic aspects of reality.

Where negative elements simply cannot be avoided, we have developed an incredible culture, or better, cult of linguistic conventions. A whole rhetorical technique prevents the person who is being told the truth from actually experiencing it. What is 'bad' is turned into 'not yet good'. If people have been working badly, this is turned into the need 'to do even better work'. The words 'even' and 'increasingly' are everywhere made to work their magic. Even the demand not to talk things up ends up like this:

> We need to strengthen our resolve even more increasingly to start with the facts in order to provide the public with an even more realistic initiation into the correctness of our path, victorious on the one hand but on the other of course still displaying flaws and weaknesses that are increasingly being overcome, so that the way our development conforms to law becomes even more apparent, increasingly helping us to avoid defeats ...

Such apparent pacification of the public, meant to ensure peace but in reality causing unrest, is a matter not just of dubious taste but of politics. For if undeniable problems do appear unannounced in (so-called) 'sudden about-turns', the public is completely unprepared for them. Then art is ushered in, in the hope that that old magic formula will prevail whereby if art gives its blessing to the existing order, people will accept this order as a blessing where in actual fact it would be a blessing to change it.

It is tempting here to return once more to theory, to one indeed that is forty years old, so as old as the GDR. In the famous debate between Friedrich Wolf and Bertolt Brecht as to whether Mother Courage has to learn from her experience in order for the spectator to learn, Brecht explained that it was precisely Courage's inability to learn that serves as a lesson for the spectator. Courage's inability to learn anything from her participation in the war should not only provide the spectator with insight but also shock him into realizing that not learning from situations leads to catastrophes. But seeing as I have taken my leave of theorizing for today, I should like to let a painter speak instead. Theodor Hosemann said many years ago: 'No one has ever tried to claim that Max and Moritz[3] made children naughtier and inspired them to fill their teacher's pipe with gun-powder.'

But now to the spontaneous applause in the suburban cinema following Heike Misselwitz's film *Farewell to Winter*. Was it perhaps a case of 'clapping in the wrong direction', a smack in the state's face for the fact that the kind of thing shown in the film actually exists: the woman working in the briquette factory who has a mentally handicapped daughter, is consequently snubbed by her neighbours and is unable to find the money for a holiday for herself and her children? So was the applause spiteful? Were people perhaps clapping because the film had destroyed the good faith of those who think they live in a state that guarantees social security, and this was a source of pleasure to the dissenters? The people I asked had quite different answers, which they expressed in various ways: the film had opened doors. Doors behind which problems can be seen, problems that do really exist but which are often hidden from people out of fear that they are not mature enough to understand them. The film took the spectators seriously. It created the impression of allowing them in, of asking and trusting them to help solve these kinds of problems. Because only when you are aware that there are problems can you find the knowledge and strength to overcome them. That was more or less what the spectators replied on this Sunday afternoon. For me, it brought unusual clarity to the phrase that not only a political but also a great human force resides in truth: an aspect of poetry becomes a human motivation. And that beauty not only comes from beauty, but above all from truth – including hard truths – when you are entrusted with it.

Postscript

As we pushed our way out of the cinema, our thoughts still with the film, we saw the projectionist pinning up a poster announcing the next film. It was *Die Kommissarin* (*The Commissar*), a film that for no apparent reason had disappeared from our picture-theatres. But now it was back. Openly correcting a decision in such a manner, showing a state's ability to learn from its mistakes, could significantly increase people's confidence in the state. I perceived this in the murmurs of approval around me, as people took note that this excellent Soviet revolutionary film had been re-approved. And I enquired when exactly the film would be back in the major cinemas so that lots of people could see it and welcome the correction. The projectionist's response: it had been stipulated that the film should only be shown in the small cinemas on the edge of the city.

'Yes, it is strange that people, who in their theory speak precisely of how circumstances and people can be changed, in practice have so little confidence that providing people with insight into their actual situation really will allow them to be changed,' says Christa Wolf in an interview in one of the most recent editions of *Sinn und Form*. I would like to apologize for not giving a celebratory speech on this double fortieth anniversary and speaking instead of work. And as a justification I do not want to start referring yet again to Brecht's *The Carpet Weavers of Kujan Bulak*, but I do believe that constantly re-informing ourselves about our situation and the work we do is even more necessary today than ever before if we do not want to fall victim to that crippling sense of self-evidence that entails stasis, and thus relapse. Old Brecht's suggestion still prevails: 'Change the world, it needs it.' But also: 'Real advancement is not about being advanced, but advancing.'

ON THE OPENING OF THE ACADEMY FOR PERFORMING ARTS IN DELITZSCH IN MARCH 2008

The common-sense approach of this new academy and its sense of realism, both essential to the performing arts, can already be seen in its decision to limit opening speeches to five minutes. I am going to stick to that, even though the occasion tempts me to say a lot more. For something incredible is happening here: a cultural institution is being opened, not closed. And this at a time when three successful theatres not at all far from here are threatened with closure. Even as we are opening this new academy, an institute in Marburg that was founded after the Second World War by the great political scientist Wolfgang Abendroth and became an international centre for political science is disappearing without ceremony, for none of this could prevent it from – as it is known in the 'East' – 'being wound down'. But enough of that, five minutes really aren't long enough for such a topic. And because I do want to stick to the five minutes, I shall get straight to the point: to studying theatre, and from there to me and the kinds of experiences I have had with it.

Arts colleges – and particularly drama schools – have a tendency not met in other professions: they want to be godlike. The gods are called 'tutors', and they share with the gods a demand that their disciples believe in them, especially when they can't understand them. For, as the Bible tells us, the Lord works in mysterious ways.

I came upon this kind of 'godlike' school as an eighteen-year-old. It was 1949 and the school wasn't at all far from here, in an attractive park where Goethe liked to take a turn. They were so modest there as to want nothing more than to 'renew German theatre' (not just the Deutsches Theater in Berlin, but German theatre as a whole). Their point of reference was Konstantin Sergeievich Stanislavski, the great Russian theatre reformer, but they were only familiar with his early works, which by this stage he had long since revoked. But they didn't know this. The lessons consisted, rather like church services, primarily of exercises that were called 'études'. The attractive parkland served us here, as the loving couples of each respective play had to spend at least an hour preparing for their scenes by embarking on silent perambulations around it. Thus one saw Ferdinand and Luise, Thekla and Max, Romeo and Juliet, Penthesilea and Achilles – even Faust and Gretchen were spotted. The walks took place at dusk, when there was least likelihood of distraction, and served the purpose of 'fully feeling your way into the character', so behaving as if one actually were Romeo and Juliet, Faust and Gretchen, and so on. For only through empathy – or, in the language of the godlike – 'through complete identification with the character', was it believed possible to discover emotions hidden deep within ourselves. For example, what is generally called 'love' and is already well known. But here the students looked for it under the rustling trees of the beautiful park, at dusk, for a good hour.

I cannot really say how successful the silent perambulations were, as I did not personally experience them, I failed the entrance exam. But this much I know: of all the drama schools, this one chalked up the greatest number of births.

For me, however, it was all a little less pleasurable, as I failed – as I said – the entrance exam, for I possessed, as was duly recorded by the godlike, absolutely no artistic talent. I was advised against theatre, teaching was after all also a nice job. I was a newly qualified teacher at the time. When the Nazi teachers were eradicated from the schools, teachers were in short supply and so I completed a nine-month teaching course after my school exams and became, as it was known at the time, a 'new teacher', in mathematics, which, along with the practice of theatre, I greatly enjoyed. The entrance exam that quickly ruined my theatre plans consisted of a single 'étude'. After I had, as required, auditioned in three roles, including the Templar from Lessing's *Nathan the Wise*, and believed myself to have been 'on good form', I was informed that the entrance exam was nowhere near over, in fact it was only just beginning. For, as I was told, everyone can hide behind the great Lessing's text, but here they were looking for 'personal intuition'. And I would have to prove this with the following 'étude': 'Imagine', one of the godlike said, 'you have managed to exchange your camera on the black market for two sausages (that was about its value at the time). You are desperately in love with a girl, and in order to win her favour you lovingly lay a table in your house with candles and serviettes, serve the hot sausages on a china plate and await the arrival of your loved one with great inner excitement. The bell rings, you rush to the door, but it is only the gasman who wants to read your meter. When you come back, you see that your cat has eaten the sausages. What do you do?' I had to retreat to an empty room and was given two hours to consider what I would do. Probably two hours was too long, because after I had mentally raged and wept all I could it occurred to me that cats do not eat hot food. That was to be the undoing of me. For after I had acted out the 'étude' up to the arrival of the gasman, thoroughly identifying with my character all the time, I did not scream out in horror when I discovered the missing sausages (my original intention), but rather (and this was the 'intuitive solution' I arrived at during the two hours) I frantically applauded the cat for its sensational achievement of having eaten two hot sausages against its instinct. Instead of the hearty laughter I had expected there came a long pause. Then I was solemnly told that I had absolutely no artistic talent. I was lacking 'inner life', as I clearly found superficial details like the dietary habits of cats more important.

My second experience with drama schools and teachers came about in a rather more convoluted manner, for the godlike from Goethe's park had thoroughly undermined all my daring and desire for theatre. I returned to my precious mathematics, but could not renounce my other vice, theatre, for long. We had founded an amateur drama group in Köthen right after the war because we wanted to escape the lethargy that was spreading like wildfire among us. We performed Hofmannsthal, Terence and Plautus, Evgeny Schwartz and produced our own plays, when one day we came across a text by a certain Bert Brecht. Of course the name was familiar to us by then, but not much more, for the Nazis had been very effective. They had made sure that up until 1945 names like Heine, Brecht, Thomas Mann, Feuchtwanger, etc., were completely unknown. We loved this play by the name of *Senora Carrar's Rifles*, set in the Spanish Civil War, with its irresistible realism and thrilling complexity. We decided to do it immediately. But we had no one to fill the male lead, the worker and militiaman Pedro. We turned for help to a metal worker whom we had seen at a plant and who had made quite an impression on us. Following his return from Soviet captivity he never missed a chance to recite Pushkin, very loudly but by no means badly. But he dismissed us out of hand. He abhorred the pretence of theatrical performance, he was always just himself, and that was that! But that wasn't that, because we tempted him to our rehearsal, supposedly in order to hear more Pushkin. We did listen to his Pushkin for about an hour, and then asked him to try reading us just one other text as a parting gesture, by a certain Bert

Brecht. He did this, fantastically by the way, for here too he was 'always just himself', and in the end he was our Pedro. As the premiere approached we thought about what might be the most appropriate way of honouring our work of the last half year. We were young, so modesty wasn't our thing. It was obvious, if we were going to put on his play, then the author should be there.

We put an announcement in the paper, an invitation to the premiere, adding: 'The author Bert Brecht will be present'. We cut this out, sent it to 'Bert Brecht, Berliner Ensemble', and waited to see what would happen. Our reasoning: If he is a great man, as was always claimed, then he will have a sense of humour and come, if he doesn't come, then in our eyes his greatness is just a rumour. He didn't actually come himself because he purportedly had a cold, but he sent two buses from the Berliner Ensemble for us to get on and perform the thing to him in Berlin. We got on and probably wouldn't have uttered a single word on the rehearsal stage at the Berliner Ensemble, if we had known who was sitting in the audience: Ernst Busch, Helene Weigel, Erwin Geschonneck, Therese Giehse, Hanns Eisler, Paul Dessau, all the actors from the Berliner Ensemble, Helene Weigel had even invited Berlin theatre managers and critics. But we – completely in the dark – acted as if our lives depended on it, and earned great applause, as everyone was so impressed that young people from the provinces had worked for almost a whole half a year … etc. Only one person took us seriously: Brecht. He criticized us and immediately began working with the group, and this he did until nearly midnight. For we had thought that, as the play was about Spaniards, Spaniards must always be like they are in *Carmen*, i.e., excited. Brecht thought that was too 'misty' and went into detail on how to turn our 'Carmen' Carrar into Carrar the Fishwife. Our Pedro however, who rejected all pretence, was here too – as he repeatedly said – 'always just himself', and Brecht liked that so much that he immediately offered him a contract. The reason: he had enjoyed watching him. So by midnight our Pedro was a member of the Berliner Ensemble. (Incidentally, he later went on to become one of the most popular film actors in the GDR, and a club in Berlin still bears his name today.) I was really annoyed, for after all I was the director and had 'put it all together'. The following day, just as we were getting back on the buses, I met Brecht going in to rehearsal. He must have noticed my frustration, because he turned back round in the doorway and said he had seen that I still had a lot to learn. And now I expected the line that always comes in such situations: 'Come back when you have learned a bit more.' But the line I could hardly believe I was hearing was another: 'And seeing as you have to learn, it's best you stay and do it here.'

So much for the prologue. And now my reason for telling you all this in the first place. If the godlike of Goethe's park once undermined all my daring and desire for theatre, Brecht's Berliner Ensemble was a completely different experience for a beginner. Although I really had expected 'gods' here (for Brecht was something of a god for us back then), it was in fact all very down-to-earth, for we quite simply got straight down to work, or better, collaboration. And this instantly gave you the most important things for making theatre: daring and desire. When we – 'my' Pedro and I – arrived, suitcase in hand, at the rehearsal stage of the Berliner Ensemble, Brecht, to our surprise, interrupted the rehearsal, came over to us as we stood reverently rooted in the doorway, shook our hands and said, 'Sit in on the rehearsal and write down all your objections'.

With these words I should like to end the stipulated five-minute opening speech. If I now add on some further remarks, they no longer have anything to do with the opening speech, for I am moving on now to the everyday business of this academy. My thoughts are rather like the beginning of an introductory seminar on the question: 'What do you have to learn in order to learn all about theatre?' The line with which Brecht received us beginners reflects his opinion that the best way of getting to know theatre is to make it. That might lead one to the widely held misconception that talent alone suffices, everything else comes from 'gut-feeling'. Brecht's instruction to sit in on the rehearsal right away and start collaborating without further ado is of course only half the story: because this is exactly what you have to learn. Of course it was fantastic that I, hardly a full three days at the Berliner Ensemble, was already sitting right next to Brecht and was allowed to work as his assistant on the production of *Mother Courage*. But by the same token all assistants were given the strict order (which was rare for Brecht) to attend the lectures held by the youngest and most idiosyncratic professor of philosophy at the time, a certain Wolfgang Harich, twice a week before rehearsal, starting at about 7:30 a.m. Brecht simply held ignorance of Hegel and Marx's dialectics to be 'immoral'. So there is a lot to learn (and not only with Brecht) about the theatre and above all about the world. For without knowledge nothing can be shown, or how else is one to know what is worth knowing? This is roughly what Brecht says in his *Short Organum for the Theatre*.

Nevertheless, I do not want to end this little session with theory, when Brecht is often purported to be far too theoretical (which only proves how little those who make such claims know Brecht). I would like to present Brecht here as a practical man for a change, caught up in the everyday work of rehearsal. For even Marcel Reich-Ranicki[1] once said of him:

> Brecht was not just a theatre practitioner he was also a theatre expert. Of course the songs with which he interrupts his plays provide social and political criticism, but he, like his colleague Nestroy, also knew that when every now and then a song comes along, people won't run away.

So here is a rather less well known 'practical' Brecht, taken from his *Elementary Rules for Actors* (1951):

> There is no need to adopt an affected voice for the old woman, the villain, and the fortune-teller.
>
> Characters with depth should be developed. Pavel Vlassov in *The Mother* becomes a professional revolutionary. But at the beginning he is not yet one, and so cannot be played as if he were one.
>
> Heroes should not be characterized as never frightened and cowards as never brave, etc. One-word characterizations like hero or coward are very dangerous.
>
> When speaking quickly, you should not also become loud, when speaking loudly you should not start invoking pathos.
>
> If the actor wants the spectator to be moved, it is not enough for him merely to be moved himself. Realism will always lose out if the actor 'plays for sympathy' or enthusiasm, etc.
>
> Most characters on the German stage are not taken from life but from theatre. Theatre's old man mumbles and dodders, theatre's youth is all fired up and childishly exuberant, theatre's flirt speaks with a husky voice and swings her hips, theatre's petit-bourgeois rants and raves, etc.
>
> Social awareness is indispensable for the actor. However, it cannot replace an understanding of social circumstances. And understanding social circumstances cannot replace constantly studying them. Every character and every situation and every statement requires studying afresh.
>
> For a century, actors were chosen according to temperament. Now, temperament is necessary, or better: vitality, but not in order to carry the spectator along with you, rather in

order to exaggerate characters, situations and statements sufficiently for the stage.

Sometimes in average plays it is necessary to 'make something out of nothing'. But in good plays you must not try to squeeze out more than is already there. The unexcited must not be made exciting, the lacklustre must not become gripping. There is a natural ebb and flow in works of art – in this they are living organisms. They should be left as such.

Concerning pathos: if you are not representing a pathetic person, then you should be very careful with pathos. Bear in mind the advice: 'If you hadn't climbed up, you wouldn't have to come down.'

Illustration 12 Manfred Wekwerth co-directing with Brecht in rehearsal of *Caucasian Chalk Circle*, Carl Weber on left (1954). (Photograph by Horst E. Schulze in possession of Manfred Wekwerth.)

I have chosen this possible beginning of a lesson in theatre performance in order to indicate that I am sure this new Academy for Performing Arts that we are opening in Delitzsch today will belong to that class of 'down-to-earth' schools that take people and what matters to them, and not false gods, as their starting point. For this, let me heartily wish you all in good theatre fashion to 'break a leg!'

5

ENJOYING THE FINAL FRUITS

Rather than provide a summative conclusion, in the spirit of scepticism and irony – and in the light of rightwing attacks on himself – Manfred Wekwerth ends with some playful comments on the release of Brecht's FBI file and on the press coverage of the fiftieth anniversary of Brecht's death.

AH

THE SECRET SERVICE'S OPEN SECRET

Thoughts on the 'Brecht file', Now to be Made Public by the FBI by Order of the Supreme Court of the USA

Actually I would advise anyone who wants to find out something about Brecht against reading the Federal Bureau of Investigation's 'Brecht file'.[1] For everything that FBI agents hoped to find out by conspiratorially rummaging through the 'subject's' (Brecht's) waste-paper baskets or diligently working day and night tapping his telephone conversations and keeping a constant watch on everyone who entered and left the 'subject's' house in Santa Monica could have been established with less effort and considerably less cost in, for example, Brecht's play *Saint Joan of the Stockyards*, which is even available in English: 'Where ever violence prevails, the only help is violence itself.' Is there any stronger proof that the 'subject' really was planning to 'violently overthrow' capitalism? This one simple sentence would have sufficed to replace a whole 371 pages of transcripts. For it delivers something the mountains of paperwork could not: proof that the 'subject' was a communist.

The Federal Bureau's mammoth task, as senseless as it was costly, yet again proves right clever people like Graham Greene, author of the stunning spy novel *Our Man in Havana*, when he calls the world-wide activities of secret service agents an 'indispensable perpetuum mobile of high-paid acts of futility'.

For the Federal Bureau of Investigation is – as Graham Greene suggests – not at all interested in what is in the files. They contain nothing that you couldn't have found out at the nearest street corner or news stand. What they do *not* contain is far more significant. What, as was then generally suspected, they possibly could contain. And because they do not contain anything, you can suspect the worst. So this is not about what is in these files, but rather the simple fact that such files exist and that everyone knows it. Because they have not been made public, they may concern everything and everyone. The authorities are concerned not with factual certainty but rather with the uncertainty factor. Actually the files of the Federal Bureau are not at all intended for those cases where someone really has already done something, but rather for indicating what he must absolutely not do in the future. They are hidden warnings to the disloyal, or to those who are thus made disloyal. In short: perhaps the professional pointlessness of the secret service is its very point: people should fear it without knowing why. And the greater the uncertainties, the more certain the fear. God, who watches everyone, pursues those who sin publicly and so contravene fixed commandments that have been generally known since Moses. The FBI by contrast, who also watches everyone, pursues them right into their wastepaper baskets and marital beds, without their ever finding out why. And that creates the right atmosphere so conducive to fear and denunciation.

In this respect, the FBI files do actually make a good read. For the very emptiness that can be discerned within them, recorded with professional monotony over the course of constant round-the-clock observations, produce the desired effect. It is precisely that pointlessness they display that makes the 'subject' feel insecure, because he is constantly looking for the point, that is to say for the thing he is supposed to have contravened. It is a perfect war of nerves. And the less proof, the greater the opportunity to build on suspicions. The law of *in dubio pro reo* (in case of doubt, believe the defendant) is given a completely different interpretation here: in case of doubt, increase surveillance on the person concerned. Here innocence makes you all the more suspicious, because it could be a disguise.

The Federal Bureau of Investigation has been successful with this approach, and still is today. Admittedly it failed to 'investigate' the threat posed by the Japanese bombers as they headed unnoticed towards Pearl Harbour in their hundreds to destroy the USA's Pacific fleet, but the FBI did manage to divert another threat from the United States of North America: the actor Charlie Chaplin, who had long been the target of 'intense operative treatment' by the FBI, fled the country to settle in Switzerland. From then on the USA was safe from Charlie Chaplin.

Brecht himself left the USA in 1947, after he had narrowly escaped McCarthy's persecution. But the FBI nevertheless had one success: the American occupying forces threatened 'the communist Brecht' with arrest should he attempt to cross the American zone when the 'subject' wanted to travel to East Berlin on his return from emigration. As a result, the 'subject' had to travel through Austria and Czechoslovakia instead.

However, it is virtually imperative to read the 'Brecht file' if you want to find your way through the state-conditioned jungle of contemporary, home-grown secret services that successfully extended their web of 'sources' (the Christian-Democratic term for an *Informeller Mitarbeiter* [informal collaborator in the GDR]), to include journalists and children – and today even liaise with well known companies like Deutsche Telekom, Lidl, Siemens, etc. Just like the Federal Bureau of Investigation they only want what's best: ensuring the 'security' of the company by making its members feel insecure and thus bound to obey.

PARTY GAME[1]

The galas, events, and parties that were laid on to celebrate the 50th anniversary of Brecht's death in August 2006 were over, things quietened down again for the 'Goethe of the twenty-first century' (Jan Knopf[2]). He went back to the same place that the Goethe of the nineteenth century can be found: the bookshelf. For one whole month 'our dramatic Himalaya' (Claus Peymann[3]) was top of the charts, then normality set in again, meaning Brecht was once again 'cast aside like an old operetta' (Claus Peymann). The time for making profits from Brecht was over; it was once again profitable to read Brecht.

There was a game that Brecht used to play to pass away the long Scandinavian afternoons. His preference for the scholarly led him to call it 'On reconstructing truth'. The rules of the game are simple: you take, for example, the 'Christmas message from the Führer's deputy' (Rudolf Hess), draw two columns, and write the Christmas message into the left-hand one, its correction in the right-hand one. Slogan: 'In times when deception is demanded and mistakes are the order of the day, the thinking man endeavours to correct everything he reads and hears.' For fun, I am going to play this game from 1934 with a few publications from Brecht's anniversary in 2006:

Frankfurter Allgemeine, 9 July 2006:
But what, many a voice will now ask,
has become of all the seriousness, of
the Brecht who wanted to improve the
world? There is perhaps no need to
mention again that he acted
opportunistically with the socialist
authorities... And Frieda Grafe has
finally burst the bubble of pathos around
Brecht the social visionary. In 1931 the
film *Kuhle Wampe*, scripted by Brecht,
was produced, and its moral lesson can
be easily reduced to the closing dialogue:
'Who should change the world?' asks a
petit-bourgeois man. And the proletarian
woman answers: 'Those who don't like it.'
In an essay about cinema of that time
(and making reference to one of the Nazis'
propaganda films) the critic Frieda
Grafe continues this logic: 'Did the
SA-man Brand[4] like the world? And didn't
he change it?'
Here (to quote B.B. one last time) she sadly is
quite right.

No comment

Reader's Digest, August 2006:
Bert Brecht, born 1898 in Augsburg: the
greatest German writer of the twentieth
century and equally its greatest opportunist?
Even 50 years after his death in August 1956
his image still remains ambivalent. He was
short and ugly, his mousy face full of spots,
and he didn't smell good. Everybody around
him turned up their noses, from his school
days right through to his time as 'boss' at the
Berliner Ensemble. This 'boss', as everyone
knew, didn't care too much for personal
hygiene...

I am one of those affected, because as an
assistant and later as a co-director I always
had to sit fairly close to the 'boss'. And I
remember very well: he smelled of sulphur.
And the mousy face didn't just have spots, it
had two fangs and the undeniable beginnings
of two little horns. I do however also
remember that the 'boss' was always very
short with you if you came to rehearsal
unshaven, overtired or with a lingering smell
of liquor. 'Bedrozzled'('Verschwiemelt'), as
he put it, 'you can neither think nor direct'.
He also needed daylight and always had all
the blackout curtains pulled up on the
windows in the rehearsal space. In a poem
'On the pleasure of beginning' he even
describes his morning toilet: 'The first splash
of water / On my sweaty face! The fresh /
Cooling shirt! / ...And the first draw of smoke
filling my lungs! And you / New thought!'

Frankfurter Allgemeine, 9 July 2006:
There is in any case no doubt that Brecht's
grey worker's outfit was, ever since he could
afford it, made from the finest material and
tailored to fit. Furthermore it's a safe bet that
his Mao caps were produced by the best Mao
cap maker in town. And his nickel spectacles
with their prescription frames were really
made of titanium and incredibly expensive…
Which naturally reminds us contemporaries
(as Mr B. would call us) of the Sex Pistols,
who likewise didn't get their rags and old
clothes … from the charity clothing collection
but from Vivienne Westwood's fancy
boutique. Or of the Ramones with their
artfully ripped jeans… In short, whoever
takes a look back today will spot Brecht
sitting alongside those popular stars for
whom painstakingly posing as outsiders was
always an integral, if not substantial, part of
their work… First came his mug, then his
morals. And here it should be noticed that
even a shoddy kind of dandyism always tends
towards the totalitarian: why not form the
world in your own image.

The 'bespoke tailor' was called Gleichfeld
and he worked in the men's section of the
costume workshop at the Staatsoper, which
was also where the costumes were produced
for the Berliner Ensemble. He earned a little
on the side by taking on private commissions,
which worked out well not only for Brecht
but also for us assistants because he only
asked for his hourly pay for these jobs on the
side, and the cloth was also affordable. I
actually only came across 'Mao caps' on
stage, where Brecht kitted out the rather
dopey attaché in his play *Mr Puntila* with
such a cap. He usually bought his own caps,
typical Berlin, soft-peaked caps, after lengthy
rummaging in small shops that still stocked
such a thing. I have disappointing news about
the titanium medical-assistance frame as well:
for what I sometimes had to pick up from the
floor when the 'boss' had once again acted
something out for the cast a little too
vehemently and knocked off his glasses was –
unlike my own exclusive 'rimless' glasses –
made of horn. And the point about the
'worker's outfit' that he always wore is also in
need of a little correction. Brecht, like all of
us, liked these 'light, wide jackets', and he
didn't wear them in order to look like a
labourer, but because they were
comfortable (labourers would have refused
to wear such an 'overall' outside their place
of work). Brecht liked to call himself, as far
as clothes were concerned, 'the inventor of
the movable male neck', as he rejected
stiff collars on the grounds of comfort.
But whoever wants to check up on the
titanium spectacles himself: Brecht's
heirs are currently selling all his
glasses and walking sticks on the
internet.

Frankfurter Rundschau, 10 August 2006:
The sights were trained on the 'womanizer'
and 'Stalin Peace Prize winner', the 'fair-
weather Confucian' and the 'talented
monster' (Thomas Mann): in 1998 (Brecht's
100th birthday, MW), Brecht seemed more
evil than ever before, as if his evil had to be
emphasized in order for the man to be
remembered at all. People relished in the
gruesome image of this 'eternal welfare
dependent' (Manthey), and Elfriede Jelinek[5]
pronounced him to be a man of extreme
orality, 'who constantly wedges his beak open
and untiringly stuffs in everything that is
thrown his way'.

No comment.

Reader's Digest, **August 2006:**
The war is over... But Brecht will always be Brecht: In me you have someone in whom you can't trust... First he applies for admission to the West. He is refused. A shrug of the shoulders. And, with the Czech citizenship up his sleeve that he obtained a little earlier with the help of Egon Erwin Kisch, off he goes to East Berlin.

An application for admission to the West with the aim of settling there, as well as a Czech citizenship cannot be found even in Brecht's inherently meticulously documented FBI files. By contrast, these files do contain a letter from the 'stateless subject Berthold Brecht' (FBI files) to an American general, where Brecht protests against the Americans' refusal to let him travel through West Germany (the West zone) on his way to Berlin, 'where he is intending to work in the (East) Berlin Deutsches Theater' (FBI files): 'I fear [...] that your officers are now [...] not only not supporting many of the members of the German resistance movement against Hitler, but hindering them, and this because of their social views' (Brecht, September 1948). Brecht had to travel via Salzburg and Prague. In Salzburg, the composer von Einem guaranteed the 'stateless man' an Austrian passport for all eventualities if he wrote a new *Dance of Death* for Salzburg. The *Dance of Death* that Brecht drafted was rejected as 'too socially critical', but Austrian bureaucracy carried on working away unperturbed, until Brecht, by now a citizen of the GDR, to his surprise also became a citizen of Austria.

Der Tagespiegel, **14 August 2006**
(the anniversary of Brecht's death)
Erich Mielke and the writer's heart attack – Was Brecht intending to bring charges against Stasi bosses? Was that why he had to die? Following up a strange sound recording.
A dead Brecht, glossed over and misunderstood as a socialist classic, was a more comfortable prospect for the state powers in the GDR of 50 years ago than a living Brecht. And for the State Security? Of course, there is no such thing as a Brecht file in the Gauck-Birthler-Institute[6] [...]. But there does exist a [...] hitherto unknown speech by the head of the Stasi, Erich Mielke, that mentions Brecht's death in a tone of final reckoning: '... and that the well known writer (pause) and, er, dramaturg Brecht wanted to press charges against a leading functionary of the State Security.' Here Mielke pauses briefly ... and carries on in a Berlin dialect, with poor grammar and placing special emphasis on the second word: 'And **then** Brecht succumbed to a heart attack.'[...]

In early August 1956 Brecht and I were working in Buckow on the preparations for the premiere of *The Days of the Commune*. We were working alone, as Benno Besson was late returning from holiday. Brecht was recovering from a viral illness, which was why he could only work for two hours at a time, but he was working intensively and enjoying it. When he grew markedly weaker I suggested interrupting our work, but he refused. He claimed he knew about medicine, he had studied it for two semesters after all. He drove the car himself when we travelled back to Berlin for a rehearsal of *The Caucasian Chalk Circle* that was about to go on tour in London. Brecht asked the actors over a stage microphone not to ask him how he was; when he was feeling better, he would let them know himself.
When he deteriorated on the following Sunday, Helene Weigel tried in vain to reach Professor Brugsch, head doctor at the Charité at the time. Early on Monday morning Brecht rang me up and cancelled the day's work. He wanted to ring early on Tuesday, the 14th August, to rearrange another meeting as a matter of priority, because he was intending to travel to Dr Schmitt's spa in Munich on Tuesday evening.

But Werner Hecht, long-time head dramaturg at the Berliner Ensemble in the years of the GDR, [...] who knows more about Brecht's life and impact than any other mortal, simply says in surprise: 'I've never heard of this speech [...] I too can imagine that they wanted to get rid of Brecht. And of course it would be a coup, especially in this anniversary year, if secret triumph about some sort of Stasi-planned euthanasia could be read into Mielke's comments and then actually proved!'[...]

A study by the doctor Hans Karl Schulten that examined Brecht's medical records from 1956 in 2000 showed [...] that Brugsch (and others) should have given Brecht in the days before he died 'a sufficiently high dose of antibiotics instead of dietary advice and an immunization that even then was considered obsolete. [...] In any case it certainly stands out that the head of the Stasi, who in his speeches often spoke with brutal openness of his role as a political killer who made 'short work' of 'villains' and 'scumbags', should refer so specifically to the 'er, dramaturg Brecht' and his heart attack months after his death.

Early on Tuesday Besson, Peter Palitzsch and I were at Elisabeth Hauptmann's to make our plans for Brecht's absence. When we still hadn't heard anything from Brecht by midday and nobody answered the phone in his apartment in the Chauseestrasse either, we asked the theatre doctor, Dr. Tsouloukidse, to check on Brecht. Dr. Tsouloukidse immediately rang us back to tell us that Brecht had had a heart attack, which, because it had been painless, was probably already four days old. He got in touch with the governmental hospital, that immediately sent doctors and equipment, and Dr. Tsouloukidse asked us to get particular medication in West Berlin that was not available in East Berlin. Besson, who owned a car, set off at once and, because he didn't have any papers for crossing the border, he told the border guard at the Brandenburg Gate: 'Comrade Brecht is in mortal danger.' He was allowed through immediately, got the medication, but the help came too late. Incidentally, Werner Hecht was never the head dramaturg at the Berliner Ensemble. He managed the Brecht archive. He never knew Brecht personally.

NOTES

Introduction by Anthony Hozier

1 Co-directed with Palitzsch and Tenschert respectively.
2 Again with Tenschert.
3 Daughter Barbara, with her husband, Ekkehard Schall.

Preface by Manfred Wekwerth

1 Wekwerth here uses one of Brecht's favourite words, 'Spaß'. [Ed.]
2 Alongside Brecht's achievement of using science to reinvigorate theatre, he also had a scientific achievement independent of theatre. Although he never formulated a philosophical system, his systematic contribution to the Marxist thought of his time is comparable to that of other great philosophers. Wolfgang Fritz Haug has impressively analysed this in his book *Philosophieren mit Brecht und Gramsci* (*Philosophizing with Brecht and Gramsci*), published in 2006 by Argument-Verlag.

1 BRECHT'S THEATRE – AN EXTENDED OVERVIEW

Brecht's Theatre Today – An Attempt in Seven Days

1 The text is based on lectures that I gave in the Swedish Institute for Film and Theatre in Stockholm. This version dates from 2007/2008.
2 'Wissenschaft' and 'wissenschaftlich' have a broader meaning in German than the English 'science' and 'scientific'. Where in English 'science' commonly refers to the natural sciences, in German 'Wissenschaft' can include the social sciences and, particularly for Brecht, Marx's 'materialist conception of history'. In the translation of this book 'scholarship', 'scholarly' or 'academic' have frequently been used where the words 'science' and 'scientific' would have too narrow a meaning. On the occasions that Wekwerth, following Brecht, talks of 'das Theater des wissenschaftlichen Zeitalter' this has been rendered, as in other translations as 'theatre for a scientific age'. [Ed.]

3 The very second production at the newly founded Berliner Ensemble was Gorki's *Vassa Zheleznova*, and this was followed by *The Tutor* by J.M.R. Lenz and Hauptmann's *Biberpelz und roter Hahn*. Later on too for each Brecht play there were three to four plays by other authors.

4 Born 1936. Professor at Freie Universität Berlin, editor of the journal *Das Argument*, founding member of the Left Party in 2007. [Ed.]

5 A term used by Brecht to refer to the sterile form taken by institutionalized Marxism. [Ed.]

6 East German philosopher (1923–95). Associate of Brecht. Imprisoned for counter-revolutionary activity in 1956, released in 1964. [Ed.]

7 Russian-born economic and social theorist (1910–64). [Ed.]

8 German Marxist philosopher (1885–1977), known to Brecht. [Ed.]

9 (1925–87), philosopher in the GDR. [Ed.]

10 Choosing not to tell stories in order to interpret them instead, i.e. knowingly or unknowingly confusing the appearance with the thing, is not new in art. One hundred and fifty years ago Jean Paul, the great storyteller, commented to those 'interpreters and thinkers': 'It is hopeless! Only in the atypical minutiae of daily life will you find the true path of essential truth.'

11 Alongside her equally famous 'there is no such thing as society', this stands as one of Margaret Thatcher's best-known summations of free-market neo-liberalism. [Ed.]

12 The Swedish Royal Dramatic Theatre.

13 'Haltung' has been translated throughout this book mostly as 'stance' or 'standpoint'. In Brecht's writing this key word is often associated with '*Gestus*' (discussed at length later) and refers to the (usually social) position or attitude taken by a theatre artist or by a character within a scene towards others or to their world. [Ed.]

14 '*Verfremdung*' is Brecht's term for the process of making things strange, casting them in a new light, prompting questions about cause and effect in human actions. When translated as 'alienation' it is misleadingly confused with the concept used by Marx and others ('Entfremdung') to describe the way in which workers in the capitalist mode of production are separated (alienated) from the fruits of their own labour, from their own nature, or from society. '*Verfremdung*', '*Verfremdungsffekt*'and '*V-Effekt*' have been retained in German throughout this book. [Ed.]

15 'The joy of old plays is all the greater the more we can give ourselves over to a new kind of satisfaction that is appropriate to us. In order to do this we have to make the historical sense – which we also need for new plays – into a real sensuousness. Our theatres have a habit, when they produce plays from other epochs, of blurring the division, filling in the distance, underplaying the differences. But what happens then to our pleasure in gaining an overview, and in seeing what is far away, what is different? That pleasure is also the pleasure in what is near and our own!' (Brecht)

16 The same director later produced Ibsen's *Hedda Gabler*. Here too people wrote (in the nineteenth century, after all!) on laptops, but the 'historical field' remained perfectly intact. Hedda is not driven to suicide by a constructed catastrophe, but by the boredom of a normal bourgeois existence that plays itself out in ordered and repetitive processes. Even Hedda's

suicide does not upset bourgeois normality: it happens 'like an aside' and is hardly noticed by the others.

17 See also 'The Uncertain Thing about Certainty' later. [Ed.]

18 Brecht is supposed to have heard the term 'ostranenije' on his visit to Moscow in 1932, which literally translates as 'to make noteworthy or strange' ('vermerkwürdigen'). Brecht's friend, the writer Sergej Tretjakov is believed to have suggested he translate it with 'verfremden'. [The translation of this short passage follows Wekwerth's German text using 'Verfremdung' interchangeably with 'ostranenije'.] [Ed.]

19 'Fabel' is a central concept in Brecht's work that cannot be readily translated into English. As used by Brecht it refers both (a) to the interpretative analysis of the structure of events embodied in a playtext, and also (b) to the freshly re-interpreted presentation of the play's events in production in all their contradictions and from a historical materialist point of view. None of the words available in English adequately embraces Brecht's meanings: 'story' (John Willett), 'plot' (for 'mythos' in most translations of Aristotle), 'fable' (older translations of Aristotle). 'Narrative' suggests the active process of arranging events for an audience, but Brecht and Wekwerth separate the concept of 'narrative' from 'Fabel', talking of 'narrating the Fabel' ('die Fabel zu erzählen'). To retain Brecht's specialist usage the word has been left in German in this book. [Ed.]

20 A well-known Swedish theatre school.

21 English has diversified its theatre vocabulary since Shakespeare's time, using 'actor' in preference to 'player', 'theatre' instead of 'playhouse', 'game' for structured 'playing'. In German, words compounded around the shared root 'spiel' retain a flexibility which can seem ambiguous when translated as 'play' in English. Sometimes – as in the present context of paralleling the spectator's and actor's imaginative worlds – that ambiguity can be fruitful. At others alternative words must be used. [Ed.]

22 A keyword formulated by Brecht, not easily translated, and retained in the book in German. Manfred Wekwerth goes on to explain the concept in detail below. [Ed.]

23 This is the only time that the dramaturgical term is mentioned in this book. It is central to the analysis of a play text and to the development of the Fabel in rehearsal. Identification of the 'turning point' assists in intensifying the polarity between both aspects of the 'Not–But' and contributing to the overall Verfremdungseffekt of a scene. [Ed.]

24 In order to avoid this, Helene Weigel, when she played Mother Courage, included a V-Effekt that was also a great theatrical idea. As she was cursing war, she checked the quality of the goods that her daughter had brought to her under her instructions. She spoke the sentence 'A curse on war!' with great forcefulness, but at the same time her hands let the flour run though her fingers, apparently automatically, and her fist expertly tried out the sound of the new drum. The audience's applause that could usually be expected when war was cursed faltered at the very start because people wondered how it was that Mother Courage did not have any sense of responsibility for her daughter's misfortune. No matter how much sympathy they felt for the mother, the audience could now no longer comprehend the business woman and were dismayed at how blind war can make even such a realistically minded woman as Mother Courage.

25 Translated from 'gestisch' and rendered here as 'gestic', but, like the noun 'Gestus', Brecht's term is without an English equivalent. Here it is anglicized but italicized. [Ed.]

26 Nevertheless, Gestus is not, as is claimed, a linguistic term like 'speech act' or 'speech strategy', but rather a practical theatre one.

27 Christlich Demokratische Union, the right-wing Christian Democratic party of West Germany at the time. [Ed.]

28 Junge Union, the youth organization of the CDU and the CSU (Christlich-Soziale Union). [Ed.]

29 ' "Mein lieber Herr Gesangsverein!" or "Großer Gott" ' (literally, ' "My dear Mr Singing Group" or "Good God" '). These expressions are untranslatable in this context. Explaining this episode in a discussion in the UK in 2000, Manfred Wekwerth with his translator roughly paraphrased the expressions as 'Good Lord! Come, come, my good man! Come, come!' [Ed.]

30 'That the scenes should first simply be played in order and with the experiences one gains from life, but without much care for what comes next or even the overall meaning of the play, has great significance for the way a proper Fabel comes about. This then develops in a self-contradictory fashion, the individual scenes retain their meaning, create (and draw upon) a variety of ideas, and the whole thing, the Fabel, is properly developed, with twists and leaps, and we avoid that banal pervading-idealization (one word leads to the next) and the need for subordinate, purely functional individual details reliant on an end that resolves all.' (Brecht)

Brecht's Simplicity

1 Draft of a paper for the 2006 International Brecht Conference in Berlin.

2 The occasion was Ernst Bloch's The Heritage of our Times, which was published in Zurich in 1934. [One year after Hitler came to power and Brecht himself went into exile. Ed.]

3 i.e. 'serious formality'. [Ed.]

4 Manfred Wekwerth is referring to Abschied (directed by Jan Schütte), usually shown in English as Farewell, Brecht's Last Summer. The title appears in various forms in both German and English. [Ed.]

5 Benno Besson (1933–2006), Swiss theatre director, also an assistant to Brecht. [Ed.]

6 Karl Valentin (1882–1948), cabaret and silent film comic actor. [Ed.]

7 The conference was opened with the recitative The Manifesto, Brecht's verse rendering of the Marx/Engels' Communist Manifesto. The music for piano, drums and two speakers was written by the young composer Syman, the speakers were Renate Richter and Hendrik Duryn. The papers were interspersed with 'interludes' by the actors and entertainers Peter Sodann and Peter Bause, consisting of stories about Brecht and improvisations. The conference closed with an act entitled In der Sünder Schamvollem Gewimmel (In the Shameful Throng of Sinners). This line, originating from 'Baal's hymn', was the title of a Brecht programme, in which the actors Renate Richter and Hendrik Duryn, under the by-line 'A Rock Band remembers Brecht', performed early guitar songs, diary entries by the young Brecht and ballads from the Manual of Piety (Die Hauspostille) together with the rock band Emma-Männlich.

8 'My love of clarity comes from my inability to think clearly. I became a little doctrinaire because I was badly in need of teaching. My thoughts are easily confused, I am not at all concerned about saying this. Confusion calms me. When I have discovered something, I immediately strongly contradict it and in my grief question everything all over again, even though I had just childishly rejoiced that at least one thing seemed certain enough, as I told myself, for my modest demands. Sentences such as the proof of the pudding is in the eating, or even that life is the existence of protein, have an incredibly calming effect on me, until I get into trouble again. Likewise, I actually only note down scenes that occur between people because I would otherwise have only a very hazy recollection of them.' (Brecht, *Work Journal*, 1938)

Brechtian Theatre

1 Opening lecture at a Brecht colloquium for Latin American directors and actors in Havana in 2004.
2 From comments made by Brook in an interview with *Neues Deutschland*. [Ed.]
3 Stalin. [Ed.]
4 Brecht wrote his personal notes in lower case. [Ed.]
5 Marx. [Ed.]
6 Manfred Wekwerth's comments here are similar to those in Misconception Number Two of 'Brecht Today' above, and points of repetition have been cut. While acknowledging that theatre itself can't change society, Wekwerth discusses the theatre's potential influence on people's political awareness. [Ed.]
7 Manfred Wekwerth includes a slightly longer quotation in 'Brecht's Simplicity' earlier. [Ed.]

2 POLITICAL PERSPECTIVES

The Left's Difficulties with Culture, or The Practical Use of Brechtian Slogans

1 Contribution to the XIII International Rosa Luxemburg Conference, Berlin 2008.
2 German Marxist philosopher (b. 1927). [Ed.]
3 DKP: *Deutsche Kommunistische Partei*, formed in the FRG in 1968. [Ed.]
4 German Marxist (1846–1919).
5 Erich Mühsam (1878–1934), radical, writer and performer. Died in Oranienburg concentration camp. [Ed.]
6 Freie Deutsche Jugend: Free German Youth organization of the GDR. [Ed.]
7 Ludwig Ganghofer (1855–1920), conservative writer on German themes. [Ed.]
8 Already quoted in 'Brechtian Theatre – An Opportunity for the Future', and, because *Galileo* is such an important play for Brecht and Wekwerth, repeated here.

The Uncertain Thing about Certainty

1 Eulogy on the eightieth birthday (2007) of Uwe-Jens Heuer, Professor of Law, and, after reunification, member for the German Bundestag for the PDS.
2 Quoted in full in 'The Left's Difficulties with Culture'. [Ed.]

3 THEATRE MAKING – THE *FABEL*

Keyword – *Fabel*

1 Extract from the draft for a book *Das Berliner Ensemble und die achtziger Jahre* (*The Berliner Ensemble and the Eighties*).
2 Bertolt Brecht, *Saint Joan of the Stockyards*.
3 A reference to the play *Johanna von Döbeln* (*Joan of Döbeln*) that premiered in the Berliner Ensemble in 1968.
4 An argument over Beckett has once more broken out in leftwing literary criticism, as his 'ontological irrationalism' ostensibly precludes any sense of progress. Now it is well known that Brecht in his last years still wanted to produce Beckett's *Waiting for Godot* because 'this play serves as a brilliant echo for a society that no longer achieves anything anymore'. The clownery, as a mediating form, could highlight the actual content here: namely that nothing happens any more because here we have people waiting for something that they themselves will no longer do. Once again, literary criticism has omitted the theatre when judging theatrical works.
5 Concerning the central nervous system. [Ed.]
6 In one of our last conversations, Brecht answered my question about what he thought the theatre of the future would be without hesitation: *The Measures Taken*. In this play a 'control chorus' examines whether the behaviour of a group of agitators was right or wrong on their return from pre-revolutionary China, where they were spreading revolutionary propaganda and had shot a comrade. Had he been successfully identified, their cover would have been blown. The situations are acted out in a reconstruction. Today it is claimed that Brecht's comment on the theatre of the future referred solely to 'the theme', shooting a comrade, and was therefore 'Stalinist'. Brecht meant, when he spoke of theatre of the future, above all the mediating form: a 'control chorus' examines the party functionaries' behaviour by reconstructing events as a play. In so doing, it asks the spectator to judge. *The Measures Taken* proposes that all political decisions be subject to 'control from below' and is – in contrast to Stalin's views and practices – a hymn to socialist (participatory) democracy.
7 Heinrich Heine, who valued this play above all of Shakespeare's works, deemed it 'unperformable' in the theatre of his day because first 'a new aesthetics must be invented for it'.
8 The fine Shakespeare scholar Robert Weimann (*Shakespeare and the Popular Tradition in the Theater: Studies in the Social Dimension of Dramatic Form and Function*) suggests that the heroes in this play should not be demolished, as for example Offenbach does in his operettas, but that the 'the act of demolishing be rendered heroic'.
9 Attempts to modernize theatre and create a 'theatre without a *Fabel*' even failed where they were successful: in the Theatre of the Absurd, which

owes its success to the fact that the *Fabel* continues to drive theatre where supposedly no 'Fabel', i.e. drive, exists. Here the lack of a *Fabel* actually becomes the *Fabel*. Thus the uneventful stasis in Samuel Beckett's *Waiting for Godot* was to have just such an impact.

10 These titles differ from the English-language editions. [Ed.]

11 Usually the opposite approach is taken. A character's personality is fixed (sometimes before rehearsals even start) and this is then used to justify all of the character's actions within the play.

12 Deutsche Film-Aktiengesellschaft, film studios in the GDR. [Ed.]

13 Ministerium für Staatssicherheit: State Security in the GDR.

Translation, Adaptation, Dramatization

1 The Remscheider version was commissioned by the WTT (Westdeutsches Tourneetheater / West German Touring Theatre) for the fiftieth anniversary of the Rittersaalspiele at the castle of Burg an der Wupper. The premiere was in September 2000, with music by Richard Strauss / Deodato, Georg Friedrich Handel, Modest Mussorgski; stage design: Manfred Grund; costumes: Ursula Wolf; direction: Manfred Wekwerth. Hilmar Eichhorn was 'Everyman'. Further performances in: Theater im Dom (new theatre) in Halle; direction: Wekwerth; stage design and costumes: Rolf Klemm; Everyman: Hilmar Eichhorn; premiere Whitsun 2002. Guest performances in Germany, Switzerland, Austria, Basel Open-Air festival, premiere 2004.

2 Hans Sachs's prologue to his own comedy is omitted in this English edition. [Ed.]

3 After the premiere Hugo von Hofmannsthal and the director Max Reinhardt converted to Catholicism.

4 The 1999 premiere on the occasion of the tenth anniversary of the Theater des Ostens in the Lessingtheater, Wolfenbüttel. Music: Jean-Baptiste Lully / Paul Dessau; direction: Wekwerth; stage design: Reinhard Zimmermann; costumes: Ursula Wolf; with Vera Oelschlegel, Barbara Dittus, Rose Vischer, Ingolf Gorges and company; guest performances in Germany, Austria, Switzerland. Further performances: 2002/2003 Studiobühne, Bayreuth; Pyrmontertheater Compagnie; Kellertheater, Heilbronn; 2004 Gymnasium, Alsdorf; 2007 Team-Theater, Munich; 2008 Gruppe Rosenblut, Cologne; 2008 Theater 'Die Tonne', Reutlingen.

5 The preface to the first edition of Choderlos de Laclos's epistolary novel of 1782 has been omitted in this English edition. [Ed.]

6 Premiere at the WTT (Westdeutsches Tourneetheater / West German Touring Theatre), 52nd Rittersaalspiele, Burg Castle; direction: Wekwerth; music: Syman; Stage design and costumes: Joachim Vogler; Lead role: Renate Richter.

7 The Prefatory poem by Rojas has been omitted in this English edition. [Ed.]

8 Director: Manfred Wekwerth; Music: Hans Dieter Hosalla; Script: Elisabeth Hauptmann, Isot Kilian, Manfred Wekwerth; Design: Karl von Appen; with Renate Richter, Hilmar Thate, Rolf Ludwig, Günter Naumann, Bruno Carstens, Norbert Christian, Peter Kalisch, Hermann Hiesgen, Stefan Lisewski and company.

9 (1940–79) Leader of student movement, and later associated with Greens. Influenced by western Marxist theorists like Gramsci. Survived assassination attempt in 1968, but subsequently died as result of injuries sustained. [Ed.]
10 Film director in the GDR (1925–82).

4 TWO SPEECHES

On the reopening of the Berliner Ensemble after six months of Reconstruction Work in September 1989

1 A game show with teams from several European countries. [Ed.]
2 West German politician, journalist and broadcaster, for a period engaged in German East–West liaison. [Ed.]
3 Two children's characters created by Wilhelm Busch in the nineteenth century who engage in outrageously naughty behaviour. [Ed.]

On the Opening of the Academy for Performing Arts in Delitzsch in March 2008

1 Literary critic. [Ed.]

5 ENJOYING THE FINAL FRUITS

The Secret Service's Open Secret – The FBI Brecht File

1 Filed under the rubric 'Subject Bertolt Eugen Friedrich Brecht, Document File #100–119o707'. [See http://foia.fbi.gov/foiaindex/brecht.htm; as accessed 20/08/10. Ed.]

Party Game

1 First published in *Ossietzky: Zweiwochenschrift für Politik/Kultur/Wirtschaft*, 2007, Ausgabe 3.
2 Director of the Arbeitsstelle Bertolt Brecht at the University of Karlsruhe. [Ed.]
3 Present director of the Berliner Ensemble. [Ed.]
4 *S.A. Mann Brand* was a Nazi propaganda film made in 1933. [Ed.]
5 German literary scholar and Austrian writer, respectively. [Ed.]
6 Archive of the records of the State Security Service of the former GDR. [Ed.]

MANFRED WEKWERTH
CHRONOLOGY AND KEY
PUBLICATIONS

This chronology includes principal productions (at Berliner Ensemble unless specified).

1951   After training as a teacher in Köthen, MW takes his amateur production of Brecht's *Senora Carrar's Rifles* to Brecht in Berlin. Brecht invites Wekwerth to train at the Berliner Ensemble.

1953–56   Directs Brecht's *The Mother* in Vienna. Assistant to Brecht on Strittmatter's *Katzgraben*.

Illustration 13 (l. to r.) Carlo Ponti, Sophia Loren, Vittorio de Sica, Wolf Kaiser, Kurt Bork, Manfred Wekwerth, Helene Weigel (Berlin, 1963). (Photograph by Karl Leher, courtesy of Tassilo Leher.)

	Co-director with Brecht on *The Caucasian Chalk Circle* and Becher's *Winterschlacht*.

1956–57   After the death of Brecht leads the directorial team under Helene Weigel. Directs Brecht's *The Days of the Commune* with Benno Besson, in Karl-Marx Stadt, Vishnevskiy's *Optimistic Tragedy*, and film version of Brecht's *The Mother* (with Helene Weigel).

1959–60   Directs Brecht's *The Resistible Rise of Arturo Ui*, with Palitzsch. (Production, with Ekkehard Schall in the lead, receives the Théâtre des Nations prize and critics' award in Paris.)

Directs film of *Mother Courage* with Palitzsch (with Helene Weigel).

1961   Becomes principal director of the Berliner Ensemble.

1962–69   Productions include: *The Days of the Commune*, Brecht's version of Shakespeare's *Coriolanus* (with Weigel and Schall); Kipphardt's *The Matter of J. Robert Oppenheimer* with Tenschert; Brecht's *St Joan of the Stockyards*, with Joachim Tenschert; Baierl's *Johanna von Döbeln*.

Guest productions of the Berlin Ensemble in Paris, London, Moscow, Venice, Frankfurt, Prague, Budapest, Vienna, Warsaw.

1969   Leaves Berliner Ensemble.

1970   Awarded doctorate by Humboldt University.

Illustration 14 With Helene Weigel in canteen of Berliner Ensemble (1965). (Photograph courtesy of Vera Tenschert.)

1970–77	Freelance productions include: Gorky's *Yegor Bulytchov*; Shakespeare's *Richard III* at Deutsches Theater, and Brecht's *The Good Person of Szechwan* at Schauspielhaus Zürich (with Renate Richter as Shen Te).
	Guest performances in Sweden, Finland, France, Austria.
1971	Invited by Laurence Olivier to direct (with Tenschert) *Coriolanus* at the National Theatre, London (with Anthony Hopkins in title role).
1971–77	Directs films for television including: Vishnevskiy's *Optimistic Tragedy* and 'Dorothy Lane's' *Happy End.*
1974	Director of the new Institut für Schauspielregie (Institute of Theatrical Direction) in Berlin.
1977–91	Returns as Director of the Berliner Ensemble.
1977–82	Productions include: Brecht's *Galilei* (Danish version) with Tenschert; Volker Braun's *The Great Peace* with Tenschert; Brecht's *Turandot or the Whitewashers' Congress* with Tenschert; Brecht's *Threepenny Opera* with Kern; Eisler's *Johann Faustus* with Tenschert.
	Guest performances in: Toronto, Vienna, Caracas, Rome, Bari, Milan, Venice, Jerusalem, Paris, Mexico City.
1982–90	President of the Academy of Arts of the GDR.

Illustration 15 (l. to r. facing camera) Hilmar Thate, Manfred Wekwerth, Paolo Grassi, Giorgio Strehler, Helene Weigel (Venice 1966). (Photograph in possession of Manfred Wekwerth.)

1986–89	Member of the Central Committee of the SED.
1983–92	Productions include: Schiller's *Wallenstein* in Burgtheater Vienna; Shakespeare's *Troilus and Cressida*; Fo's *Elizabeth – By Chance a Woman* with Alejandro Quintana; Brecht's *The Mother* with Tenschert (with Renate Richter); Erdman's *The Suicide*; Brecht's *Schwejk in the Second World War*; Kleist's *The Prince of Homburg* at Berliner Ensemble and Schauspielhaus Zürich.
1989	Resigns position as President of the Akademie der Künste.
1991	Leaves the Berliner Ensemble.
1992–2002	Freelance productions include: Fallada/Dorst's *Little Man, What Now?* and *The Good Person of Szechwan* in Meininger Theater; Brecht's *Mr Puntila and His Man Matti* and *Richard III* in Neues Theater Halle; Brecht Revue *Denn wie man sich bettet, so …* ; adaptations of Goethe's *Iphigenia auf Tauris* and Laclos's *Les Liaisons*

Illustration 16 Manfred Wekwerth (c.) with Helene Weigel, Helmut Baierl and Joachim Tenschert at the Brecht/Weigel house in Buckow (1967). (Photograph courtesy of Vera Tenschert.)

	Dangereuses in Theater des Ostens; von Hofmannsthal's *Jedermann* and Rojas's *Celestina* for WTT Remscheid; and Marlowe's *Dr. Faustus* in cathedral, Halle.
2002	Awarded Honorary Fellowship of Rose Bruford College, UK.
	Lectures and Workshops in Havana, Istanbul, Leipzig and Graz.
2005–9	Directs *Stars*, musical by Diether Dehm with Rock Band EMMA.
2006–8	Directs Brecht version of *Communist Manifesto*, with music and text at the International Brecht conference October, 2006, Berlin with Renate Richter and Hendrik Duryn.
2006–9	Directs *In der Sünder schamvollem Gewimmel – eine Rockband erinnert sich an den jungen Brecht*, with the Rock band EMMA with Renate Richter und Hendrik Duryn.

Illustration 17 Manfred Wekwerth at the Brecht/Weigel house in Buckow (2006). (Photograph courtesy of Angelika Haas.)

Books (numerous articles not included)

(1960) *Theater in Veränderung,* Berlin: Aufbau-Verlag.

(1959) *Regiearbeit mit Laienkünstlern,* Leipzig: Hofmeister-Verlag. Translated (French) as (1971) *La Mise en scène dans le théâtre d'amateurs,* Texte français de Béatrice Perregaux, Paris: Arche. Translated (Spanish) as *Dialogo sobre a Encenação: Manual Direção Teatral,* Editora: Hucitec.

(1966) *Notate – über die Arbeit des Berliner Ensemble 1956 Bis 1966,* Berlin: Aufbau-Verlag; (1967) Frankfurt/Main: Suhrkamp-Verlag.

(1975) *Arbeit mit Brecht – Schriften zum Theater,* Berlin: Henschelverlag.

(1975) *Theater und Wissenschaft* (Doctoral Thesis), München: Hanser-Verlag.

(1976) *Brecht? Berichte – Erfahrungen – Polemik,* München: Hanser-Verlag.

(1982) *Theater in Diskussion – Notate, Gespräche, Polemiken,* Berlin: Henschelverlag.

(1994) *Im Gespräch mit Hans-Dieter Schütt,* Frankfurtan der Oder: Editionen.

(2000) *Erinnern ist Leben – Autobiographie,* Leipzig: Verlag Faber & Faber.

(2004) *Mit Brecht in Havanna,* Berlin: Spotless-Verlag.

(2009) *Mut zum Genuß: Ein Brecht-Handbuch für Spieler, Zuschauer, Mitstreiter und Streiter,* Berlin: Kai Homilius Verlag.

Lang, Joachim and Wekwerth, Manfred (2010) *Neues vom alten Brecht: Manfred Wekwerth im Gespräch,* Berlin: Aurora Verlag.

Plays

(1999) *Gefährliche Liebschaften,* Scenes from Choderlos de Laclos, München: Drei Masken Verlag.

(2002) *Celestina,* from the novel by Fernando de Rojas, München: Drei Masken Verlag.

Translations, Adaptations

(1966) Libretto for *Puntila-Opera* by Paul Dessau, with Peter Palitzsch

(1970) *Leben und Tod König Richard des Ditten,* by Shakespeare, München: Drei Masken Verlag.

(1972) *Jegor Bulytschow und die anderen,* by Maxim Gorki, München: Drei Masken Verlag.

(1973) *Zement,* screenplay after the novel by Fjodor Gladkow.

(1974) *Die unheilige Sophia,* screenplay after the novel by Eberhard Panitz.

(1976) *Happy End,* Screenplay after the comedy by Dorothy Lane (Elisabeth Hauptmann).

(1985) *Troilus und Cressida,* by Shakespeare, München: Drei Masken Verlag.

(1986) *Elisabeth – zufällig eine Frau,* by Dario Fo.

(1989) *Der Selbstmörder,* by Nikolai Erdman.

(1992) *Der Florentiner Strohhut,* by Eugène Labiche, München: Drei Masken Verlag.

(2000) *Jedermann,* by Hugo von Hofmannsthal, München: Drei Masken Verlag.

(2003) *Die Tragische Geschichte des Doktor Faustus,* by Christopher Marlowe, München: Drei Masken Verlag.

FURTHER READING

English titles have been given where they are available.

Anders, Günther (1962) *Gespräche mit Brecht*, Zürich: Verlag Die Arche.

Aristotle, *Poetics* (many editions available).

Artaud, Antonin (1971)*The Theatre and its Double*, in *Collected Works*, trans. Victor Corti, vol. 4, London: Calder and Boyars.

Barthes, Roland (1972) *Mythologies*, New York: Hill and Wang.

Benjamin, Walter (1955) *Schriften*, Frankfurt am Main: Suhrkamp Verlag.

——(1998) *Understanding Brecht*, trans. Stanley Mitchell, London: Verso.

Bloch, Ernst (2009) *The Heritage of our Times (Weimar and Now: German Cultural Criticism)*, trans. Neville Plaice and Stephen Plaice, Cambridge: Polity Press.

Brecht, Bertolt (1993) *Große Kommentierte Berliner und Frankfurter Ausgabe*, Frankfurt am Main and Berlin: Suhrkamp Verlag and Aufbau-Verlag.

——(1993) *Journals 1934–1955*, trans. Hugh Rorrison, ed. John Willett, London: Methuen.

——(1978) *Brecht on Theatre*, ed. and trans. by John Willett, London: Methuen.

——(2002) *The Messingkauf Dialogues*, ed. and trans. by John Willett, London: Methuen.

Chomsky, Noam (1998) *Profit over People: Neoliberalism and the Global Order*, New York: Seven Stories Press.

Defoe, Daniel (2004) *Robinson Crusoe*, Harmondsworth: Penguin.

Deppe, Frank (1999) *Politisches Denken im 20. Jahrhundert*, Hamburg: VSA-Verlag.

Derrida, Jacques (2006) *Spectres of Marx*, London and New York: Routledge.

Diderot, Denis (1994) 'The Paradox of the Actor', in *Selected Writings on Art and Literature*, ed. and trans. Geoffrey Bremner, Harmondsworth: Penguin.

Eisler, Hanns (1975) *Gespräche mit Hans Bunge*, Leipzig: Deutscher Verlag für Musik.

von Goethe, Johann Wolfgang (1927) 'Rules for Actors', trans. Arthur Woehl, *Quarterly Journal of Speech* (Routledge), Volume 13, Issue 3 June: 243–64.

Gorchakov, Nikolai M. (1973) *Stanislavsky Directs*, trans. Miriam Goldina, Westport, Conn.: Greenwood Press.

Harich, Wolfgang (1971) *Zur Kritik der revolutionären Ungeduld*, Basel: Edition Etcetera.

Haug, Wolfgang Fritz (2006a) *Neue Vorlesungen zur Einführung ins 'Kapital'*, Hamburg: Argument-Verlag.

——(2006b) *Philosophieren mit Brecht und Gramsci*, Hamburg: Argument-Verlag.

Hermann, István (1982) *Probleme der heutigen Kultur*, Budapest: Akadémiai Kiadó.

Heuer, Uwe-Jens (2004) *Marxismus und Politik*, Hamburg: VSA-Verlag.

Kebir, Sabine (1997) *Ich fragte nicht nach meinem Anteil – Elisabeth Hauptmanns Arbeit mit Bertold Brecht*, Berlin: Aufbau-Verlag.

Klaus, Georg (1968) *Die Macht des Wortes*, Berlin: Deutscher Verlag der Wissenschaften.

Kofler, Leo Zur (1974) *Theorie der Modernen Literatur*, Düsseldorf: Bertelsmann Universitätsverlag.

Lukács, Georg (1980) *The Destruction of Reason*, trans. David Fernbach, London: Merlin Press.

——(1983) *The Historical Novel*, trans. Hannah Mitchell and Stanley Mitchell, Lincoln: University of Nebraska Press.

Lyotard, Jean-François, (1993) *Libidinal Economy*, trans. Iain Hamilton Grant, Bloomington: Indiana University Press.

Marcuse, Herbert (2002) *One-Dimensional Man*, London and New York: Routledge.

Marx, Karl (1973/1993) *Grundrisse: Foundations of the Critique of Political Economy*, trans. Martin Nicolaus, Harmondsworth: Penguin.

——(1977) *Critique of Hegel's Philosophy of Right*, trans. Annette Jolin and J. O'Malley Cambridge: Cambridge University Press.

——(1992) *Capital: A Critique of Political Economy*, Vol. 1, trans. Ben Fowkes, Vols 2 and 3 trans. David Fernbach, Harmondsworth: Penguin.

Morris, Charles William (1971) *Writings on the General Theory of Signs*, The Hague: Mouton.

Shklovskij, Viktor (1998) 'Art as Technique', *Literary Theory: An Anthology*, ed. Julie Rivkin and Michael Ryan, Malden: Blackwell Publishing Ltd.

Strehler, Giorgio (1974) *Per un Teatro Humano: pensieri scritti, parlati ed attuati*, Milan: Feltrinelli.

Wolff, Friedrich (2005) *Einigkeit und Recht*, Berlin: Edition Ost.

INDEX

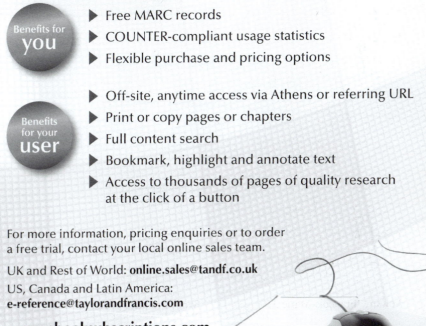